"Leadership Matters?"

In recent years, we have seen what could be described as a moral meltdown in the corporate corridors of power. Few sectors have escaped high-profile scandals, with public officials and leaders guilty of malpractice, duplicity, fraud and corporate malfeasance. Conventional leadership theories appear to be inadequate to equip those with power to act ethically and responsibly. At a more macro level, many of the social and environmental problems we face in the 21st century could, in fact, be described as spiritual in nature, rooted in a flawed human condition.

"Leadership Matters?": Finding Voice, Connection and Meaning in the 21st Century brings together an eclectic mix of authors of different faith traditions and philosophical standpoints to explore what this spiritual and cultural transformation might look like. For too long, we have relied on external codes of conduct, which are, at best, blunt instruments for creating ethical practice. So, chapter by chapter, this book examines our interior lives from the perspective of mind, body and soul.

The unashamed premise of this book is that true and influential leadership comes from the inside with each chapter presenting what it means to lead respectfully, critically, responsibly and humbly in the gritty reality of the twenty first century workplace. This volume will be of keen interest to academics and practitioners in the field of leadership and the related disciplines.

Chris Mabey is a Chartered Psychologist and Professor of Leadership at Middlesex University Business School, UK. He has held a career-long interest in leadership development as a counsellor for a Christian charity, an occupational psychologist for British Telecom, a management trainer at Rank Xerox and a consultant to a wide range of private and public sector organizations.

David Knights is a Professor in the Department of Organization, Work and Technology in Lancaster University Management School, UK. His research interests are broadly in the area of Organization Studies and Management with a particular interest in leadership, power and identity, gender and diversity, the body and ethics. His current research has been on academics and business schools, the global financial crisis, the body and embodiment and, most recently, on veterinary surgeons.

Routledge Studies in Leadership Research

"Leadership Matters?"
Finding Voice, Connection and Meaning in the 21st Century

Edited by Chris Mabey
and David Knights

Routledge
Taylor & Francis Group

LONDON AND NEW YORK

First published 2018 by Routledge

2 Park Square, Milton Park, Abingdon, Oxfordshire OX14 4RN

711 Third Avenue, New York, NY 10017

Routledge is an imprint of the Taylor & Francis Group, an informa business

First issued in paperback 2018

Copyright © 2018 Taylor & Francis

Library of Congress Cataloging-in-Publication Data
A catalog record for this book has been requested

ISBN: 978-1-138-57205-8 (hbk)
ISBN: 978-1-138-36884-2 (pbk)

Typeset in Sabon
by Apex CoVantage, LLC

Contents

Contributors

Karen Blakeley's formative experience was working in the City of London during the deregulation of the banking sector. Following the collapse of Barings Bank, she appeared in the press and TV discussing the factors behind irresponsible leadership in banking. She went on to work as a leadership development consultant for clients such as British Airways, Barclays Bank, Pizza Express, PricewaterhouseCoopers and the Home Office. She now heads up the Centre for Responsible Management at Winchester Business School, a UK champion school for the UN *Principles for Responsible Management Education*. Karen is currently researching the roles of action learning and spirituality in the development of responsible leaders. She pursues her own spirituality by blending her Christian faith with Gurdjieff Fourth Way practices.

Mervyn Conroy is a Senior Fellow at the Health Services Management Centre, University of Birmingham, UK. His work at the center spans teaching, consultancy, research and PhD supervision. He first worked in the health and social care sector as a counselor and later in mental health services as a manager and researcher. His research formed the basis of a briefing paper on *Alternative Approaches to Healthcare Reform* to the UK Department of Health. He currently leads a three year Arts and Humanities Research Council (AHRC) funded project on *Phronesis and the Medical Community*.

Sara De Marco is an Italian, married to a New Zealander born in Africa with three young daughters. She grew up in the Dolomites mountains of northern Italy with a keen desire to learn English and travel abroad. Following her MA in Linguistics in Lancaster University in the UK, she worked in management consulting as a key account manager for the financial sector where she faced multiple ethical challenges and had to learn from her own mistakes on how to lead her own self as a woman from another culture. While at Middlesex University Business School, she worked with the ESRC team exploring and researching Ethical Leadership and has become a passionate apprentice.

Hugo Gaggiotti lectures in Organisation Studies at the Faculty of Business and Law at the University of the West of England, UK. He received his PhD in Anthropology from the University of Barcelona and his PhD in Management Studies from ESADE Business School. He was a foreigner at birth and has remained displaced all his life. He is currently leading a British Academy financed Advanced Research Grant conducting fieldwork in industrial assembly plants in the USA-Mexican borderlands. He has been working for the last four years on the book *Redefining Professional Cultures*. He is reluctant to finish because he is also interested in things he shouldn't be, like organizational time, space, images and death. To avoid tedium, he prefers to write with friends.

Tim Harle lives at the interface of business and faith. He has worked at senior levels in service sector organizations, ranging from a FTSE100 company to a family owned SME. Earlier in his career, he worked with UK government ministers and now combines this experience with insights from academic disciplines in the field of leadership and organizational studies. Tim leads the Centre for Leadership Learning at Sarum College, situated in the historic grounds of Salisbury Cathedral (www.sarum.ac.uk). He is also a Visiting Fellow at Bristol Business School.

Andrew Henley is a Professor of Entrepreneurship and Economics at Cardiff Business School, Cardiff University. He has also been Director of the EU-funded LEAD Wales program, which provided leadership development to small business and social enterprise owners across Wales. He has served in a number of advisory and consultancy roles, including for ten years as an appointed member of the First Minister of Wales' Economic Research Advisory Panel. He has published extensively on research in entrepreneurship, leadership, small business and in regional economics and has a particular interest in Christian belief and economic ethics.

Phil Jackman is a spiritual entrepreneur, leadership consultant, musician and would-be change agent. This millennium, he has taught forgiveness to American businessmen and British Head Teachers, designed and delivered the personal growth course "Habits of the Heart", based on Hebrew wisdom, to over 200 individuals and led a team towards the establishment of Changing Tunes Midlands, running music workshops to reduce reoffending in prisons. He has a special interest in the connections between moral courage, storytelling and resilience and loves to get people talking and listening well about things that matter.

Sally Jeanrenaud is a Senior Research Fellow in Sustainability, Business School, University of Exeter, UK. She has worked in Nepal, Rwanda, Cameroon and Europe in field-based and international leadership positions. She led IUCN's Future of Sustainability Initiative, co-founded the Green Economy Coalition and helped establish Exeter's One Planet MBA and OPEN for Business. She researches innovation in sustainability philosophies and practices, teaches Exeter post-graduates and is a Visiting Professor at Audencia School of Management in France. She is a Trustee of the Fintry Trust, which is dedicated to Integral Wisdom, and a qualified Mindfulness (MBSR) teacher.

Jean-Paul Jeanrenaud is a Senior Advisor to WWF Switzerland. During his career, he worked as a forester and Director of development projects in South Asia, Africa and Europe. He worked for WWF International for 26 years as Director of the International Forest Programme, Director of Corporate Relations and Director of Business Education. He co-founded the Forest Stewardship Council (FSC); One Planet Leaders; the award winning One Planet MBA; and OPEN for Business (One Planet Education Networks). He is a Visiting Professor at Audencia School of Management, Nantes, France. He has been a student of universal and integral wisdom for 40 years and is a qualified Mindfulness (MBSR) teacher.

David Knights is a Professor in the Department of Organization, Work and Technology in Lancaster University Management School, UK. His research interests are broadly in the area of Organization Studies and Management with a particular interest in leadership, power and identity, gender and diversity, the body and ethics. His current research has been on academics and business schools, the global financial crisis, the body and embodiment and, most recently, on veterinary surgeons. He jointly created and edited the international journal *Gender, Work, and Organization* from 1994–2016. Besides publishing, research and teaching, he worked closely with management practitioners in establishing a research center and a forum for academic-industry collaboration in the financial sector between 1994 and 2011.

Chris Mabey is a Chartered Psychologist and Professor of Leadership at Middlesex University Business School. Chris has held a career long interest in leadership development as a counsellor for a Christian charity, as an occupational psychologist for British Telecom, a management trainer at Rank Xerox and as a consultant to a wide range of private and public sector organizations. More recently he has researched, taught and written on knowledge management and leadership and heads up the ESRC-funded Seminar Series on Ethical Leadership (www.ethicalleadership.org.uk). With his wife, he provides leadership development and counseling for a family-focused community church in the UK and a small Bible college in Yangon.

Simon Mitchell was, until recently, CEO of a leading IT company, LinuxIT, which he and the team built over 15 years. During that time, while undertaking an MBA, he was awakened to a deeper sense of self-awareness and applying learning from his newfound passion, LinuxIT, successfully replaced its fear-based operating systems with a values-led approach. This not only yielded better results but also created a fulfilling workplace of trust, vision and commitment. After taking the company to acquisition, he is now about to launch a coaching business that will allow him to engage and evolve this passion while hopefully helping other soul-searching leaders in transition.

Edwin Ng, PhD, is a Lecturer in Media and Communication Studies at the School of Communication and Creative Arts, Deakin University, Australia. He also describes himself as an unemployed author and cultural theorist who is healing from the trauma of a decade of precarious livelihood in Australian academia. He is the author of *Buddhism and Cultural Studies: A Profession of Faith* (2016; Palgrave) and is currently working on his second monograph, *Buddhist Critical Theory: The Critique of Mindfulness and the Mindfulness of Critique* (under contract with Bloomsbury).

Ron Purser, PhD, is a Professor of Management at San Francisco State University, where he has taught the in the MBA and undergraduate business programs, as well in the doctoral program in the College of Education. His recent research has been exploring the challenges and issues of introducing mindfulness into secular contexts, particularly critical perspectives of mindfulness in corporate settings. His article *Beyond McMindfulness* (with David Loy) in the *Huffington Post* went viral in 2013. He enjoys writing critical social media pieces which have appeared in *salon.com*, *AlterNet* and the Buddhist Peace Fellowship's *Turning Wheel Media.*

Clare Rigg is a Senior Lecturer in Management at the University of Liverpool where she currently leads the Doctorate in Business Administration program, working with managers in pretty much every sector across the world. Her teaching and research interests intermesh through her concern with managers' engagement with and in scholarly practice and the facilitation of management learning through phronesis. Her particular research interest at present is in managers' self-care and resilience, through an exploration of the critical potential of engagement with mindfulness integrated in leadership development. She is editor of the *Journal of Action Learning: Research and Practice.*

Peter Simpson is an Associate Professor in Organisation Studies at Bristol Business School, University of the West of England. Throughout his career, he has held a range of leadership roles within a university setting. As an academic, he has actively engaged with private, public and voluntary sector organizations, which has included consulting to senior managers on strategic change as well as facilitating executive development programs. He studies leadership through the theoretical lenses of spirituality, philosophy, complexity and psychodynamics and has published widely in this field. His current interests include the importance of quality of attention in effective and ethical leadership practice and how this might be enhanced through the development of Negative Capability.

Leah Tomkins is a Senior Lecturer in Organization Studies at the Open University, UK. Prior to entering academia, Leah held a range of corporate and central government leadership positions, including being responsible for the People Strategy for the UK Civil Service in the late noughties. Much of her writing now involves trying to bridge the divide between academics and practitioners, and find ways to surface and explore the lived experience of work for the human beings who occupy both professional domains. Her research draws on the philosophies of hermeneutics and phenomenology to try to make sense of organizations and the people who inhabit and lead them, critiquing popular notions of *authentic leadership* and *the caring organization* for downplaying the difficulties of organizational experience in its day-to-day, un-heroic moments.

Catherine Turner-Perrott is a hard-working, ambitious mother. She left school early with few qualifications but flourished in her career as Business Development Manager for Global Change Management Consultants DBM plc. After a brief stint at Scripture Union as Children & Youth Campaign Manager, she left the corporate and charity world to become a mother and retrain as a Personal Trainer and Nutritional Advisor. Catherine is now committed to her business venture *Dotty's Kitchin*, currently working with restaurants to create fun, tasty and healthy children's menus, as well as developing a *Little Chef* online training qualification to tackle fussy eating.

Zack Walsh is a PhD candidate in the Process Studies graduate program at Claremont School of Theology. His research is transdisciplinary, exploring process-relational, contemplative and engaged Buddhist approaches to political economy, sustainability and China. His most recent writings provide critical and constructive reflection on mindfulness trends, while developing contemplative pedagogies and practices for addressing social and ecological issues.

1 Introduction

"Leadership Matters?"

David Knights and Chris Mabey

Key Questions

What is the moral compass in your life that guides the way you lead?
Where do you turn for inspiration as a leader?
How much attention do you give to the nurturing of your spirit?
What do you relate to in your life that is in some way "bigger than you"?

In recent years, there has been something of a moral meltdown in the corporate corridors of power. Few sectors have escaped high profile scandals, with public officials and business leaders guilty of malpractice, duplicity, fraud and corporate malfeasance. There are clearly important leadership matters surrounding these moral crises and we can see that leadership therefore matters to us all. Conventional leadership theories appear to be inadequate to equip those with power to act ethically and responsibly. According to the 2014 Edelman Trust Barometer—a survey conducted across 27 countries with more than 33,000 respondents—overall trust has significantly declined across countries and sectors around the world, with CEOs ranking second lowest at 43% and government officials the lowest at 36% as credible spokespeople. It seems that in the eyes of a majority of the population, business is eroding rather than building trust, thereby threatening to undermine the very idea of leadership.

This breakdown in trust not only damages relations between leaders and those they seek to lead as well as other important stakeholder relationships (e.g., customers, suppliers, regulators and the communities/societies in which they are located), but also stands in the way of the risky but necessary innovations that could contribute to solving the problem of sustainable and equitable social and economic development. A number of business leaders, scholars and other observers have suggested that one response to this crisis is to move towards a world in which business is "purpose driven" beyond the goals of profit. For example, initiatives like *A Blueprint for Better Business*[1] are drawing on insights from the "great faith" and philosophical traditions to argue that both our society and the firms within it are more likely to flourish if we can reframe business to reflect important deeply held social values, moral purpose and broader responsibilities to society.

As authors of this introduction and as editors of the book we need to say something about our collaboration. In terms of some of the issues this book encompasses, it could be argued that the two of us are at opposite ends of a spectrum that runs from philosophically grounded ethics, at the one extreme, todeep Christian convictions, at the other. This book represents only one of our responses to the ethical problematic in leadership—we, with two other colleagues, have also edited a special issue of an international ethics journal which focuses more specifically on philosophical treatments of the topic.[2] It was partly for this reason that we came together to edit this book because we wanted to allow multiple and often-contentious voices to mingle if not merge. In the process of contributing to and editing the book, we believe that the continuum can be seen more like a globe where on many issues we coincide, even though we may start from distant positions and may channel our end thoughts in diverse directions. This is perhaps the opposite of what is tending to occur through social media where we live in self-contained and self-reinforcing bubbles in which our ideas are forever confirmed and reconfirmed rather than subjected to some level of challenge. The remainder of this chapter is organized as follows: while traditionally ethics has been treated as an outlier or an additional issue to contemplate almost as an after-thought in the study of leadership, we first consider developing an integrative idea of ethical leadership where moral matters are embedded in leadership, which, in turn, is an embodiment of ethical practice. Second, this theme of holistic and integrated thinking is applied to the popular notion of leading with integrity. Third, we provide the reader with a summary of the guiding assumptions of the book, and these are not just a vehicle for helping the reader to navigate the different chapters but essentially have provided us as authors with a sense of moral purpose in writing our separate contributions. Fifth and finally, we outline the book through a summary of the rationales behind each of the three sections: Voice, Connection and Meaning, although we leave a synopsis of the separate chapters and the invited vignettes to the Introduction within each section.

Developing Ethical Leadership

What is the response? Scholarship on business ethics is extensive, and there is a growing recognition by business schools that this is an important topic, yet frequently, it is treated merely as an optional module tagged on to the end of the syllabus. Given the corporate and finance scandals outlined above, is it not somewhat scandalous that ethical matters are seen as peripheral or viewed as less than essential within business education? Equally problematic, however, is the limited way in which writing and teaching about business ethics falls short in a number of ways: it draws upon a very limited philosophical base, usually restricting itself to rule-based or utilitarian understandings of ethics; it is inclined to focus on corporate social responsibility (CSR), which usually means demonstrating how business ethics is "good for business" and profits to the exclusion of it being a good in itself; it tends to propound a universal, one-size-fits-all approach, which is unrealistic given the situational ethics of international business; and it focuses upon specific issues like bribery, human rights and legal requirements rather than surfacing the ethical threads in everyday thought and action. It is no surprise that there are questions as to whether leadership can be a reflection and development of, rather than merely marginally constrained by, ethical values?

In responding to crises such as that of global finance in 2008, government and policy makers tend to resort to the law and regulatory rules as a way of curbing misdemeanors or ethical shortcomings despite similar regulatory frameworks failing to address the recalcitrant ethos, which led to malpractice in the first place. This partly reflects how regulatory agencies, accreditation schemes and audit bodies become institutionalized and readily are transformed into self-generating industries that claim a monopoly over their domain, thus providing steady remuneration for consultants and advisers (see Box 1.1).

Despite the global chaos created by the 2008 global financial crisis (GFC), it was concluded by an International Monetary Fund review several years later, that the financial reform agenda is still only half-baked.[3] Moreover, after a decade of austerity instigated by the major economies in large part to recover their finances from the devastating effects of the crisis, it is surprising how so little leadership imagination and innovation there has been to try and

---

Box 1.1   Scandals

Despite the global chaos created by the 2008 financial crisis, it was concluded by an International Monetary Fund review several years later by, that the financial reform agenda is still only half-baked at best (Claessens and Kodres, "The Regulatory Responses to the Global Financial Crisis: Some Uncomfortable Questions", *IMF Working Paper*, March 2014).

In the UK National Health Service, two public inquiries into the Mid Staffordshire hospital scandal (where it was estimated that between 400 and 1,200 people died unnecessarily in a four-year period) carried out by Robert Francis QC, identified a range of performance management problems that persisted. He concluded that a focus on achieving externally set targets had largely left a culture of bullying and secrecy untouched.

In 2017, global shares in British Telecom tumbled 20%, in part due to fraud among senior leadership at BT Italy, with reported collusion by the highly respected auditors PricewaterhouseCoopers.

prevent a repetition of the problems. This again can be attributed to the failure of ethics to be integral not only to business education but also to the very idea of leadership that is the most frequent port of call when things go wrong in organizations or society more broadly[4]

As has been observed, the idea that morality is merely about being obedient to a set of rules has long been discredited.[5] The emphasis now is upon the kind of person each of us has a capacity to become, and the aesthetical and ethical leadership that this evokes, rather than complying with rules, the universality of which preclude any personal moral engagement. These are inescapably important matters for the theory and practice of leadership whether in the private, public or civil society sectors; from financial services to education and IT; from multinational to Small and Medium-sized Enterprises (SMEs); and from local catastrophes to global terrorism.

Given that few countries have escaped their own leadership scandals, it is timely to question the reliance on regulatory responses to poor leadership ethics since practitioners are invariably one step ahead and thus readily able to avoid the intentions of the regulators.[6] It also prompts us to ask: why are business schools frequently failing in their original mission to be capitalism's conscience, to ask questions other institutions are afraid to ask, to promote multi-disciplinary dialogue and to use their educational skills to provoke deeper self- and other-awareness? One possibility is that our business schools are locked into a collusive cycle with other stakeholders where few appear to be prepared to confront this stultifying inertia. At its most cynical, it could be argued that performance-driven, parents, schools, employers and the media encourage students to concentrate almost exclusively on the instrumental goals of academic grades, a phenomenon that becomes self-fulfilling as academics seek to please in order to secure good student evaluations. This is reinforced further when students encounter career-minded academics that are driven, albeit often reluctantly, by elitist accreditation and ranking; the result is overprescribed, risk-free research and uncontentious teaching, that is unlikely to generate the innovative thinking essential to a modern economy. And so the collusive cycle continues. It seems each of the players in this cycle is unable or unwilling to break rank to challenge the consequences, but there may be ways to unlock the stalemate for business schools.[7] For example:

- To engage in more adventurous theorizing, breaking the unholy silence between competing discourses and disciplines in search of effective and ethical leadership; an example is a growing rapprochement between philosophy, theology (hitherto often entrenched in universalist and foundationalist thought), and organization studies (typically naturalist and empiricist with little time for the classics or "outdated" religion).
- To recover their moral authority, not by pushing a particular brand of ideology or spirituality, but by creating dialogue between disparate belief systems and world-views; by decreasing a reliance upon tired

methodologies and models and exploring more human as well as post- or neo-humanist qualities such as embodied engagement, affect, celebrating difference and not just diversity, judgment, wisdom and ethics. Given the multi-ethnicity of most student groups, the opportunity to do this is readily available.

We hope this book will start to do these things.

Leading With Integrity

The Future of Work unit at ESADE, Spain, recently reported on ten trends resulting from the powerful, parallel forces of globalization, digitalization/virtualization and knowledge creation-innovation.[8] The authors characterize the contemporary work space as being: "a continual search for quick fixes and lives that are distanced—while causing us to give up the 'high-touch' aspects of life that give our lives meaning, hope, fear and longing, love, forgiveness, nature and spirituality". Given the technological focus of the paper, it is noteworthy that many of the questions of leaders in the future have an ethical dimension:

- How will I develop whole-person relationships with people and teams with the heavy reliance on technology-based relationships?
- Is my own mix of daily activities contributing to effective accomplishment of my tasks as an executive? Is my work providing me with job, career and life satisfaction?
- How am I building values, ethics and relational/emotional intelligence skills into my human resources and organizational culture, given the prevalence of portfolio employment?
- How can our employees learn and operate with and from values of compassion, trust and care—bridging technology-based relationships with human-based interactions?
- How is my company using the full potential of our physical spaces to flexibly adapt to specific and changing work environments?
- Do jobs create meaning and allow workers and employees to realize their full potential in creating something they care about?
- Are staff able to pursue their passions and allowed the space to make a social impact?

It is no coincidence, then, that those researching and writing in the area of leadership are expressing a growing interest in how to promote ethical approaches to leadership. Three levels of analysis can be discerned. First, at an *organizational practice* level there is increasing pre-occupation with ensuring that corporate credentials are morally and environmentally defensible. But given the ineffectiveness of regulation and compliance (see Box 1.1), there is a marked growth of workplace interest in mindfulness, meditation, emotional intelligence, ethics and the like. For example, many organizations across the world now incorporate meditation as a means for promoting health and improved performance, including Google which developed a meditation training program, *"Search Inside Yourself"*, that has evolved into a Leadership Institute. Yet over recent years, Google, along with other major household names, such as Amazon, Apple and Starbucks, has paid tax bills that are a fraction of what would be expected given the size of their revenues.[9] In Google's case, it is heavily ironic in that apart from the meditation program, its "founders—bright eyed and fiercely intelligent maths PhDs—were inspired by the force for good their algorithm could become. And so it has. Perhaps more than any other company, Google has changed the way that humanity engages with information".[10] This paradox should not then lead us to be wholly condemning of the hypocrisy because we have to recognize that global corporations are complex organizations that cannot guarantee to speak with one voice. Nonetheless, the place of meditation in business has increasingly become a focus of attention and academics have scrutinized its effects on, for example, ethics, stress management and performance. And long may such scrutiny continue since we should not be either *for* or *against* meditation but just always watchful of its dangers because everything is dangerous no matter how "good" or "bad" it may appear.[11]

Second, although not always apparent, such practices are associated with particular *theories and discourses*. So there is a range of approaches informed by a rainbow of disciplines (from economics to theology, from Greek philosophy to organizational behavior, from anthropology to neuro-science) which seek to discern the moral roots of effective leadership. Two observations may be made about this level. Because our favored discourses feel as natural as the air we breathe, we often take them for granted, assume others "share the same air" and rarely question their validity. This leads to a second facet: dialogue with those not disposed towards our pet theories and preferred discourse is tricky. Consider for a moment:

- Why do businesspeople often think that academics ask the wrong questions and over-complicate their answers?
- Why do academics routinely find businesspeople preoccupied with technical, pragmatic or profit directed solutions?

But beneath this there is a third level, because our attachment to certain discourses and theories does not happen in a vacuum or by chance; it arises from our view of the world, our *belief system* and our historical and biographical experiences. Again, this may or not be conscious and well-articulated, but each of us inhabits a world-view which guides our life, our deep (sometimes unuttered) choices, shapes our values and is the bedrock of our relationships. It is our contention therefore, that if we are to unpack the notion of leadership—particularly its ethical basis—we need to dive down to this level and *not* paddle exclusively in the arena of contemporary practices and discourses, important though they are.

Guiding Assumptions of This Book

At this point, it might be helpful to set out some guiding assumptions for the book. In the spirit of what we have just said, these will inevitably reflect the world-views of the authors, but hopefully they will be inclusive enough to bring most readers along with us, if only to sample what is on offer.

- *We live in a work-world of individual economic self-interest and instrumental rationality* and a kind of mindless materialism (which is actually profoundly disrespectful of the material world[12]). This is destructive and 'thin' in terms of understanding individual, organizational and institutional life on a global scale. Of course, there are examples of leaders and organizations treading more noble paths, but there is sufficient dissatisfaction with the waywardness and ineffectiveness of current corporate leadership to fuel a search for more fundamental remedies than those generally on offer.
- *Leading with integrity.* This involves individual and collective efforts, organizational initiatives and the nurturing of culture and creativity such as those propounded by Positive Organizational Scholarship[13] or affective and embodied leadership.[14] For too long, we have relied upon leadership development programs which engage the mind but not the soul, and upon external codes of conduct, which at best, are blunt instruments for generating ethical practice.
- *We can all ask the question about depth and value in life.* We all have some worthwhile non-instrumental commitments and values, regardless of whether we have anything to do with the world of the "spiritual" and "religious". The problem is that most of us are so absorbed in a vortex of ever-improved performance we don't have the time, energy or space to ask these questions. As it happens, to address the perceived moral vacuum in leadership studies, scholars are increasingly drawing upon philosophical (existentialist, humanist, post or neo-humanist and secularist) approaches, or faith-based approaches to leadership (for example, Judeo-Christian and Buddhist).[15] The problem here is that these approaches are untested in terms of their application to the workplace.
- As resources to make this quest towards leading with integrity, it is helpful to venture beyond our own own favored *discipline*: in other words, to facilitate a dialogue, we will usually forestall by closed minds and bodies, ignorance or, sometimes, prejudice. For example, for many social scientists invoking spirituality involves a retreat from rational thinking. Below an apparently innocuous commentary belies a fundamental misconception that reason and spirituality are mutually incompatible (see Box 1.2).[16]
- By giving attention to the *formation of our own subjectivity* (our cultural norms, our upbringing, our personal psychology, our deeply held beliefs, including those about leadership), it may be possible to engage with an ethics of practice through attention to theories of moral imagination,

---

Box 1.2   Enlightened Thinking?

So-called post-Enlightenment thinking has left us with the unquestioned norm that reason and spirituality are mutually incompatible. This is exemplified in the social sciences by this quotation from a sociology text in the early 1970s: "*it is not of great sciological significance to inquire into the factors effecting changes in systems of belief and value which are super-empirical or transcendental in their reference: since nobody could conceivably deny that significant proportions of the individuals in contemporary industrial societies have either given up or come seriously to doubt the validity of such orientations*". The arrogance of this pronouncement is as breath-taking as it has been influential on a generation of students. If we subscribe to the view that the sacred realm—comprising personal morality, worship and religion—is inherently private and separate from the public realm where science and reason is played out, then we enter a moral minefield. As a more recent scholar notes: "*modernism and the resulting sacred/secular divide simply changed our views regarding knowledge, truth and morality. Although scientific reason held out the promise of being able to explain everything, it could not resolve moral issues nor address fundamental existential questions*".

---

diverse approaches to ethics and values-based management. We recognize that this is personal territory, not usually discussed or disclosed in leadership circles; however, we believe the gains in terms of arriving at your own, thought-out approach to leadership integrity are immense.

- Though modernists like to see themselves as rational, guided by scientific reason alone, we all in fact arrive at—and inhabit—our worldview, whether of a spiritual or philosophical persuasion, *by faith*. None of us can point to incontrovertible evidence to factually confirm our worldview as correct and universal. The point being that these beliefs constitute our identity, no matter how precarious and in flux these may be at a particular point in time. It is in our everyday organizational work, that our ethics will be tested, pummeled and sifted as we reflexively bump against others with their own take on such matters; this is all part of the ongoing negotiation of power and identity in leader-follower exchange.

In short, this book offers a radical re-appraisal and way forward by exploring what is meant by a return to ethics, philosophy and "spirituality" around the theory and practice of leadership. This leads us to three USPs for this book. First, many have gone before us advocating their own particular brand of philosophy or spirituality for improving our workplace experience (witness the voluminous "self-help" industry); here, we seek to be more *inclusive* by corralling a variety of approaches. The common ground is that, in order to better explore the ethical dimensions of leadership, all authors advocate—in their different ways—moving beyond tools and techniques (which tend to have a limited shelf-life), beyond the cognitive (neither jettisoning or inflating reason) and beyond the intellectual (where it is too easy to play academic mind-games without real commitment) . . . to the philosophical, to the embodied, to the spiritual, to the corporeal, to the emotional, to the intuitive. We recognize that these are not equitable domains, but nevertheless what they share is a post-rationalist and possibly post-humanist[17] exploratory space; each author is saying something distinctive about—and inviting you into—that space of what it means to be involved with leadership ethically and not just instrumentally.

Second, we have made real efforts to access and appreciate these different understandings between ourselves. This book is, in large part, an outcome of a Seminar Series funded by the Economic and Social Research Council (ESRC) in the UK.[18] During the course of nine Seminars over a period of three years, a myriad of keynote international speakers, debates, small group discussions and conversations have taken place in which we have each wrestled with practices, discourses, philosophies and spiritualties which are both familiar and unfamiliar, mainstream and marginal. This has led to a measure of unusual trust and respect between us, not something for which autonomous academics are renowned. This is not to say each of us wholly endorses the beliefs, the views, or even the chapter texts of each other, but what we can say is that this book is a collective offering, where each chapter is the result of "iron sharpening iron", not a series of disconnected contributions.

Third, each author includes reference to why their topic or theme is important to them personally and how the seminar series has affected their lives and whether this means feeling, thinking and doing things 'differently'. In other words, rather than staying at the hypothetical level of theory and recommendation, we are seeking to close the gap between what we say and do. We each reflect on the whole experience of working together including the discomforts, the challenges and the excitement, by stating how our personal view of leading with integrity has been affected by participating in this collaborative research endeavor. Again, this degree of personal disclosure takes some bravery because it is not encouraged in conventional scholarly work,[19] but we felt it to be not just helpful but utterly consistent with a project of this nature.

Outline of the Book

The reason for the title of this book: *Leadership Matters?* is not simply to delineate the terrain we cover; it also pertains to two further levels. First and most obviously, leadership matters as a significant element of our daily lives: without effective and ethical leadership we suffer personally, socially, economically, ecologically. It matters for us also in so far as we are all *affected* by leadership not just in the simple way depicted in followership studies but in the more substantive manner in which leadership is about energizing practices of transformation that can only be enacted through collective embodied engagement. Second, much of the thrust of this book concerns the return to materiality in social science, the realization that we do not just bring our brains to work; that knowledge is not simply a commodity to be traded; that our relationships with co-workers are not simply transactions. What moves our heads is our bodies and the material contexts of their intra-action, and what moves our bodies is our souls and our relationships to the world around us. So, literally, matter does matter. Another interesting feature on this notion of what matters is Latour's[20] distinction between matters of "fact" and matters of "concern", for he felt that the latter moral dimension was frequently being chased out by the so-called factual as a result of epistemologies and methods grounded in the logical and positive sciences. In matters of leadership, the shift between "facts" and "concerns" is historical and forever in transition. Yet the question mark in our title suggests that we are not unreflective about each of these meanings and do not wish to impose them on readers but merely to offer them as points for debate, dispute, and even dismissal.

VOICE. The sub-title is also important and the three sections of the book broadly follow the substantial though rarely articulated concerns of many of us enmeshed in contemporary organizations. Although recognizing that most of us have, and continue, to work out of economic necessity, we ought to leave space to consider the value of our labor that goes beyond mere material or even symbolic accumulation,[21] how do we resist the ready-made and often vacuous "solutions" and technologies of power and leadership with which we are confronted on a daily basis? In short, how do we find *our* moral bearings, *our* unique voices? With a particular focus upon mindfulness, this is the subject of the first section.

The second deals with CONNECTION. For too long, the workplace has neglected the viscerality of our emotions, airbrushed-out diversity and difference, relegated family and non-work attachments, idolized the heroic at the expense of the here-and-now. Despite the everyday palpability of our bodies and all the signals they convey, we continue to pursue leadership in a largely dis-embodied manner, neglecting how "the mind is simply the idea of the body".[22] In doing so, the body often returns to haunt us and no more so than in our masculine driven world of winning regardless of the consequences to one's own and others bodies. In the blurring of boundaries between work and non-work, it is attention to the latter (and all the care and commitments this carries) that gets sacrificed. Also, despite the constant babble about "leadership" in the media, in sport, in corporations, in politics, the Englishness of this narrative (with all the mono-linguistic imposition and limitation that this implies) goes unquestioned. Furthermore, in the pre-occupation with fantasized ideals of heroic leadership, this mythology massively underestimates the mundane, the everyday expression of leadership in ordinary acts.

The third section deals with MEANING. In the raging waters of workplace expectations, business targets and career goals, it is easy to lose our moorings. In moments of honesty and places of trust, we all—as leaders—ask of ourselves: how do I deal with the persistence of ego, reduce the credibility gap between what I say and what I do, determine what is really important, retain integrity, have fun and stay resolute to my life goals? And in relation to leading with others, we ask: how can we find a moral compass so that we lead responsibly together; how can we confront dubious practices which cause us unease; how can we empower ourselves to do what is important, not just what is urgent and how do we play *our part* in changing the world and leaving a meaningful legacy? Whether we use the language of philosophy, soul or spirituality, the common territory here is not just the desire to invest our workspace with meaning but also to recognize its presence without such investments. And finding this voice, connection and meaning will surely bring an ethical edge to the way we think, speak and behave as followers and leaders.

Notes

1. It supports five principles around: Honesty, Responsibility, Sustainability, Citizenship and protecting the Future; see www.blueprintforbusiness.org.
2. *Business Ethics Quarterly*, Forthcoming, 2018.
3. Claessens and Kodres (2014).
4. At the time of writing, the UK has suffered some devastating tragedies relating to terrorism and a tower block fire, and the public in each case called out for politicians and managers to show leadership, although no one is quite sure what this mantra means.
5. This view is famously attributed to Derrida (1995). Michel Foucault (2011) also notes that only when we have recovered ourselves from how we have been constituted as subjects—by previous exercises of power so as to become self-governing—can we contemplate ethical approaches to leadership. These previous exercises of power include the traditional deontological, consequential and virtue discourses on ethics.
6. Knights and McCabe (2015).
7. This collusive cycle and how to break it is explored in Mabey, C. and Mayrhofer, W. (2015) *Developing Leaders: Questions Business Schools Don't Ask*. London: Sage. They invited contributors to address one question that they felt business schools were failing to ask—or answer. In response they received a rich mix of ethical and spiritual resources including Heideggerian philosophy, McIntyre's virtue, classical Greek philosophy, Hebrew wisdom tradition, Christian spirituality and the Maori notion of *wairua*.
8. The work of the Centre is reported in a paper by Dolan et al. (2015) It probes what is needed to develop people, companies and ecosystems to flourish in a high tech, high touch and high growth work reality while resisting the possibilities of strategic implosion. It is symptomatic of many reports that are beginning to question driving for performance without considering the human, social and environmental costs.
9. See *Huffington Post*, available from: www.huffingtonpost.co.uk/chuka-umunna/ed-miliband-google-speech-tax-avoidance_b_3320561.html
10. *Huffington Post* ibid.
11. See Foucault (1984).
12. Chapter 2 in this book also takes up this theme more fully.
13. Of particular note in this regard is Positive Organizational Scholarship (POS), summarized as follows: "By focusing on the generative dynamics of human organizing, POS provides an expanded view of how organizations can create

sustained competitive advantage . . . and collective capability". (Cameron et al., 2003, p. 11). There is much to help the aspiring leader in their book and the POS literature more generally, but note the weaknesses of this approach advanced in Chapter 3 (Mabey).

14. See Chapters 2 (Sally and Jean-Paul Jeanrenaud), 5 (Knights) and 6 (Tomkins and Simpson) in this book.

15. See Chapters 3 (Mabey) and 10 (Henley) for Judeo-Christian approaches and Chapters 2 (Jeanrenaud) and 4 (Purser) for those referring to the Buddhist tradition. See also a Yale initiative which looked at management learnings from the world's Wisdom Traditions: www.efmd.org/blog/view/375-can-managers-learn-to-be-wise-inspiration-from-religious-and-philosophical-traditions.

16. The first of the quotations in Box 2 comes from Robertson (1971) and the second from Kim et al. (2012).

17. See Wolfe (2010), Braidotti (2013).

18. Grant Reference: ESRC ES/M0018571/1, see www.ethicalleaders.org.uk

19. The usual advice from academic journal editors and even book publishers is to locate what you say in the current literature, to reference extensively, to support statements with hard empirical evidence (whether quantitative or qualitative), to avoid personal pronouns and unsubstantiated opinions. While this promotes good "science", such advice can also leave large tracts of important territory (in our case, relating to leadership integrity) uncharted.

20. Latour (2004) This distinction was mobilized as an analytical resource for studying an industrial protest against redundancies in a university in Knights and McCabe (2016).

21. We recognize that given the relentless pressure and the economic necessity of work, creating this space can be extraordinarily difficult.

22. Spinoza (1677 [1994]).

Bibliography

Braidotti, R. (2013) *The Posthuman*. Malden: MA: Polity Press.

Claessens, S. and Kodres, L. (2014) *The Regulatory Responses to the Global Financial Crisis: Some Uncomfortable Questions*. IMF Working Paper, March.

Derrida, J. (1995) *The Gift of Death*, trans. David Wills. Chicago: University of Chicago Press.

Dolan, S., Makarevich, A. and Kawamura, K. (2015) Are you and your company prepared for the future of work? *European Business Review*, July–August, pp. 5–12.

Foucault, M. (1984) What is enlightenment? In Rabinow, P. (ed.) *The Foucault Reader*. Harmondsworth: Penguin, pp. 32–50.

Foucault, M. (2011) *The Courage of Truth: Lectures at the College de France 1983–4*. Basingstoke: Palgrave Macmillan.

Khurana, R. (2007) *From Higher Aims to Hired Hands*. Princeton, NJ: Princeton University Press.

Kim, D., McCalman, D. and Fisher, D. (2012) The sacred/secular divide and the Christian worldview. *Journal of Business Ethics* 109, pp. 203–208.

Knights, D. and McCabe, D. (2015) 'Masters of the Universe': Demystifying leadership in the context of the 2008 financial crisis. *British Journal of Management* 26, pp. 197–210.

Knights, D. and McCabe, D. (2016) The missing masses of resistance: Employing insights from actor network theory to enhance our understanding of resistance. *British Journal of Management*, early on line, forthcoming.

Latour, B. (2004) Why has critique run out of steam? From matters of fact to matters of concern. *Critical Inquiry* 30(2), Winter, pp. 225–248. The University of Chicago Press.

Mabey, C. and Mayrhofer, W. (2015) *Developing Leaders: Questions Business Schools Don't Ask*. London: Sage Publications.

Robertson, R. (1971) Belief: Basic problems of definition, in an Open University set text. In Thomson, K. and Tunstall, J. (eds.) *Sociological Perspectives*. Harmondsworth: Penguin Books.

Spinoza, B. de. (1677 [1994]) *The Ethics and Other Works*, trans. E. Curley. Princeton, NJ: Princeton University Press. Ethics II Proposition 13.

Wolfe, C. (2010) *What Is Posthumanism*. Minneapoli, MN: University of Minnesota Press.

Part I

Voice

Is Leadership All in the Mind?

Although in this section, we neither deny the importance of the mind or the necessity of intellectual knowledge, we do argue that knowledge *about* things is very different from intimate acquaintance *with* things. Our preoccupation with extant thoughts, wise words, descriptive writing (all representations of reality) serve as a poor substitute for first hand immersion in the actual experience. We maintain that for the development of ourselves and others as leaders, this kind of knowledge cannot be taught or imparted. What we can do is create the space for experience in the present moment in a compassionate and non-judgmental yet critical manner. And this is the essence of mindfulness.

Jean-Paul and Sally Jeanrenaud consider what it takes to achieve corporate and social change which is just, compassionate, collaborative and ecologically sustainable. They propose that what is required is ethical and radical leadership, and that mindfulness can play a key part in bringing about this transformation on three levels. Drawing upon interviews with ten leaders with a mindfulness practice, they propose that personal, interior work is a key, but generally unrecognized, dimension, shaping transformations at organizational and then at a wider systems level. In other words, a well-being economy ultimately emerges from the inside-out.

Chris Mabey explores some of the ways in which individuals and corporates have attempted to overcome an in-built bias toward selfish motives and amoral attitudes. He reflects on the way mindfulness as a way of life, rather than as a technique, can help us to "wake up" to our senses to become more fully aware of our own experience in the present moment and, as a result, become more sensitized in the workplace to moments of celebration on the one hand or murmurs of unease or disquiet on the other. As discovered by those in the contemplative Christian tradition, this leads very naturally, for those of faith, into making space for God and the divine. This, in turn, can have profound effects on how and why we exercise leadership.

The practice of mindfulness has conjured up a range of caricatures in the popular press, which are unhelpful, misleading and do a dis-service to the roots of this approach. **Ron Purser** and colleagues help to dispel some of the myths. With reference to original Buddhist teachings, they link mindfulness to an ethos of *response-ability* where we all invite from, and gift to, one another mutual recognition, respect, care and concern in order to grow and thrive as communities in a precarious world.

This may seem a strange way to start a book on leadership ethics. However, we trust that you can see how leading is merely a verb. It is a vehicle if you like and irrespective of the mode of transport, it all depends on who is leading, who is following and how worthwhile is the destination. We may or may not have leadership in our job titles, we may hold senior positions in our organization or be influencers in our community, but until we have reflected on who we are, what is important to us and why, our leading is unlikely to have an ethical edge. Yes, our heads and minds play a part, but only as far as they allow us to be truly attentive to the present moment, to develop the capacity to perceive things differently, to resist premature problem-solving and to relish the holistic experience of mind in connection to body and spirit.

To illustrate this integrative approach to leadership, we conclude with two very different stories, one corporate and one more family and community based. Both contributors faced personally daunting circumstances and both had to find moral courage from within.

Simon Mitchell is the CEO of LinuxIT, a thriving IT company and the UK leader in its field. When he took over, the organization was struggling. It was in financial and cultural ruin and needed a miracle to survive. The fact that it did, he puts down to a journey of spiritual transformation in his own life and, following on from this, the discovery of a newfound personal balance and meaning in the organization.

Sara de Marco relates some of the challenges facing her following the birth of her children when she became a full-time parent and volunteered actively in many fundraising activities for schools and families in a multi-ethnic network of people in north east London. Having a child with dyslexia also offered her a significant opportunity to bring her Christian beliefs to bear on issues of inclusion and justice in her community, which is more religious than spiritual. For her, this raised important questions about ethical leadership, now heightened by her family's recent relocation to Italy, which she describes as a collision of cultures.

2 The Mindful-Promise

Leading With Integrity for a Sustainable Future

Sally Jeanrenaud and Jean-Paul Jeanrenaud

Key Questions

Does mindfulness offer a radical way of leading with integrity for a sustainable future?

What are the leadership benefits and challenges of practicing mindfulness?

What are the opportunities, benefits and challenges of bringing mindfulness into the workplace?

Introduction

Scientists claim we are facing a "perfect storm" of interconnected social, environmental and economic challenges.[1] And, countless analysts are calling for responsible leadership and an urgent transition to a sustainable economy. These challenges relate to:

Planet

We currently use 1.5 planet's worth of resources to fuel our economic growth and consumption, generating risks for business.[2] Our fossil fuel based, linear, take-make-waste economy creates climate disruption, biodiversity loss, water shortages, resource scarcity and mountains of waste. The "ecological disconnect"[3] between people and nature is destroying our life support systems.

People

Wealth is not trickling down. Just eight men own the same wealth as the 3.6 billion people who make up the poorest half of humanity.[4] Power and privilege are skewing the economic system, increasing extreme inequalities, and creating a "social disconnect" between the rich and the rest. This is unethical, unjust, socially divisive, politically corrosive and ecologically and economically damaging in the long term.

Profit

The financial sector is unstable, favoring speculation and "phantom wealth" over investment in real wealth.[5] This "economic disconnect" is driving boom and bust cycles, creating debt, holding governments hostage to financiers and undermining efforts to invest in a sustainable economy.

Power

Corporations spend billions of dollars a year on lobbying governments, international trade and financial institutions and influencing decisions relating to taxes, subsidies, trade deals and legislation. These support private gain at the expense of people and planet and threaten democratic processes.

Person

Rates of stress and depression are increasing worldwide. Some one million people die by suicide each year, and it is the leading cause of death among young people.[6] Materialistic values and consumerism generate chronic dissatisfaction, do not fulfill our human potential and create an inner "spiritual disconnect".

A "better world" is often presented in terms of "sustainable development" or "sustainable business". But sustainability, which addresses the environmental, social and economic "problems out there", is struggling to achieve lasting results at scale. Are there any new ways of thinking and leading that can make a difference?

The Mindful-Promise

This chapter explores the notion that "*Mindfulness has the power to change the world, one person at a time, from the inside out*" (attributed to Joseph Goldstein).

The mindful-promise shifts the focus of **WHAT** we need to change to transform the world for the better. Sustainable development focuses on change for good, but sustainability theory and practice traditionally prioritize the outer, ecological, social, economic and technological dimensions of change. While such approaches have generated many innovative ideas (e.g., ending subsidies to fossil-fuels to support renewable energy), they usually only address external conditions. This outward focus is crucial, but we believe that it is only part of a deeper story. We argue that leading with integrity for a sustainable future needs to explore the "inner dimensions" of change.

These inner dimensions are the innate human faculties of mind, heart and will and their powers of consciousness, aspiration and intention. We rarely examine the content of our thoughts, longings and purposes in the sustainability context and lack an understanding of their role in manifesting and shaping external conditions. Inner change involves discovering the power of these innate faculties and aligning them to higher, universal ideals of truth, beauty and goodness. We are not alone in proposing the need for engaging these inner dimensions and cultivating higher values. There is a growing sense that this interior work might provide the missing link in the quest for a sustainable future; see Box 2.1.

The mindful-promise proposes radically different technologies for **HOW** to change the world. It emphasizes the role of contemplative practices in transforming individuals, organizations and systems, rather than promoting technical fixes, economic reforms or political revolutions. Mindfulness, which is a form of meditation, has been defined as *"paying attention, on purpose, in the present moment, non-judgmentally"*.[7] The word describes engagement in a practice, as well as a cultivated state of awareness. Mindfulness techniques provide a key for opening the door to deeper levels of consciousness and presence, and for bringing the transformative power of this awareness back into everyday life. However, we lack an in-depth understanding of how change takes place from the "inside-out".

The mindful-promise provides a fresh perspective on agency, or **WHO** changes the world, founded on the premise that transformation starts with the individual and then ripples out to effect change in the world. Individual-interior change involves people working on their deep, inner structures of attention, attitude and intention to develop conscious awareness, compassion and higher purpose. This is a prerequisite, and enabler of social change for good, which could not take root without it. While the internal dimensions of human experience have long been studied (e.g., psychology and leadership), we lack theories and insights to help understand the connections between the individual-inner dimensions of change and organizational or wider systems change (see Box 2.1).

Box 2.1 Propositions

I used to think the top environmental problems were biodiversity loss, ecosystem collapse and climate change. I thought that with 30 years of good science we could address these problems. But I was wrong. The top environmental problems are selfishness, greed and apathy. And to deal with these we need a spiritual and cultural transformation. And we scientists don't know how to do that.

(Speth, 2013)

Without deep change on yourself, how will you avoid re-creating your own internalized oppression in all that you do? So often we see the same abuses of power, the same organizational dysfunctions among social change activists as in the institutions they seek to change. Unless we have also done transformational work on ourselves, we will remain products of the very same civilization we seek to transform. We need to change our habits of thought, beliefs and doing as well as change our systems. Each reinforces the other.

(Eisenstein, 2013)

In the past, changing the self and changing the world were often regarded as separate endeavours and viewed in either-or terms. But in the story of the Great Turning, they are recognized as mutually reinforcing and essential to one another.

(Macy and Johnstone, 2012)

The mindful-promise underpins our proposition that leaders who realize the benefits of contemplative practices, and introduce mindfulness into organizations and projects, help catalyze positive changes in cultures, which may provoke changes in macro-economic systems.

We explore the benefits and challenges of adopting mindfulness practices; how change from the "inside-out" is experienced at the level of Self, Organization and System (SOS) and their interconnections. We draw on recent conversations with ten well-established leaders: five women and five men from four continents who have a personal mindfulness practice and who are introducing mindfulness into various organizational and system-change initiatives. The quotes in double italics, and in the boxes, are drawn from these interviews.

Overview of Mindfulness

Mindfulness has its roots in the contemplative practices of many of the world's wisdom traditions, including mainstream religions—Vedanta/Hinduism, Buddhism, Judaism, Christianity and Islam. These provide inspiration and practices for inner transformation and harmonious living. In its current form, mindfulness is most closely related to the self-observation techniques of Buddhist meditation, although it is also an inherent human capacity,[8] outside any particular religion.

Mindfulness includes both formal and informal practices. Techniques include focusing on breath and body sensations; labeling emotions and attitudes; witnessing thoughts; deep listening; deep looking; and compassion training, as well as mindfulness of everyday activities such as eating, walking and bathing. Such techniques reduce "automatic-pilot" reactions, draw attention to layers of conditioning and connect to deeper sources of knowing and being.

There are thousands of scientific studies assessing the effects of mindfulness,[9] indicating how it positively affects brain structure and function. Research into brain neuroplasticity reveals the brain as more flexible, adaptable and resilient than previously thought. Even short periods of mindfulness can have significant impacts on attitudes and behaviors and alter epigenetics.[10]

Mindfulness is the basis of many new streams of clinical practice and research, such as Mindfulness-Based Stress Reduction (MBSR)[11] and Mindfulness-Based Cognitive Therapy (MBCT),[12] where it is known to reduce anxiety, stress, depression, pain and chronic illness and to boost the immune system.

Human-centered development initiatives, such as the "U Lab" projects facilitated by faculty at MIT, Boston, "Caring Economics" at the Max Planck Institute and some "Engaged Buddhist" projects also integrate mindful approaches. Mindfulness and compassion training affect motivation, emotion and social cognition, shaping more caring models of economic decision-making.

Mindfulness also serves leadership development[13] and organizational performance. It improves concentration, focus, resilience, creativity, emotional intelligence and productivity. However, the instrumentalist adoption of mindfulness, where it is coopted to serve business as usual, is controversial, and this is critically explored by Purser et al. in Chapter 4.

An Integral Perspective

"Integral theory"[14] offers a useful approach to exploring links between mindfulness and personal, organizational and systems change for sustainability. It provides a comprehensive map—known as the Integral Framework—of major disciplinary areas relating to any theme or issue. Through integral theory, disciplines that are usually isolated from each other can be considered together to address particular issues and challenges holistically.

At its simplest level, the Integral Framework proposes four lenses of analysis on different but important dimensions of reality. These Four Quadrants, include the "I", "It", "We" and "Its", which reveal the "interiors" and "exteriors" of individuals and collectives; see Figure 2.1. These areas are traditionally studied under different disciplines. The quadrants are not rigid categories; rather, they offer unique ways of looking at the same thing, revealing different dimensions and interconnections.[15]

Used to analyze sustainable development, the Framework reveals that most sustainable development theory has privileged the ecological, social and economic aspects of reality, or "systems", in the Lower Right quadrant.[16] Even the most influential and progressive sustainability literature neglects the psychological dimensions of change in the Upper Left quadrant. Thus, there is a gap in our understanding of how the "I" dimension functions, how the dynamics between the quadrants are framed and how they interact in particular contexts.

Our conversations with leaders provided insights into the dynamics between these quadrants. Or in integral theory terms, how "I" mindful practices are involved in, and influence the "It", "We" (organizations) and "Its" (systems) in relation to leading with integrity for a sustainable future.

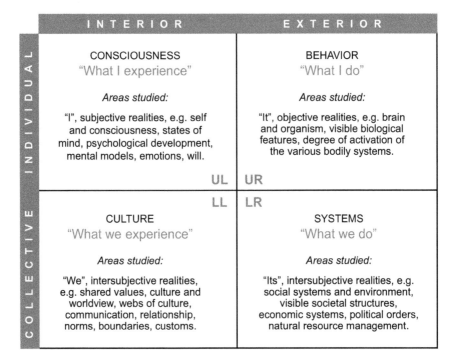

	INTERIOR	EXTERIOR
INDIVIDUAL	**CONSCIOUSNESS** "What I experience" *Areas studied:* "I", subjective realities, e.g. self and consciousness, states of mind, psychological development, mental models, emotions, will. UL	**BEHAVIOR** "What I do" *Areas studied:* "It", objective realities, e.g. brain and organism, visible biological features, degree of activation of the various bodily systems. UR
COLLECTIVE	LL **CULTURE** "What we experience" *Areas studied:* "We", intersubjective realities, e.g. shared values, culture and worldview, webs of culture, communication, relationship, norms, boundaries, customs.	LR **SYSTEMS** "What we do" *Areas studied:* "Its", intersubjective realities, e.g. social systems and environment, visible societal structures, economic systems, political orders, natural resource management.

Figure 2.1 The Four Quadrants of Integral Theory

Transforming Self

This section focuses on the "I" quadrant of integral theory. It highlights the subjective experience of mindfulness; how it alters states of mind, heart and will and transforms our relationships with others.

The leaders we interviewed use many different techniques, including both formal and informal practices (see section 3), and meditate for between a few minutes to several hours. However, whatever the type or length of practice, leaders find it essential to commit to regular daily practice. As one put it: "*It's like training my mindful muscle. Having a regular practice helps me through the bad times as well as the good. Even when I least feel like it, spending time in meditation helps me come back to my centre, and see things in a non-judgmental way, making it easier for me to cope with personal challenges. If I didn't practise everyday, I think I would lose the ability to get back to my still centre*" (INT.9).

A key benefit of mindfulness is often described as "*waking up from automatic pilot*". This involves standing back from particular thoughts, emotions or situations, and taking the time and space to skillfully respond, rather than react. It has been described as "*time slowing down*" (INT.7); "*being able to witness emerging thoughts and emotions*" (INT.3); and being aware of one's *"buttons getting pushed"* (INT.7). It is considered a huge step forward to be able: *"to look at their own experiences . . . and just ask the question what am I thinking? What's my relationship to my thinking?"* (INT.4). Being able to create a space between stimulus and response—the "sacred pause"—offers a moment of freedom from particular thoughts, wherein new solutions and less damaging reactions to oneself and others can emerge.

While some leaders highly value formal meditation practice, or *"sitting on the cushion"* (INT.7), others choose to focus on mindfulness in everyday life (eating, walking, bathing, etc.). As Jon Kabat-Zinn says, *"life becomes the Curriculum"*. For most practitioners embodying mindfulness in day-to-day routines, particularly in encounters with others, was the challenging *"growing edge of practice"*. One reflected that it boils down to *"how do I treat my wife? Or how do I relate to my son when he tells me something I don't like?"* (INT.4). Another agreed that: *"Meditating on the cushion is easy, practising off the cushion is more challenging"* (INT. 2).

One long-term meditator stressed that mindfulness is not well understood, particularly within corporate settings, and that without an ethical dimension and right intention, mindfulness may become *"attention training"* (INT.2), which can be used for unethical ends. Thus, mindfulness practices need to be balanced with compassion or loving-kindness practices (see Box 2.2).

Several leaders recognized that practising mindfulness can be quite disturbing at first: *"when you start meditating, it is deeply uncomfortable, and actually makes you much more agitated . . . you start to notice all the things you're doing . . . your impact and . . . what you do. I found that very hard . . . I think it's one of the obstacles people have around meditation"* (INT.6)

Box 2.2   Balancing Mindfulness With Compassion Practices

Mindfulness practice and compassion practice are not the same. They are two different practices, and I think they have to be combined. Ultimately, if you come to a very high level of true mindfulness, then not only have you trained your attention, but you are also aware of the consequences of your actions; aware of what happens inside you and around you. You start to see the effect of 'karma' and things like that. But it takes a long time for people to achieve this level of awareness—where they can really have a perception of what the consequences of their actions on the world and others will be. While if you train mindfulness and compassion in parallel, you lay an ethical foundation of the right intention. Because a lot of it has to do with intention. . . . Somebody may start practising mindfulness with the intention to be more efficient at doing something wrong. . . . A sniper has to be very mindful; otherwise he will miss his target. . . . So a sniper has fantastic concentration but it's not linked with an altruistic compassion motivation.

(INT.2)

Some noticed meditation changed their sense of "self" over time; their *"egos calmed down"* (INT.1), they were *"less reactive"*, *"less blaming of others"* (INT.3). They recognized how previously, their *"aversions, cravings, and attachments had made them feel more secure or important"* (INT.1). Mindfulness helped them overcome what some described as the traits and patterns of *"the insecure ego"* (INT.1). Many spoke of becoming more forgiving and accepting of themselves and others (INT.3). These observations resonate with Mabey's idea that integrity and moral power may be derived from reduced defensiveness, discussed in Chapter 3.

Many leaders mentioned a growing appreciation of nature. Long-term practitioners report that as concentration stabilizes, consciousness expands into an awareness of the interdependent nature of existence. One practitioner explained: *"this does not mean that there is no experience of 'self' anymore. Rather there is a distinction between being egotistical and self-centred, and having strong self-consciousness, which is more altruistic, compassionate and aware of connections with other beings"* INT.2)

Greater awareness and compassion, fostered through mindfulness, may translate into better relationships. Mindfulness cultivates listening skills, more thoughtful use of language, greater understanding of others' difficulties, forgiveness as well as a stronger sense of interdependence. Improving relationships through mindful practices is challenging; does not happen overnight; requires dedication and discipline and the integration of formal practices into the "tests of life". Indeed, it is practicing in real-life situations that creates transformational moments, which bring to life abstract concepts.

To summarize, self-transformation, or the *"definite need to sort yourself out first"* (INT.4), establishes the essential foundations for human wellbeing and for leading with integrity.

Transforming Organizations

This section relates to the "We" quadrant of integral theory. It explores some motivations, experiences and challenges of bringing mindfulness into the workplace. Mindfulness in the "We" quadrant goes beyond *"getting one's own house in order"* to *"taking it on the road"* (INT.5).

Several leaders were motivated to introduce mindfulness into their workplaces after realizing personal benefits they wanted colleagues to experience, particularly to help them cope with workplace stress (INT.5). However, several respondents faced resistance and put this down to false preconceptions about mindfulness (INT.5). The language of mindfulness usually has to be adapted to particular audiences, and leaders are often careful to make it secular and avoid words like "meditation" in program descriptions (INT.7). However, making it more appealing to business *"risks it becoming a means to end"* and getting coopted *"to serve business as usual"* (INT.8).

Some leaders have delivered formal mindfulness programs within their organizations, such as an eight-week face-to-face MBSR program within a

University (INT.8); an eight-week bespoke mindfulness program for leaders within a corporation (using the internet to convene participants remotely) (INT.7); or a week-long face-to-face, business-leaders program at a government institution (INT.2). Organizers highlighted how the development and delivery of such programs involve much thought, time and commitment: arranging logistics, venue, technologies, cost structures, advertising, preparatory health interviews and/or questionnaires with participants and the development of course materials, including feedback surveys.

Participants in formal programs reported multiple benefits: less anxiety, better sleep, improved family and work relationships, improved focus, creativity and performance. However, formal programs generate a number of common challenges for course participants; "*some are so agitated they can't sit still*" (INT.8); others find the inner experience emotionally challenging, and drop out (INT.7). Some "*expect a quick-fix*" (INT.7) and are disappointed when they don't get it and stop practicing. Others challenge the course format, and the length of sessions. Leaders needed to continually adapt without losing the essential program objectives.

Some took a different approach, integrating mindfulness into everyday work practices, rather than introducing formal sessions (see Box 3.3)

Box 3.3 Mindful Work

A lot of what I teach from a mindfulness perspective is very much about: How do you bring this into your day? How do you use informal practice even if you never sit on the cushion? How do you have mindful-meetings? How do you eat mindfully? How do you walk mindfully? This is stuff you have to do anyway, so you may as well do it mindfully. And if this is all you do, that's a big shift. . . . So while some people are purists . . . I'm not like that at all. I'm literally like one minute, when you sit in a meeting: 'sit, feel into your feet, feel your hands'. That's mindfulness you know, cultivating that tiny bit of awareness every single day.

(INT.6)

In the corporate environment, it's 'how do I make it simple? How do I make it accessible? How do I bake it into their lives?' It's organic as opposed to: 'Here's one more thing that you have to do. You're supposed to go to the gym. You're supposed to eat healthily. You're supposed to have everything done. . . . Let's put another thing on the end of your "to do list"'. People respond by saying 'I'm sorry—but I don't have time to meditate'. And I say: 'You have to eat, right, so just eat mindfully. You have to go from meeting to meeting, so just walk mindfully. You go to meetings, you sit down, just take a breath mindfully that's all you have to do, I'm not asking you to add one more thing on your 'to do list'.

(INT.6)

Integrating mindful-approaches into meetings can help create more spacious, respectful and constructive exchanges. Adopting enquiry-based approaches and modeling mindful attitudes in group encounters (rather than imposing points of view or ways of behaving) can help create a safe environment in which people find *"the space to grow for themselves"* (INT.3). It can be frustrating for those who expect answers and to be told how to behave, but such exchanges are often transformative for both individuals and organizations.

Mindfulness also helps leaders cultivate inner strengths and new behaviours. It enables them to observe their patterns when facing challenging situations, to set personal boundaries, have more assertive conversations, deal with interpersonal problems and make difficult ethical choices. Some leaders mentioned that dealing with these outer problems is an ongoing process that is never ultimately resolved, because each new situation generates different challenges. One leader emphasized that *"ethics is not always about being nice"*, but *"doing the right thing"* (INT.4), which can be tough and requires courage.

Introducing mindfulness and compassion practices into business can be provocative, since it may challenge dominant corporate cultures or be seen as threatening to the corporate work ethic. For example, some employees resisted practices that *"fly in the face of the received wisdom that you have to be ruthlessly competitive to get ahead in the 'dog-eat-dog' corporate world"* (INT.6).

To summarize, bringing mindfulness into work, either formally or informally, can generate many personal and collective benefits. It can also transform dominant corporate cultures. However, there are also many challenges in bringing it into work, and it risks getting coopted to promote "business as usual".

Transforming Systems

This section highlights the "Systems" quadrant of the Integral Framework or in integral theory terms, "how the I and We influence the Its". It examines how social and economic problems and solutions are understood from the standpoint of consciousness or mind and explores the implications for system change projects.

Some leaders reflected that they had not considered the impact of mindfulness on macro-level systems (INT. 5); others saw obvious connections between self, organization and systems transformation (INT.3). Practically, people talk about mindfulness influencing their food choices, their consumption habits, their waste disposal, the type of work they do and their relationships with nature. All these choices have an effect on wider systems.

Philosophically, mindfulness is rooted in ancient theories of consciousness that give the mind a role in shaping matter. For example, in contrast to the scientific materialism of much western philosophy and science—which assumes that matter is the only reality and that the mind is merely an epiphenomenon of the brain—Buddhism sees the world from the point of view of the phenomenology of consciousness. Some adherents regard life as the creation of the mind and the body as a form of materialized consciousness.[17] In other words, it is mind that creates matter, rather than vice versa. Significantly, post-materialist science is also rediscovering the links between mind and body and the importance of these connections in the conscious evolution of human civilization.[18]

This focus on consciousness has significant implications for how sustainability challenges and opportunities are framed. If material problems are manifestations of the mind, the most profound way of changing them is to change the consciousness. From a Buddhist perspective, the main drivers of unsustainability are "the three poisons of the mind": ignorance, greed and fear. These need be transformed, through mindfulness, into their opposites: wisdom, contentment and compassion. Interestingly, this perspective chimes with systems-theorists who claim that one of the most powerful levers of systems change is changing "mindsets".[19] Changing mindsets is considered more powerful than transforming anything else in a system, such as resource flows, incentives or metrics (see Box 2.4)

This inner focus also had profound implications for understanding the purpose of the economy itself. While the goal of Western economics is to increase growth, measured by GDP, Buddhist economics seeks to increase human happiness and well-being over time. These reflect contrasting means and ends. In Western economics, people are seen as the means and the increasing value of goods and services as the ends. In Buddhist economics, this instrumentality is reversed; the economy exists to serve the people, and not the people to serve the economy. Development is about people and not about objects.

One leader explained how the Buddhist theory of causality (sometimes called co-dependent arising) makes a link between personal mindful practice and wider systems change. According to this theory, everything in existence is interrelated; everything continually changes and conditions everything else. Mindfulness enables practitioners to see the bigger picture, to bring awareness to the destructive tendencies of prevailing mindsets and values

---

Box 2.4   Change the Consciousness, Change the System

Buddhist psychology starts from the inside-out. It begins with the mind, viewing any system or structure as a projection of consciousness. Economic systems, political systems or social systems, are not God-given; they are products of human consciousness and human interaction. As such, they reflect the way we think, speak, behave, and relate. Therefore, any change in structure that is not connected to a change in consciousness, will not have a long-lasting effect. You can have a revolution, but it just means that another elite is on top. . . . The new regime can have different names and forms, but basically things like exploitation or inequality, do not change, if the consciousness hasn't changed.

(INT.2)

on systems (INT.1). The ability to envision new, more harmonious forms of development emerges from purified intentions and higher purpose.

The emphasis on *"starting from the inside"* also informs several secular streams of new economics. To some, the history of the economy and of modern economic thought is the product of an evolving human consciousness. We need a new economic framework and narrative that is based on transforming the patterns of economic action and thought from "ego-system to eco-system awareness".[20] However, we cannot transform systems unless we transform the quality and awareness applied to actions within these systems.

Theory U, a social change process developed by faculty at MIT in Boston,[21] facilitates groups to co-sense and co-create solutions to particular system problems. It uses "open mind, open heart, and open will" techniques, which help people reclaim their attention and intention and enable them to be more fully present in the moment. Such techniques draw attention to habitual patterns of individual and collective consciousness and behaviors that reproduce current negative system conditions. They help shift the inner places from which people operate, allowing them to outgrow habitual ways of thinking and reacting that are no longer effective. Such practices help evolve new mindsets, values and skills that are needed to develop wiser, more creative outcomes and may help shift system conditions as a whole.

Conclusion

In conclusion, we offer some reflections on the implications of the mindful-promise for leading with integrity for a sustainable future.

Leading With Integrity

If practiced diligently mindfulness facilitates deep reflection and generates self-awareness—of body, thoughts, emotions, and intentions, and how these shape behaviors. Mindfulness highlights the impermanence of thoughts, emotions and even pain, expressed in phrases such as *"you are not your thoughts"* or *"thoughts are not facts"*. Growing awareness helps liberate from old reactive patterns, and patiently removes layers of psychological and social conditioning. It fosters greater equanimity, presence and resilience and creates the space for innovation. Combined with compassion practices, mindfulness enhances emotional intelligence, helping leaders relate more skillfully to others. We believe that these characteristics are essential ingredients of leading with integrity.

We also offer another perspective on leading with integrity. In addition to its ethical dimension, *integrity* implies *integrating* self, organization and system perspectives, or "seeing the bigger picture" and "connecting the dots" between leadership decisions and their effects on wider systems. The Integral Framework is a guide to understanding the dynamics between mindfulness at the level of self, organization and system. However, more research is required to understand these dynamics in detail, and to model these connections in the context of the mindful-promise.

Contribution to a Sustainable Future

The "mindful-promise" clearly embodies a very different approach, with a number of new contributions and benefits for sustainable development.

- Philosophical: Mindfulness highlights the role of "consciousness" in understanding systemic problems and solutions. It recognizes that sustainability problems are not "out there" but "in here". Social systems are seen not as fixed in immutable laws, but as products of the human mind, which can be changed.
- Planet: Practitioners report how mindfulness has influenced their consumption patterns as well as their connection to nature. Long-term practitioners speak of a profound experiential awareness of their interdependence with all beings.
- People: Practitioners report how their relationships have improved at home and at work. They develop more skillful ways of dealing with difficulties and are more likely to respond compassionately to people in need. Many leaders are involved in collaborative projects, which facilitate co-creative solutions from the bottom-up.
- Prosperity: Mindfulness helps draw attention to sub-conscious impulses and reactions, including fears, aversions, greed and craving that fuel destructive economic behaviors (e.g., the hedonistic treadmill). The cultivation of courage, equanimity and wisdom can provide powerful antidotes to these impulses, paving the way for new economic objectives and narratives to emerge (e.g. well-being economics).
- Power: Waking up from "automatic pilot" helps reveal the dominant mindsets and cultural stories, often supported by powerful vested interests, shaping current unsustainable systems. Some practitioners report that mindfulness leads them to challenge the status quo with alternative worldviews, within their organizations.
- Personal: Ultimately, mindfulness is a radical act. Mindfulness turns inwards, not outwards to find solutions. It harnesses the source of inner power to overcome destructive emotions and thoughts and to develop equanimity, wisdom and happiness—vital for healing and psychological well-being.

However, given the scale and urgency of the global sustainability challenges, it is legitimate to ask whether we have time to "change the world, one person at a time, from the inside out". We argue that personal transformation is a missing dimension of sustainability theory and practice and that outer changes need to arise from inner ones for lasting transformation. However, mindfulness on its own is not enough. Change must happen simultaneously from the inside-out, and the outside-in, mutually reinforcing each other.

Finally, our research suggests that transformations at the level of Self—Organization—System are interconnected, co-creative, co-emergent and co-evolutionary. Transformation of these domains can be encapsulated in the acronym "SOS"—an urgent "cry for help". We propose SOS as a radical, cutting edge approach to leading with integrity, for a sustainable future.

Personal Reflections

Our UK University motto was "Do Different". As students we often pondered on the grammatical correctness of this motto, but nevertheless recognized its call to "have the courage of your convictions". We valued "Do Different" not for the sake of just being different, but as a prerequisite for stepping out of the crowd to work for a higher purpose—which usually involved courage to do things very differently.

Courage has a fascinating etymology. It stems from the Latin "cor", meaning "heart", and is implicit in the French word for heart, "coeur". The English word courage comes from the old French "corage". It embodies the idea of "whole-heartedness"; the idea of involving the heart, mind and will in action. Definitions of courage usually explain it as action in the face of danger. As Mark Twain says: "Courage is not the absence of fear, but it is action in spite of it".

The world's Ancient Wisdom Traditions are another source of insight into courage as well as other key attributes of leadership. In the Chinese Taoist Tao-Teh canon, Chapter 67, it outlines The Three Treasures of Tao:

> *I have three treasures which I prize and hold fast.*
> *The first is called compassion.*
> *The second is called economy.*
> *The third is called humility.*
>
> *Through compassion I exhibit courage.*
> *Through economy I can freely give.*
> *Through humility I become a vessel for the highest honor.*
>
> *But men forsake compassion and seek courage.*
> *They forsake economy and seek profusion.*
> *They forsake humility and seek precedence.*
> *The end of such is death.*

The second quote is from the Indian spiritual text, *The Bhagavad Gita*:

> If you want to see the courageous, look to those who can return love for hatred. If you want to see the heroic, look to those who can forgive.

The wisdom traditions emphasize that the profound roots of leadership qualities, such as courage, generosity and honor, are fruits of living a life in conformity with an ideal, rather than as goals themselves. They are, paradoxically, associated with self-forgetting, rather than self-aggrandizement, and are cultivated through altruistic service, rather than selfishness.

But how does one free oneself from one's ego-centeredness in order to be open to a deeper wisdom? From our own experience, within the context of the *Mindful Promise*, we have discovered that it takes real courage to "look within". Far from being a "fluffy", self-indulgent activity, mindful practices require stoical courage to sit and observe one's uncomfortable thoughts, emotions, sufferings and inner demons with equanimity, without getting caught up in them, ruminating or walking away. Acknowledging and transmuting the suffering we have inflicted on others and ourselves, as well as that which others have inflicted on us, requires courage and persistent practice. While mindful practices gradually deepen our perspectives, resilience, and compassion, results are not achieved overnight.

Similarly, we have found that *Leading with Integrity for a Sustainable Future* and trying to make a difference "out there", despite continual setbacks, requires persistent effort and a certain amount of courage. We have been fortunate to volunteer and engage in the field of sustainable development for over 30 years, in Asia, Africa and Europe. And we have worked on a diversity of projects including sustainable forest management, community forestry, nature conservation and business management education, co-founding the One Planet MBA. But have the trees survived? Are the local communities any better off? Is nature now valued and protected? Are new business leaders adopting one planet approaches? Has the original vision and intention been maintained? Yes, sometimes but certainly not in all cases. It is hard not to be discouraged by disappointment and failure, to let go of success and to resist the compulsion to shape outcomes.

Perhaps one of the hardest lessons we have to learn is spiritual "impartiality", that is, non-attachment to outcomes, rather than the kind of impartiality that is unfeeling or uncaring. To us, this requires a subtle kind of courage. Yes, it requires whole-hearted commitment to a higher good, implied by our earlier definition; but paradoxically, it suggests the wisdom of knowing when *not* to act and of letting things be. It implies *inaction* in action; *non-doing* in doing.

Spiritual impartiality acknowledges that we are not in control of everything. It lets the higher purpose or intention of a work prevail, and resists the impulse to unnecessarily interfere and mold the results. It doesn't get caught up in the effects, and has faith that ultimately, all things will be turned to the Good. This is the wisdom of Wu Wei, of non-striving, or the Middle Path, which is an important balance to the focus on the courage of action. For many busy and agitated leaders, such a perspective implies a need to "Be" different, as well as "Do Different".

> Actions affect not Me, neither in Me is there desire for action's fruit: he who knows Me thus, is not bound by works. He whose every effort is free from the impulse of desire, whose work is transformed by the fire of wisdom, he is called enlightened by the wise. There is no purifier like unto wisdom in all this world, and he who seeketh it, shall find it—being grown perfect—verily in himself.
>
> Bhagavad Gita

Annex 1 Ten Interviews with Mindful Meditation Practitioners 2016

INT	Role	Country	Gender	Years of Practice
1.	Sustainability academic working in a University*	Australia	F	10+
2.	Program Director of a Government Institute*	Bhutan	M	40+
3.	Psychologist working in a University	Ireland	F	6+
4.	Founder and Co-Director of a Mindfulness Training Center*	Spain	M	30+
5.	Foreign Service Mental Health Practitioner	USA (in Iraq)	M	5+
6.	Business Consultant and Leadership Coach	Ireland	F	10+
7.	Business Consultant in Leadership Development	UK	M	18 months
8.	Company Director of Sustainability Business	UK	F	30+
9.	Senior Advisor for a Global NGO	Switzerland	M	30+
10.	Communications Director of a Government Institution	Puerto Rico	F	2

*Buddhist Mindfulness practitioner

Notes

1. Jeanrenaud et al. (2017).
2. WWF (2016).
3. Scharmer and Kaufer (2013).
4. Oxfam (2017).
5. Korten (2010).
6. WHO (2014).
7. Kabat-Zinn (1991).
8. The Mindfulness Initiative (2016).
9. Brown et al. (2007).
10. Davidson et al. (2003).
11. Kabat-Zinn (1991).
12. Segal et al. (2013).
13. Marturano (2015).
14. Wilber (1997).
15. In addition to the quadrants, the AQAL (All Quadrants All Levels) Integral Framework includes development levels (or stages of development); development lines (intelligences), states (of consciousness) and types (e.g., personality or gender types). The other elements are not explored in this chapter.
16. Brown (2005).
17. Govinda (1960).
18. Beauregard et al. (2014).
19. Meadows (1999).
20. Scharmer and Kaufer (2013).
21. Ibid.

Bibliography

Beauregard, M., Schartz, G.E., Miller, M., Dossey, L., Moreira-Ameida, A., Schlitz, M., Sheldrake, R. and Tart, C. (2014) Manifesto for a post-materialist science. *Explore: The Journal of Science and Healing* 10(5), pp. 272–274.

Brown, B.C. (2005) Theory and practice of integral sustainable development: An overview. *AQAL Journal* 1(2), Spring.

Brown, K.W., Ryan, R.M. and Creswell, J.D. (2007) Mindfulness: Theoretical foundations and evidence of its saluatary effects. *Psychological Inquiry* 18, pp. 211–237.

Davidson, R.D., Kabat-Zinn, J., Schumacher, J., Rosenkranz, M., Muller, D., Santorelli, S.F., Urbanowski, E., Harrington, A., Bonus, K. and Sheridan, J.F. (2003) Alterations in brain and immune function produced by mindfulness meditation. *Psychosomatic Medicine* 65, p. 564.

Eisenstein, C. (2013) *The More Beautiful World Our Hearts Know Is Possible*. Berkley, CA: North Atlantic Books.

Govinda, L.A. (1960) *Foundations of Tibetan Mysticism*. London: Rider and Company.

Jeanrenaud, S., Jeanrenaud, J.-P. and Gosling, J. (2017) *Sustainable Business: A One Planet Approach*. Chichester, UK: Wiley.

Kabat-Zinn, J. (1991) *Full Catastrophe Living: Using the Wisdom of Your Body and Mind to Face Stress, Pain, and Illness*. New York: Bantam Books.

Korten, D. (2010) *Agenda for a New Economy: From Phantom Wealth to Real Wealth*. San Francisco: Berrett-Koehler.

Macy, J. and Johnstone, C. (2012) *Active Hope: How to Face the Mess We're in Without Going Crazy*. Novato, CA: New World Library.

Marturano, J. (2015) *Finding the Space to Lead: A Practical Guide to Mindful Leadership*. London: Bloomsbury Press.

Meadows, D. (1999) *Leverage Points: Places to Intervene in a System*. Hartland, VT: The Sustainability Institute.

The Mindfulness Initiative. (2016) *Building the Case for Mindfulness in the Workplace: The Mindfulness Initiative*. Private Sector Working Group. Available from: www.themindfulnessinitiative.org.uk

Oxfam. (2017) *An Economy for the 99%*. Oxfam Briefing Paper, January 2017.

Scharmer, O. and Kaufer, K. (2013) *Leading From the Emerging Future: From Ego-System to Eco-System Economies. Applying Theory U to Transforming Business, Society and Self*. San Francisco: Berrett-Koehler Publishers.

Segal, Z., Williams, J.M.G. and Teasdale, J.D. (2013) *Mindfulness-Based Cognitive Therapy for Depression*. New York: The Guildford Press.

Speth, G. (2013) *Former Dean Professor, Yale School of Forestry and Environmental Studies, USA*.

WHO. (2014) *Preventing Suicide: A Global Imperative*. Geneva: World Health Organization.

Wilber, K. (1997) An integral theory of consciousness. *Journal of Consciousness Studies* 4(1), pp. 71–92.

WWF. (2016) *Living Planet Report 2016: Risk and Resilience in a New Era*. Gland, Switzerland: WWF.

3 Can Ethical Leadership Be Developed?

Chris Mabey

Key Questions

How effective are conventional leadership development methods in building ethical leadership?
How might mindfulness assist?
What could a greater awareness of spirituality bring to the process of leading with integrity?

Introduction

With a few exceptions, managers do not drive to work with the avowed intention of making life hell for their staff. Leaders rarely sit down to devise strategies to demotivate those they lead. Yet workplaces are commonly experienced as inhuman, de-spiriting and even hurtful places by the people who work there. Senior executives (like those at FIFA, VW, WorldCom) presumably set out with plans to be judicious and prosper the organizations they are entrusted with, yet by the close of play on some days, they have become complicit in dubious activities, fraud, malfeasance, nepotism and the like. How can we explain this, and does this have to be the story of all leaders?

Commonplace though such scandals have become, it seems to me that conventional, and even critical, leadership theories are struggling to lay the basis for the practice of ethical leadership in organizational life. Well-packaged remedies, often academically endorsed, come and go in the world of leadership, but little appears to change in the corridors of power. Indeed, the corruptible nature of power by those in senior roles (whether corporate or political) becomes ever more flagrant and breath-taking. But this is not simply a theoretical issue to be debated in the MBA classroom, it also has become a personal and increasingly urgent imperative for me. Over the years as I have worked in a variety of organizations: as a counselor with a charity, as an organizational psychologist with British Telecom and Rank

Xerox and, latterly, as a teacher and researcher of leadership at several UK business schools. As I reflect on these episodes of my career, I admit to often being disappointed not only with the ethical behavior of others but also with myself. Ok, this has not been at the level of a Lehman Brothers or Ponsi scandal. But there have been times where I have allowed dubious work practices to go unchallenged, where I have colluded in ill-conceived strategies, where I have not spoken up when others were treated unfairly, where I have somehow compartmentalized things, such that I say one thing but do another. To put this is in more noble language: like many others, I have frequently failed to live up to standards of ethical practice that, in a public forum we would probably all agree to be beneficial to healthy organisations and sustainable society. In this chapter, I want to confront this lack of congruency in myself. I hope it will help you do likewise.

First, I explore mindfulness as an alternative approach to developing self- and other-awareness as a step towards more ethical leading. This takes us away from more skills-oriented and technique-based leadership development to a focus on our bodies and spirits. Then, I explore what a greater awareness of spirituality might bring to the process of leading with integrity, specifically adopting a Judeo-Christian lens. In the last section, I reflect on what this means for me in my day-to-day work.

What Does Mindfulness Have to Offer Us as Developing Leaders?

Mindfulness might be defined as being more *fully aware of my own experience in the present moment in a non-judgmental way*. Immediately we see that how each aspect of this way of being runs counter to the grain of post-modern living. First, *awareness* suggests becoming more intentional, choiceful and resisting the urge to respond to situations in unconscious autopilot, to make knee jerk decisions or to default into habitual patterns of response. Mindfulness moves us to a mode of waking up, by coming—literally—to our senses and seeing afresh what was always there. Second is the immediacy of *experience*: to counter the brain's tendency to over-analyze at the expense of our visceral emotions and inquisitive spirits and to learn a different way of perceiving and attuning to what is in and around us. Then thirdly is the notion of *the present moment*: many of us are so consumed by past history and missed opportunities, or conversely, anxious and agitated about what is to come next week or next month that we miss the pleasure of enjoying, tasting, savoring what is right here now. Finally, the *non-judgmental* aspect is important, as in our hurry to state an opinion or rationalize, there is a tendency to repress deeper issues—like emotional wounding, shame and embarrassment—which, if surfaced, make them available for healing.

One reason why I am not confident that a lot of leadership development really delivers on its promise of producing effective and ethical leaders is that the methods, techniques and approaches of much training and development fail to account for our human condition, a basic condition which is exacerbated, I believe, by the post-modern age in which we live and work. It is here that mindfulness can be so helpful and, as a Christian believer, I find a reassuring connection between taking a mindful approach and practising my personal faith. Perhaps I should not be surprised at this since there has been a long and rich contemplative dimension in the Christian tradition, influenced to be sure by Eastern spirituality.[1] For me, this begins to bring together some of the loose ends and address some of the unfulfilled promise of much-hyped leadership development initiatives.[2] So in this section, I aim to explore the potential contribution of mindfulness to the way we develop as leaders. This is built on the premise that as humans we are constantly prone to divide, to disaggregate and to compartmentalize our lives.[3] There are at least four ways in which this propensity to divide manifests itself.[4]

We Divide Ourselves From Ourselves

At one level, it seems entirely natural to compartmentalize our lives. It helps us avoid internal interrogation, repress that which is uncomfortable and promote the more pleasing parts of ourselves. So-called "celebrity" leaders often rely on image management, hashtag stories and the pretense or fiction that they are in control. We all have a tendency to separate our minds and bodies, placing more emphasis on the mind as real and evidence-based while relegating, even denying the material body as somehow inferior and our emotions as untrustworthy.[5]

There is no other place any of us can operate other than through the flesh and blood of our material bodies and no other way of living other than in and through the material world. This sounds obvious when we say it, but as the chapter by David Knights reminds us, so much activity in the workplace airbrushes out the body, reducing leadership to a series of cerebral calculations and skilled but impersonal transactions. Mindfulness places a strong emphasis on the body, not as something that is constraining my leadership awareness and frustrating my spiritual progress but as a place to be celebrated and honoured. As a Christian, inheriting a view of the flesh as somehow dubious and unreliable, this comes as both a revelation and a liberation. In recent years, I have learnt to validate and reconnect with my imagination and intuition more fully, recognizing that God reveres these as much, if not more than my intellect and theorizing. Rather than relegate my feelings, suppress my emotions and repress my instincts and drives, I am learning to listen to the signals they are sending. Some of these messages may be uncomfortable, surfacing insecurities and fears that have become buried. But it is only as they are exposed that the opportunity for healing can begin.[6]

We Divide Ourselves From Each Other

A common tenet of leadership skills development is to create an environment whereby we move from unconscious to conscious incompetence, which then acts a spur to become consciously—and, finally, unconsciously—competent. Mindfulness operates in a similar way, gradually allowing what is hidden and unconscious to become apparent to the conscious mind, *but at a far deeper level.* I begin to see that I have choices and that I am not at the mercy of events around me and/or the drives within. For example, my company may have an unwritten rule that work iPads stay on 24/7, or I may have an urge to take a work call during a family dinner. If, however, I have been working at developing my sense of awareness, I may become better at recognizing the inner voice, the first stirrings of this "compulsive behavior" such that the automatic pattern is at least questioned, if not overruled (see Box 3.1)[7]

We Divide Ourselves From the Rest of Nature

Another benefit of mindfulness is that it discourages us from elevating ourselves from that which is "not us", such that we spoil, exploit and damage the finely balanced ecosystem of which we are part. Jean-Paul and Sally Jeanrenaud expand on this more fully in Chapter 2. This is more than gathering information, or using my network for market intelligence; it involves entering another's world, not to exploit or position myself to influence or even to offer solutions. This is true empathy. One of the most powerful exercises I use in leadership development is also the simplest: active listening. Giving full, non-judgmental and compassionate attention to another has a profound affect. It builds trust, invites honesty and paves the way for disclosure. For those who believe in God, this is part of the divine gaze: the confidence that, for all my fickleness, my inability to retain perspective, my

---

Box 3.1   The Power of Noticing

In his book, *The Power of Noticing: What the Best Leaders See*, Max Bazerman notes that even with his expertise in behavioral psychology, he only recently realized that his own noticing skills were 'truly terrible'. '*Hired a few years ago as an expert witness for the Department of Justice in what was to be the largest-ever lawsuit against the tobacco industry, Bazerman says that just before he was due to testify, he felt pressured by the government to water down written testimony he had submitted to the court in which he recommended structural changes to the tobacco industry. While the request seemed odd and vaguely unsettled him, Bazerman, distracted by other stresses and uncertain whether the request was corrupt, didn't act on those feelings at the time. It wasn't until six weeks later, after reading that another expert in the case said that he too had been pressured to alter his testimony, that he realized he had failed to notice that the gravity of the situation — possible witness tampering — had called for decisive action*'.

tendency to get carried away with experience, God holds me in his gentle and sovereign gaze, seeing me from an eternal reference point, valuing every part of me as unique person he created and loving me without judgment. This is so different from the kind of prejudicial critique we so readily apply to others and even ourselves.

We Divide Ourselves From the Present

By allowing the past, with all its golden memories and successes as well as its regrets, mistakes and griefs, to crowd our current thoughts, we get distracted from the eternal now. Likewise, it is easy to become preoccupied with the plans, dreams, anxieties and fears of tomorrow. Why do I find it so hard to be truly present? I am trying to write a report that needs to be handed in tomorrow, I am in a meeting that is dragging on, I am in a tedious conversation with a colleague: in these moments, distracting thoughts crowd in to entice me away to a less taxing task (psychologists call this displacement and that literally is what happens, we get divorced or displaced from the present). Of course, it is tough to constantly remain rooted in the moment, fully attentive to the emotions and senses arising in ourselves and others. Not all daily encounters require this degree of focus. But think what might occur if we manage to retain an in-the-moment (or *gestalt*) stance. Perhaps our gut tells us that something is wrong, a sensory signal that the pending report is yet another step towards collusion in an ethically flawed strategy. The temptation is to suppress our unease and tell ourselves that it is not our place to question such matters (see Box 3.1 above). But a more mindful approach may lead me to register my discomfort perhaps by calling my boss or offering a constructive counter-proposal in the report. Or in the boring meeting I might "read" the collective mood and voice a proposal: "may I ask how many of us are energized by the current discussion?" In the colleague conversation, I may seek to switch from passive distraction to active engagement. I tune into the music behind their words. I refrain from judgment, seeking only to attune to the emotions they are expressing, verbally and non-verbally. Holding them in this non-censuring, affirmative and compassionate space allows them to get in touch with their deeper concerns.[8] All these examples may seem to be a long way from a traditional leadership development program, yet we can see that "staying present" might lead to some fresh discoveries for us and those around us which are insightful and empowering. And what is this if it is not learning to lead?

What Might a Spiritual Approach to Leadership Development Look Like?

So far, I have noted the moral vacuum among those leading in organizations and the apparent inability of conventional approaches to lay the basis for ethical leadership. This tallies with my own unease about the leadership development I have "delivered" (and consumed) over the years, as a corporate leadership developer, as a consultant and as a university tutor.[9] More recently this has prompted me to turn to mindfulness, not as a new method for training leadership, but rather as a way of creating reflective space. Indeed, it is self-evident that mindfulness cannot be taught; if the "teacher" does anything, it is not to impart knowledge, but it is to create a non-judmental environment of compassion which enables us to experience the present more deeply in everyday life.[10] This is a very different way of framing leadership development. It is not to decry the value of leadership skills training, of personal development plans and MBA theorizing, but to suggest that in order to get to the heart of ethical leadership, more reflective approaches are called for that engage our bodies and spirits (and not just our minds and digital diaries).

In the previous section, I observed how mindfulness paves the way for this, and here, I want to examine more closely the spiritual dimension that was alluded to. There are many spiritual resources we could refer to in this regard and several of these are pursued in this book. The one I choose as a lens here is the Judeo-Christian discourse. It is both vaguely familiar to many (in both East and West) and yet strangely neglected in discussions of leadership (especially in the West). It is my contention that the original wisdom, contained in the New Testament scriptures and embodied in the person of Jesus, speaks very powerfully and pertinently into current leadership debates. Let me briefly touch on four provocations.

Being Prepared to Be Misunderstood

A valuable contribution of critical theory is that it sensitizes us to the unequal distribution of power in organizations and how historically, institutionally and ideologically, social control is concentrated in the hands of a few leaders, such that dissent on the part of followers becomes untenable. Recent years have seen increasing being paid to so-called spiritual leadership theory; I can see that, along with the notions of "authentic leadership" and "caring leadership", this discourse can too easily become a way of effecting a subtle form of organizational control, aligning subjectivities with corporate interests and resulting in anxiety amongst individuals who struggle and fail to achieve its lofty ideals.[11] But here I am heartened when I return to the Christian source of spirituality;[12] far from promoting this elitist discourse, much of Jesus's teaching to his followers was to prepare them for being misunderstood and persecuted—by the totalising forces around them. It could be argued that far from being conformist, conservative and protecting of the status quo, Jesus taught and modelled a radical critique of corrupt practices with a strong agenda for supporting the voiceless. This was no empty treatise. Many of his followers went to their deaths for defying local religious and political authority (Jewish and Roman), and, of course, Jesus himself led by example. This kind of spiritual leadership applied to a work setting is the antithesis of a slavish obedience to overbearing managerial interests; rather, it emerges as level-headed and very reflexive leadership-followership with a keen attention to what is just, truthful and emancipating as issues arise.[13]

Being Vulnerable

A common lament of critics is that invoking spirituality involves a retreat from rational thinking. But this assumes that reason and spirituality are mutually incompatible. A more holistic spiritual approach, encouraged by mindfulness, sees every world-view or system of thought, philosophy or religion as beginning with some ultimate purpose or principle which shapes everything that follows.[14] Again, I cannot help seeing the modern relevance of comments by Jesus on the abuse of power by those around him at the time: "*Kings like to throw their weight around and people with authority like to give themselves fancy titles. It's not going to be that way with you. Let the senior among you become like the junior; let the leaders act the part of the servant*".[15,16] Here he turns popular conception of leadership and power on its head. In the place of a domineering style, he advocates an attitude of serving others; instead of the arrogance that accompanies seniority, he calls for the humility of youth (that recognizes it has much to learn) and states that true authority comes from inner convictions rather than outward status. The wisdom of this approach to leadership has long since been recognized by advocates of servant leadership[17] and those theorists who give more prominence to followership.

Re-Framing the Notion of Work

For much of my life I have regarded spirituality and the workplace as different worlds, so incommensurate that any intersection between them is purely incidental. But as I meditate on Jesus-centered wisdom, I find myself arriving at a different place. In my more mindful moments, I see human work (of all kinds, professional, domestic, caring,[18] recreational) as potentially reflective of God's work. At best, this mind-set will address the divisions referred to in section two above. First, the unhelpful compartmentalizing of private values and public work will begin to dissolve as I see my work (from a personal perspective) as creating things which have value and endure, and (from a planet perspective) as sustaining that which already exists and (from a relational perspective) as helping to redeem that which requires healing, reconciliation and repair.[19] This is, subtly but significantly, *not* a case of spirituality being pressed into the service of an organization's mission as a means to an end; rather it is a re-framing of work—and non-work—relationships and systems as the central issue, calling for them to be mutually respectful, creative and diversity-conscious. And, coming full circle, this will begin to constitute leadership development by another name . . . in the form of more effective, energized and ethical attitudes towards leading/following.

Pursuing an Other-Centered Ethic

How does all this speak to the morality and integrity of leadership and how contemporary firms, enterprises and networks organize themselves? On the one hand, we have well-established organizational forms like bureaucracy becoming increasingly outmoded and irrelevant; while these structures are often criticized as conservative and restrictive, the dismantling of them could lead to the disastrous weakening of positive values like accountability, loyalty and rule-governed action. On the other hand, we have more ambiguous, fragmented and structurally diverse "workspaces" populated by multiple actors and agencies, each pursuing partisan interests or market-driven agendas. Even distributed leadership, which appears to offer greater democracy and participation, can disguise institutionalized power inequalities. More than ever, then, an ethically based approach to leadership is called for; to avert the promotion of partisan ideology requires the counter-balance of a belief system that is avowedly "other-centered". It is here that Jesus's dire warnings continue to have traction for present-day leadership—consumed as it is with positive PR, social control, league-tables, benchmarking and regulation: "*You're hopeless, you religious scholars and Pharisees! Frauds! You keep meticulous account books, tithing on every nickle and dime you get, but on the meat of God's law, things like fairness, compassion and commitment— the absolute basics!—you carelessly take it or leave*".[20] Jesus roundly condemns the leadership of his day. In their myopic efforts to count, to calibrate and to maintain orthodoxy, they were religiously missing the point!

In short, I am becoming more confident in a spiritual point of departure, which for me is a conviction that Jesus speaks with timeless eloquence to the issues of ethical leadership and that this is best apprehended by direct experiential encounter with His divinity. For others, their ethical reference point will be quite different, but the common ground is that spirituality—in all its forms and however expressed—has the capacity to enrich and inform our understanding and practice of leadership development.

What Am I Doing Differently?

I close this chapter on a practical note by returning to the question which has vexed me for so long. How can we—on a day-by-day basis—develop ourselves and others as leaders? How can we draw upon spiritual resources in order to lead in a more ethical manner? One way, for me at least, is contemplative prayer. This is a close companion of mindfulness and meditation, but compared to these practices, a largely neglected topic in leadership development: "*reflective practices such as prayer, contemplation and spiritual reading are virtually untouched in the fields of organizational psychology, business and leadership*".[21]

Drawing upon the philosophies of Lonergan and Helminiak, Margaret Benefiel discusses the experience of receiving a moment of revelation.

She describes five stages of individual spiritual transformation leading to a dark night followed by a new dawn, at which point, a person's ego becomes *"relativized to a higher good such that they are able to fully let go"*.[22] Whether or not we subscribe to this language, we can all recognize our inability to meet our deepest needs on our own, and this leads us to a place of humility and dependence. However, this does not have to entail a loss of our sense of selfhood and autonomy but can be an appreciation of our limitations and our need for the Other. As Walter Conn puts it (in theistic terms):

> Properly understood, one surrenders not oneself or one's personal moral autonomy, but one's illusion of absolute autonomy. But such total surrender is possible only for the person who has totally fallen-in-love with a mysterious, uncomprehended God, for the person who has been grasped by an other-worldly love and completely transformed into a being-in-love. . . . Among all the possible realizations of human potential, such cognitive, moral, and affective self transcendence is the criterion of authentic self-realization.[23]

Over time, I guess it becomes possible to live more fully in this place of "letting go", but I can only glimpse this possibility! Benefiel suggests that leaders who live predominantly in this place are more available to the needs of the people they serve and of their organizations. In a small but significant way, I am seeking to do this.

Personal Reflection

I am sitting in a classroom with no glass in the windows. Birds occasionally fly through the rafters, the monsoon rain drums the tin roof and Buddhist chants float through from loudspeakers at local temples. I am taking a breather from teaching as my wife April, a trained counsellor, is at the front trying to get across the notion of empathy to around 20 students. No mean feat in a country like Myanmar which politically has experienced a complete deficit of empathy and education for 50 years. The students are attentive and attractive in their brightly patterned longhyis; but the fresh faces deceive. Most are from deprived backgrounds and one to one conversations reveal shameful levels of humiliation, persecution and bullying. Not for the first time, as I gaze across the room I wonder what we are doing here teaching leadership and listening skills at a small bible college on the outskirts of Yangon.

April is from Burma herself, leaving with her family as the military junta took tight but shambolic control in the mid-1960s. She has many cousins still in Yangon and we take the opportunity to drop by for a chat over curry. We enjoy the natural beauty of the country and the challenge of teaching in a very different environment where the student 'fees' are a dollar a day. At a very simple level, I guess our close association with this college arises from prayer.

In no way am I claiming self-transcendence as Conn puts it, but as we have meditated on the needs of those around us and what gifts God has given us to offer, we sense a gentle divine prod to take time out each year to invest in a small group of tomorrow's leaders. And that is what they are. For all their social and educational disadvantage—indeed perhaps because of this—these students will return to their villages better equipped, better motivated and supported to make a real community impact. And, as we work alongside the principal and his few dedicated staff, we can make a small contribution to this. An understanding of the bible will help lay a moral foundation in what is a Godless, animistic environment, acquaintance with leadership training will give them confidence as they teach in schools, serve in hospitals and kick start businesses and the relationships forged at the college will provide ongoing mentoring in years to come.

In some ways it takes little courage to follow through on our convictions and be with these young people, a trip we have made six times now. Each year we ask ourselves: do we have the time, can we face the long-haul flights, can we afford it, are we really making a difference? Then there is the 'letting go' bit and our need for the Other, because—without fail—we feel inadequate for the task. Prayerful reliance on our father God gets us through. We arrive in the dry heat on the streets of Yangon, amidst the dust of massive construction projects downtown, a sea of people clinging onto clapped-out buses, stuck in incessant traffic jams and living in poor, crowded housing. As the crimson sun sets on a steamy, buzzing Yangon of pagodas, high rise apartments and palm trees, He reminds us of why we are here and what part values-based education can make in this largely forgotten country.

In this chapter, I have tried to engage in an honest conversation with myself about developing ethical leaders. In so doing, I hope to have sparked some fresh thoughts for you as the reader. Many authors in this book have argued persuasively for ethical leadership rooted in a concern with community as an *immanent* force. In contrast, here I choose a *transcendent* approach, a recognition that we need a *voice from the outside* and access to the love and wisdom of our Creator God. This makes us aware that there is more to life than the material world around us, that the material world itself is a manifestation of the deepest mystery that confronts humanity: the very fact and existence of life itself. For those that believe in divine life, there is a spiritual world beyond our senses that energizes and inspires the human soul. For those that do not believe in the divine, there is an awareness of qualities such as sublimity, beauty, joy and love glimpsed through our culture, the arts, creation and the sciences. Regular reflection upon the immanent and/or transcendent cultivates an awareness that life is not about "me" but rather about me in some energizing and self-transforming relationship with something bigger. These internal insights and external revelations provide us with a sense of joy and love without which it is difficult (some might say impossible) to embody other elements of the spiritual life, including the time spent "at work".

Notes

1. See, for example, Nataraja (2011). In her book, which recounts the development of the Christian contemplative tradition over the centuries, she refers to Christians from the Western tradition who have been influenced by general spirituality coming from the East, whether Christian, Buddhist or Hindu.
2. See Mabey and Finch-Lees (2008) for a fuller discussion of this phenomenum.
3. It is not necessary to have a belief in God to recognize this, but certainly those of Christian and Jewish faith in particular, would hold to the notion of there being natural unity in God, that we have been created as whole persons and living as integrated beings is both desirable and—within mortal constraints—possible.
4. I am indebted to Stead (2016) for the first three of these "divisions" and for many of the insights which follow.
5. An exercise called *body scanning* is a fundamental plank of mindfulness practice and has a major part to play in restoring our rightful, respectful connectedness with our bodies (Stead, 2016, p. 45).
6. Facing up to the consequences of a somewhat disciplinarian father has helped me forgive him and myself for unhealthy attitudes and become more liberated from the need to win approval from others.
7. Max Bazerman, http://news.harvard.edu/gazette/story/2014/08/missed-opportunities/ accessed 7th October 2014.
8. Note that this conversation, unlike an appraisal discussion, a performance review or even many coaching sessions, has no predetermined agenda.
9. In Mabey (2013), I review ten years of leadership development literature to show how such activities and programs can be construed quite differently, depending on one's perspective.
10. Williams and Penman (2007).
11. See Mabey et al. (2016) for a fuller discussion of Spiritual Leadership Theory.
12. The primary sources for our understanding of Jesus's leadership come from the four biblical quasi-biographical accounts. While this is, of course, a selective, theologically motivated set of accounts, it is nevertheless what I mean by a Christian understanding. When I speak of Jesus's leadership, I am therefore referring to the perceptions of Jesus's leadership among the emerging communities of his earliest followers.
13. Of course, such leadership is not confined to Christians. For an inspiring and well-researched analysis of ten spiritual leaders in the twentieth century, each having different religious attachments—or in one case, none—see Parameshwar (2005). Among the many insights about how they came to be influential, she notes that they shared the following characteristic: "*In responding to challenging circumstances, the leaders defuse ego threats by transcending their ego and by enlarging their commitment to their higher purpose rather than by protecting their ego and short changing their higher purpose*" (2005, p. 703).
14. For an explanation of how the sacred and the secular became dichotomized and the consequences of this, see: Kim et al. (2012).
15. Bible, Luke 22v 24–6.
16. Here and following, I quote the words of Jesus as recorded in the Gospel accounts (using *The Message* which is a contemporary rendering from the original languages), historically verified and recognized as the canon of the New Testament at the Synod of Hippo in 393 AD.
17. According to Liden et al. (2008), servant leadership differs from traditional approaches to leadership in that it stresses personal integrity and focuses on forming strong long-term relationships with employees, customers and communities.
18. See Chapter 6 in this volume.
19. In fact, there are a number of views concerning Christianity and society which have arisen over the centuries: Jesus in opposition to, in agreement with, in

tension with and above culture. However, the view that Jesus Christ is the transformer of culture was at the heart of Reformation spirituality and is arguably the most mainstream today. *"This attitude is characterized by the belief that although there is often a conflict between faith and work, the latter can be transformed by the former when it is recognized as being part of God's plan for humankind"* (Westcott, 1996, p. 68).

20. Bible, Matthew 23 v24.
21. Reave (2005, p. 656).
22. Benefiel (2005, p. 734).
23. Conn, W (1986:21;31)

Bibliography

Benefiel, M. (2005) The second half of the journey: Spiritual; leadership for organizational transformation. *The Leadership Quarterly* 16, pp. 723–747.

Conn, W. (1986) *Christian Conversion: A Developmental Interpretation of Autonomy and Surrender*. Mahwah, NJ: Paulist.

Kim, D., McCalman, D. and Fisher, D. (2012) The sacred/secular divide and the Christian worldview. *Journal of Business Ethics* 109, pp. 203–208.

Liden, R., Wayne, S., Zhao, H. and Henderson, D. (2008) Multi-level approaches to leadership. *The Leadership Quarterly* 19(2), pp 161–177.

Mabey, C. (2013) Leadership development in organizations: Multiple discourses and diverse practice. *International Journal of Management Reviews* 15(4), pp 359–469.

Mabey, C., Conroy, M., Blakeley, K. and deMarco, S. (2016) Having burned the straw-man of Christian spiritual leadership, what can we learn from Jesus about leading ethically? *Journal of Business Ethics* 134(1), published online 17 February 2016. doi: 10.1007/s10551-016-3045-5

Mabey, C. and Finch-Lees, T. (2008) *Management and Leadership Development*. London: Sage Publications.

Nataraja, K. (2011) *Journey to the Heart*. London: Canterbury Press.

Parameshwar, S. (2005) Spiritual leadership through ego-transcendence: Exceptional responses to challenging circumstances. *The Leadership Quarterly* 16, pp. 689–722.

Reave, L. (2005) Spiritual values and practices related to leadership effectiveness. *The Leadership Quarterly* 16, pp. 655–687.

Stead, T. (2016) *Mindfulness and Christian Spirituality*. London: SPCK.

Westcott, D. (1996) *Work Well: Live Well*. London: Marshall Pickering.

Williams, M. and Penman, D. (2007) *Mindfulness: A Practical Guide to Finding Peace in a Frantic World*. London: Piatkus.

4 The Promise and Perils of Corporate Mindfulness

Ronald E. Purser, Edwin Ng and Zack Walsh

Key Questions

Why does mindfulness practice require an ethical perspective?

What are the common misconceptions regarding mindfulness?

What is "right mindfulness", and how can leaders nurture and develop it?

How can mindfulness practices be tied to systemic change?

Introduction[1]

Mindfulness meditation has become mainstream, making its way into schools, corporations, prisons and government agencies including the U.S. military. Millions of people are receiving tangible benefits from their mindfulness practice: less stress, better concentration, perhaps a little more empathy. Almost daily, the media cite scientific studies that report the numerous health benefits of mindfulness meditation and how such a simple practice can effect neurological changes in the brain.

Needless to say, this is an important development to be welcomed—but is something missing in the midst of all the media hype?

Uncoupling mindfulness from its ethical and religious contexts is understandable as an expedient move to make such training a viable product on the open market. But the rush to secularize and commodify mindfulness into a marketable technique may be leading to an unfortunate denaturing of this ancient practice, which was intended for far more than relieving a headache, reducing blood pressure or helping executives become better focused and more productive.

Unfortunately, a more ethical and socially responsible view of mindfulness is sorely lacking. While a stripped-down, secularized technique—what some critics are now calling "McMindfulness"—may make it more palatable to the corporate world, decontextualizing mindfulness from its liberative and transformative purpose, as well as its foundation in social ethics, amounts to a Faustian bargain. Rather than applying mindfulness as a means to awaken individuals and organizations from the unwholesome roots of greed, ill will and delusion, it is usually being refashioned into a banal, therapeutic, self-help technique that can actually reinforce those roots.

Most scientific and popular accounts circulating in the media have portrayed mindfulness in terms of stress reduction and attention-enhancement. These human performance benefits are heralded as the *sine qua non* of mindfulness and its major attraction for modern corporations. But mindfulness, as understood and practiced within the Buddhist tradition (and others as well), is not merely an ethically neutral technique for reducing stress and improving concentration. Rather, mindfulness is a distinct quality of attention that is dependent upon and influenced by many other factors: the nature of our thoughts, speech and actions; our way of making a living; and our efforts to avoid unwholesome and unskillful behaviors, while developing those that are conducive to wise action, social harmony and compassion.

This is why Buddhists differentiate between Right Mindfulness and Wrong Mindfulness. The distinction is not moralistic: the issue is whether the quality of awareness is characterized by wholesome intentions and positive mental qualities that lead to human flourishing and optimal well-being for others as well as oneself.

According to the Pali Canon (the earliest recorded teachings of the Buddha), even a person committing a premeditated and heinous crime can be exercising mindfulness, albeit *wrong mindfulness*. Clearly, the mindful attention and single-minded concentration of a terrorist, sniper assassin or white-collar criminal is not the same quality of mindfulness that the Dalai Lama and other Buddhist and Christian adepts have developed. Right Mindfulness is guided by intentions and motivations based on self-restraint, wholesome mental states and ethical behaviors—goals that include but supersede stress reduction and improvements in concentration.

Another common misconception is that mindfulness meditation is a private, internal affair. Mindfulness is often marketed as a method for personal self-fulfillment, a reprieve from the trials and tribulations of cutthroat corporate life. Such an individualistic and consumer orientation to the practice of mindfulness may be effective for self-preservation and self-advancement but is essentially impotent for mitigating the causes of collective and organizational distress.

Thus far, those celebrating the mindfulness boom have avoided any serious consideration of why stress is so pervasive in corporations and society. According to *New York Times* business reporter David Gelles, author of *Mindful Work*, "Stress isn't something imposed on us. It's something we impose on ourselves".[2] The *New York Times* featured an exposé on the toxic, sociopathic work culture at Amazon.[3] A former employee was quoted as saying that he saw nearly everyone he worked with cry at their desk. Would Gelles offer his advice with a straight face to these employees of

Amazon, telling them that they have imposed stress on themselves, that they could have chosen not to cry?

Stress and misery are partly due to our habitual reactivity, but Gelles is too reductionist in his advice. His victim blaming philosophy echoes the corporate mindfulness ethos: shift the burden and locus of psychological stress and structural insecurities onto the individual employee, frame stress as a personal problem and then offer mindfulness as the panacea. Critical psychologist David Smail referred to this philosophy as "magical voluntarism", because it blames individuals for their own stress, ignoring the social and economic conditions which may have contributed to it.[4]

When mindfulness practice is compartmentalized in this way, there is a dissociation between one's own personal transformation and the kind of organizational transformation that takes into account the causes and conditions of suffering in the broader environment. Such a colonization of mindfulness also has an instrumentalizing effect, reorienting the practice to the needs of the market, rather than to a critical reflection on ultimate concerns, ethics and human values.

Many corporate advocates argue that transformational change starts with oneself: if one's mind can become more focused and peaceful, then social and organizational transformation will naturally follow. The problem with this formulation is that today the three unwholesome motivations that Buddhism highlights—greed, ill will and delusion—are no longer confined to individual minds, but have become institutionalized into forces beyond personal control.

The result is an atomized and highly privatized version of mindfulness practice, which is easily coopted and confined to what Jeremy Carrette and Richard King in their book *Selling Spirituality: The Silent Takeover of Religion*, describe as an "accommodationist" orientation.[5] Mindfulness training has wide appeal because it has become a trendy method for subduing employee unrest, promoting a tacit acceptance of the status quo, and as an instrumental tool for keeping attention focused on corporate goals and interests. Most of those in mindfulness movement believe capitalism and spirituality can be easily reconciled; they want a mindfulness that will ameliorate their stress, but without having to look deeper and wider at its social causes.

The mindfulness movement, however, need not follow the usual trajectory of most corporate fads—unbridled enthusiasm, uncritical acceptance of the status quo and eventual disillusionment. To become a genuine force for positive personal and social transformation, leaders must reclaim an ethical framework and aspire to employ mindfulness practices not only for personal stress reduction, but also towards making refuge for the other—developing situational response-ability. Civic mindfulness is a collective inquiry that goes beyond providing individual employees therapeutic interventions; it offers a way of linking individual agency with organizational and social change.

Fortunately, there have been an increasing number of scholars from the humanities and social sciences critically examining how mindfulness can be more than a private self-help technique.

They began asking critical questions, such as: what is mindfulness for? Are mindfulness-based interventions limited to a palliative for individual stress relief and mental hygiene, or can mindfulness programs develop in ways that call into question deeply rooted cultural assumptions which have been the source of so much misery, injustice and unnecessary suffering in the modern Western world?

At a time when the hype, commercialization and popularity of mindfulness is at its peak, leaders should be cautious and discerning. Leaders must be wary of decontextualized treatments of mindfulness and encourage dialogue that will take into account historical, cultural, social, political, economic, racial and ethical dimensions of contemplative practice in and around corporations. Leaders must also appreciate how everyone is implicated in the cultural translation of mindfulness and why we all share an ethical responsibility to question the values instantiated in particular mindfulness practices.

In the next section, we provide a number of guidelines for developing an ethically informed mindfulness practice, as well as principles for advancing a more socially engaged approach to mindfulness training in organizations.

Guidelines for Leading Ethically Informed Mindfulness Programs

Mindfulness Must Be Coupled With Clear Comprehension

Contrary to popular definitions, mindfulness is not merely paying attention to the present moment non-judgmentally. This is a common misinterpretation which obscures the role mindfulness plays as an integrated path, when properly cultivated and developed, can discern wholesome/skillful and healthy states of mind from those which are unwholesome and harmful to self and others. Discrimination, evaluation and judgment are part and parcel of mindfulness.

Mindfulness and clear comprehension are the tools not only for training the mind, but proper investigation of it as well. Mindfulness practitioners, whether Buddhist or secular, share a core commitment to cultivating clear comprehension. Clear comprehension has a reflexive monitoring quality. What seems self-evident often remains distorted by implicit biases, but when clear comprehension and mindfulness are cultivated together, leaders can fully grasp and comprehend what is actually taking place in one's own mind and surroundings. Developing clear comprehension involves more than simply paying attention to the breath, or concentrating one-pointedly on an object. Clear comprehension can range from basic forms of knowing to discriminative understanding, the latter of which is able to discern wholesome from unwholesome thoughts and behaviors.

Corporate Mindfulness Programs Must Diagnose and Address the Causes of Workplace Stressors

The scientific research on mindfulness has already well established the potential health benefits of mindfulness for individuals. Because the majority of mindfulness programs are designed for individual-level stress reduction and therapeutic relief, these individual-focused programs will not effectively address the structural and systemic sources of stress. Individualized mindfulness programs are not designed to take into account how stress is shaped by a complex set of interacting power relations, networks of interests and narratives.

Leaders should take note of a recent Stanford-Harvard meta-analysis of 228 studies showing that employee stress is not self-imposed nor due to a lack of mindfulness.[6] Rather, major workplace stressors were associated with a lack of health insurance, threats of constant lay-offs and job insecurity, lack of discretion and autonomy in decision-making, long work hours, low organizational justice and unrealistic job demands. These systemic and structural problems cannot be solved at the individual level of personal well-being; rather, they require collective discerning attention and action that connects the work of self-care with social and political engagement.

Mindfulness Is Not a Value-Free Practice

Mindfulness is often thought to be a value-free practice, stripped of its religious trappings and validated by science. The secular status of mindfulness often prohibits an open discussion of ethics. Those who simultaneously claim that mindfulness is value free and universally beneficial escape scrutiny by preventing any critical investigation of who benefits from mindfulness, how and why.

This laissez-faire stance toward mindfulness programs is very disconcerting. In his article, "Mindfulness at Work is Not Mind Control", Jeremy Smith admits mindfulness might not address workplace inequality and insecurity as we allege, but he rhetorically says, "is it supposed to?" Evidently not for Smith and most corporate mindfulness advocates. Instead, corporate mindfulness apologists, perhaps unwittingly, affirm a neoliberal ideology that limits such practices to forms of self-help. Taking a depoliticized view of mindfulness conveniently forecloses critical inquiry pertaining to the social, economic and political interests linked to such programs. While mindfulness programs may provide salutary health benefits to individual employees (which we applaud), such programs are also training and conditioning individual employees to see themselves as completely autonomous, fully responsible and self-regulating employees who can govern themselves.

Framing mindfulness as a self-improvement and performance enhancement technique confines the practice. This narrowing provides the ground for dismissing structural critiques, because the implicit model of organizational change is limited to individual-level behavioral change. Ethical leadership can correct this limitation by implementing mindfulness programs as a means for uprooting the sources of greed, ill will and delusion in persons *and* society. The practice of mindfulness is revolutionary to the extent that it transforms the isolated self that is haunted by a sense of lack, while overcoming our dualism and sense of separateness from the world (see also Chris Mabey's Chapter 3 and David Knights's Chapter 5). This requires a resituating of mindfulness as a part of a larger life-practice of ethical conscientiousness rather than just a mere technique for self-enhancement

Mindfulness Is More Than a Technique

Unfortunately, the stripping away of mindfulness from its ethical context, whether explicitly or implicitly, comes at a cost. Uncoupling mindfulness from its ethical roots is myopic, promoting an overemphasis on technique. Driscoll and Weibe have aptly termed this trend as "technical spirituality", where spiritual practices are extracted from their ethical context to be used as tools for improving efficiency, productivity and gaining tangible results.[7] Strong institutional structures and market pressures have the capacity to co-opt and appropriate mindfulness to their own ends.

Purser and Loy characterize this as the "McMindfulness" trend—a replica of such technical spirituality.[8] Similarly, David Forbes, in his eloquent essay, "Occupy Mindfulness", puts the matter this way:

> My concern is that mindfulness may fall victim to its own success. Mindfulness is not about stress reduction, maintaining a steady state of bliss, helping an individual act with more control or an organization run more smoothly and efficiently. Even after we're de-stressed and feeling great, we still need to ask: *how do we live now?* We're in control and are more efficient, but toward what end?

The rush to dissociate mindfulness from its ethical roots and context is not necessary in order to be palpable and acceptable to our modern sensibilities. Ensuring the ethical efficacy of mindfulness requires a willingness to view it not as simply a therapeutic self-help tool and productivity improvement technique.

The Purpose and Quality of Mindfulness is Context-Dependent

There is a widespread misconception that mindfulness is a universal, ahistorical and context-free practice, since what is being taught is allegedly the "pure essence" of what was once a religious practice. This claim is classic perennial philosophy dressed up in white scientific lab coat attire. It echoes William James's understanding of mysticism as being a direct experience of a common core essence that forms the basis for all religious experiences.

Meditation is viewed as a means for accessing a pure, unmediated and ahistorical essence of human experience that transcends sectarian boundaries and is unmediated by one's cultural and social context. This appeal to universalism and perennial philosophy isn't just a matter of decontextualizing and purging meditative practices from their cultural context and religious roots, but of recontextualizing them into the sensibilities of modernity and Western consumer capitalism.

For several decades, mindfulness-based interventions and courses were situated in clinics and hospitals—in medical and therapeutic contexts. The medicalization of mindfulnesss draws from a biomedical paradigm, where stress is understood and theorized as an individual pathology and dysfunction in managing one's habitual thoughts, emotions and mental ruminations. Psychosomatic symptoms, such as chronic stress, depression and anxiety, along with interventions for enhancing health and well-being, are seen as matters for autonomous individuals to resolve. Consequently, this frame has delimited discourse to primarily viewing mindfulness as a stand-alone practice, with a focus on internal mental-brain states measurable objective methods such as neuroscientific fMRI brain scan studies.

Recontextualizing mindfulness within an individualistic and neoliberal worldview has "overstated internal pathology while understating environmental stressors".[9] Importing a medicalized view of mindfulness into organizations disavows them from any responsibility in addressing the social, cultural and economic factors of workplace stress.

Contrary to this above myth, lived cultural contexts are inextricably interwoven and constitutive of mindfulness practices. Leaders need to appreciate that mindfulness as both a social and embodied practice situated within particular historical, cultural and economic contexts. Moving from medical centers to corporations, we are unbundling practices that is changing them in ways we do not truly understand. Mindfulness is always grounded in forms of life inclusive or individual and collective dimensions. Furthermore, mindfulness is embedded within a complex web of interdependencies, conceptual systems, aesthetic factors, social settings, motivation and aspirations, emotional factors, individual differences and temporal contexts.

Given these contextual complexities, leaders can begin to understand why context matters, and how contextual factors are constitutive of contemplative practices in terms of their transformative potential.

Beware of the Commodification of Mindfulness Programs

There is a widespread belief in the marketplace that we need not worry about corporate mindfulness programs so long as teachers are competently trained. The complexity of issues concerning corporate applications of mindfulness practices, along with the potential risks to individuals—are reduced simply to an issue of teacher competency. Such reductionism ensures it all boils down to individual personal responsibility, smoothly resonating with a neoliberal ideology. This message also assumes that corporate mindfulness offerings—the programs, practices and curricula—are just fine as they are, it's just a qualified teacher shortage that is the problem.

The booming popularity of the mindfulness movement has also turned it into a lucrative cottage industry. And it's no surprise that corporate mindfulness programs command premium consulting fees. We know of a prominent corporate mindfulness consultant whose fee for training is $12,000 USD per day. Google's Search Inside Yourself Leadership Institute (SIYLI) charges $8,000 a day minimum for its training. Clearly, corporate mindfulness trainers have a great deal to gain financially from marketing such programs as being universally beneficial and profitable to their corporate sponsors.

Yet, Barry Boyce, the editor of *Mindful* magazine, asserts in his editorial "It's Not McMindfulness", good teachers are those who "show a strong measure of independence" from their corporate sponsors.[10] But is such independence really possible? Conflicts of interest is the big elephant in the room and a matter that is almost never raised or discussed in these circles.

Can we really rely on personal testimonies that we need not worry or be concerned about issues raised by skeptics and critics when these assurances are given by trainers, consultants and teachers who have a significant financial stake in selling and sustaining their corporate mindfulness training programs?

The commercialization and commodification of mindfulness practices puts them at risk of becoming co-opted and denatured for instrumental ends. For millennia, mindfulness practices were integral to a path of spiritual liberation, for overcoming personal greed, anger, pride and an exaggerated sense of self. These methods were considered sacred, offered for free and transmitted from highly qualified spiritual monks to their disciples.

Introducing Mindfulness Requires Full Disclosure

We have repeatedly observed leading corporate mindfulness teachers declare to their corporate sponsors, especially when trying to sell a program, that mindfulness practices have nothing to do with Buddhism. But backstage, at conferences and in social media, these same corporate mindfulness teachers wax poetic about how they are "teaching the Buddha-dharma". However, deceit is contrary to the ethics of honest speech and truthfulness—factors upon which mindfulness depends.

Leaders have an ethical obligation to fully disclose that the majority of mindfulness practices being taught today are adapted from Buddhist sources. We recommend that participants in such programs should have informed consent with a choice for opting out.

Don't Over Promise and Over Sell Mindfulness Programs

Our observations suggest that most corporate mindfulness consultants are overselling the benefits of individualized mindfulness training. Going beyond individual level health benefits, proponents are promising that mindfulness can act as a "disruptive technology" reforming even the most dysfunctional companies into kinder, more compassionate and sustainable organizations. Corporate mindfulness teachers who claim that individualized mindfulness programs are subversive often evoke the "Trojan horse" metaphor. They speculate that over time, leaders, managers and employees trained in mindfulness may wake up and effect major transformations in corporate policies and practices. However, the jury is still out. It's also hard to fathom how simply training individuals to be mindful of their breathing will lead to systemic changes in corporate culture, power structures, and policies.

It remains an open question as to whether current training in mindfulness will transform corporations and society, or whether it merely amounts to individual-level employee stress reduction and a form of corporate quietism. As Farb notes, on the one hand we have those who regard the idea of mindfulness as a beneficent Trojan horse in organizations, others see mindfulness leads employees to spiral into complacency and subjugation.[11] This *open question* of what mindfulness may or may not lead to is really the rub of the matter, which asks that all parties invested in mindfulness collectively inquire into the multifarious forces of altruism *and* exploitation that might occur in organizations.

Corporate Mindfulness Programs Must Face the Question of Ethics

Many mindfulness teachers have argued that any single set of ethics would be an inappropriate imposition. Instead, ethical concerns are reduced to being contingent on the integrity of the mindfulness teacher, who serves as a model and embodiment of ethical behavior. This not only reflects the values of individualism in the mindfulness movement, but it also takes a laissez-faire, "let the market decide" attitude. In the absence of an ethical vision to guide mindfulness practice, its potential will be limited to therapeutic aims and self-improvement, without issuing any challenge to one's beliefs, values and way of life.

The legacy of our Judeo-Christian heritage, where ethics is conceived in terms of prescriptions, duties, edicts and coercive moralizing is also not appropriate for secular mindfulness programs.[12] However, rather than simply eschewing ethical principles or imposing Buddhist ethics through distorted Western lenses, we propose that leaders explore adopting a *non-normative* ethical *orientation* that may be expansive and flexible enough to serve as a guiding ethos for what we propose as the twofold task of *the critique of mindfulness and the mindfulness of critique*.

Following feminist commentators, we are guided by an ethos of response-ability.[13] This is a form of dispositional ethics which attends to *the situational capacity for responsiveness* in any given encounter, rather than the substantive terms of the encounter. The capacity for responsiveness enables mindfulness practice and is in turn strengthened by it. Within the context of formal practice, it is necessary to be repeatedly responsive, so that we may repeatedly "let go" whenever we are distracted by a stream of thought and "start again" by recollecting the task of attending to the object of contemplation, like the movement of the breath or the feeling tone of sensations. With sustained practice, this capacity of responsiveness becomes more sensitive and it may begin to serve a therapeutic purpose by helping people respond differently to afflictive habitual reactions that may be triggered by various situations. But this capacity for responsiveness extends beyond individualistic and therapeutic contexts of mindfulness practice, as we must necessarily rely on this capacity too in our social and political lives.

Regardless of whether it is an encounter with a traumatic memory co-arising with an unpleasant sensation, or a racist or homophobe abusing a passerby, or a presidential candidate spreading lies and hate about refugees and migrants or an organization callously ravaging the lands and homes of others in its drive for profit—in these different scenarios the determinate course of moral conduct to be taken must first require a degree of attentiveness towards our capacity *to be responsive*, and the degree to which we are sensitively responseable would influence the determinate course of action that is taken to respond to these challenges.

This capacity of responsiveness is necessary for ongoing response-able action, whereby we retake our decisions to repeatedly respond to the challenges confronting us, steering our decisions in a different direction if necessary to reconsider the dangers or harms that might have been overlooked. By adopting this ethical orientation of response-ability we countervail the disproportionate emphasis given to individualistic and therapeutic applications of mindfulness, supplementing existing approaches with critical and civic applications of mindfulness. With such an ethical orientation, it would be possible to take seriously the suggestive evidence that corporate mindfulness programs may help employees manage stress and even perform better at work. But it would also admit into the purview of mindfulness the systemic and structural problems that might contravene the claims of altruism and social responsibility behind corporate or other institutional programs of mindfulness.

A non-normative ethos of response-ability can thus serve as the "flip switch" that connects the critique of mindfulness with the mindfulness of critique.

Mindfulness Needs to Move Beyond the Rhetoric of Stress-Reduction, Well-Being and Happiness

In outlining these points, we are taking a step back to summarize some of the outstanding issues that the mainstream mindfulness movement largely continues to ignore. At the same time, we are laying the groundwork for charting a new course.

The *critique of mindfulness* is part of a larger movement to build new approaches for socially engaged mindfulness interventions as a corrective and supplement to the individualistic and therapeutic focus of prevailing approaches. The critique of mindfulness is thus twinned with a reciprocal task of the *mindfulness of critique*, which is the work of attuning ourselves with new modes learning, inquiry and social engagement so that we may become more responsive towards the challenges and conditionings entangling the well-being of individuals and the messy worlds we inhabit. Given the limitations of the prevailing rhetoric of "non-judgmental awareness" and focus on "happiness" or "stress reduction", we offer the guiding rubric of "refuge" as a countervailing alternative to help cultivate the mindfulness of critique.

Transforming Mindfulness: The Promise of Making Refuge

The promise of refuge is a starting premise of Buddhism. But the metaphor and ideal of refuge can be found in different religions and even non-religious lineages of understanding. The metaphorical import of refuge for a secular world can be extended to a non-doctrinal and non-sectarian principle of responsive responsibility and responsible responsiveness—*an ethos of response-ability*—which entangles the self with others and the world. We propose that ethical leadership entails the work of making refuge, beginning with the promise that all of us, human and non-humans, must invite from and gift to one another mutual recognition, respect, care and concern in order to grow and thrive as communities and habitats in a precarious world, where vulnerability to conditions beyond our choosing is a fact of life (see Box 4.1)

Moreover, refuge places an ethical demand to exercise more than simply paying attention to the present moment "non-judgmentally" and seeking

---

Box 4.1

The Making Refuge metaphor can help leaders to pay attention—to be mindful—with greater response-ability. We challenge leaders to develop a much broader vision for mindfulness, one that goes beyond the fashionable rhetoric of 'happiness', 'resilience', 'well-being' or 'stress-reduction'. The question of refuge also relates to other challenges like social justice struggles against racism or the development of ecological conscientiousness and sustainable living—because the work of addressing casual and systemic acts of discrimination and exclusion is a matter of welcoming those who are being denied certain basic conditions safety, in this broad sense of refuge. Likewise, the work of addressing ecological harm is a matter of ensuring that humans and non-humans may continue to share the planet as the only home we have. These challenges do not have any one solution which can be applied universally; but any hope of even addressing these problems must begin with leaders developing the situational capacity for responsiveness: an ethos of response-ability.

Box 4.2

Current initiatives to experiment with socially and ecologically engaged forms of mindfulness illustrate the potential of placing these practices in the broader ethical frame of Making Refuge. The Mindfulness for Social Change course developed by Paula Haddock in the U.K. provides a good example. Unlike clinical and therapeutic mindfulness programs, Haddock's program incorporates an analysis of the systemic causes of social, economic, and environmental problems, and it supports personal wellbeing through active political struggle, rather than just social or psychological adjustment. Another good example is the year-long Practice in Transformative Action course at the East Bay Meditation Center. Besides its focus on political activism, the center's focus on diversity is particularly noteworthy, because it demonstrates how its commitment to social justice is integral to its mindfulness practice. The center bars white or straight people from attending specific classes in order to allow community members to practice mindfulness in safe spaces. Affording marginalized people space to practice mindfulness in communities where white, male, middle- and upper-class, European perspectives are not the norm is an important step in decolonizing mindfulness.

calm and equanimity for only one's own benefit and well-being. Rather, refuge provides leaders the ethical and material axis around which mindfulness can be collectively articulated in a more socially engaged direction. It communicates how leaders can imagine the future and how they wish to practice mindfulness in their organizations to bring it forth (Box 4.2).

Unlike the metaphors of happiness, wellbeing, and efficiency—which bind mindfulness to the neoliberal subject—practicing mindfulness as an act of making refuge opens up space for recognizing people's vulnerability, our mutual dependency, and our ability to face an uncertain future in solidarity with one another. Whereas mindfulness for stress reduction retroactively rationalizes our present situation by treating the symptoms, rather than the causes and conditionings of our suffering; socially engaged mindfulness interventions are oriented toward a collective future of liberation, never fully realized, but nevertheless expressed in our commitment to each other: a shared promise of making refuge.

As mindfulness moves in this new direction towards an explicit social and ecological engagement, the critique of mindfulness does not end but always begins anew as the mindfulness of critique.

Personal Reflections

Ron Purser: Based on my 40 years of practice and study, I have a deep appreciation, gratitude and respect for the Buddhist tradition. Even so, the meteoric rise of the secular "mindfulness revolution" took me somewhat by surprise. I am disappointed that mindfulness has been coopted for instrumental purposes and profit-making. Secular mindfulness advocates have no qualms about flaunting Buddhism for its symbolic cultural cachet—capitalizing on its exoticness—but at the same time dismissing the Buddhist religion as saddled with "cultural baggage" that must be purged of its foreignness. Moreover, I am dismayed by the rhetoric of laying claim to the authentic essence of Buddhism to bolster branding prestige, while simultaneously proclaiming the Western scientific approach has allowed access to a "universal understanding of mindfulness" that supersedes Buddhism. This discursive habit amounts to a form of epistemic border control and cultural one-up-manship, a legacy of Western colonialism.

When corporations and the U.S. military began introducing mindfulness programs as a method of performance enhancement, I felt it was my moral duty to intervene. In 2013, I published with David Loy a blog article "Beyond McMindfulness" in the *Huffington Post* that called into question the efficacy, ethics and narrow interests of corporate mindfulness programs (Purser and Loy, 2013). To our surprise, it went viral and we found ourselves in the middle of a heated debate over the virtues and vices of this latest corporate fad.

Many of my Buddhist friends and colleagues told me privately that they were pleased that I had the courage to speak truth to power, calling into question how mindfulness practices were being coopted and adapted to further corporate interests. It seemed that our article broke the floodgates, and more critiques of secular mindfulness began to appear in the press, media and journals by Buddhists and non-Buddhists. This growing trend was labeled by the media as a "mindfulness backlash". Following this trend, I began to speak out even more, publishing in widely read outlets such as *salon.com* (e.g., see "Corporate Mindfulness is Bulls*t" and "Mindfulness' Truthiness Problem"), as well as in academic journals (e.g., see "Mindfulness Revisted: A Buddhist-Based Conceptualization" in the *Journal of Management Inquiry*).

As my social media articles went viral, so did the pushback and attacks. Petulant comments started appearing on blogs, and ad hominen arguments were directed against me. On Facebook, I faced a considerable amount of hostility and ridicule by many mindfulness teachers and even a few academics. I was even trolled repeatedly by a promiment spokesperson for Mindfulness Based Stress Reduction (MBSR) and secular mindfulness. And as the visibility of my critiques increased, I found that I was becoming the "go to critic" when journalists or conference organizers were seeking a contrarian perspective on mindfulness. I often felt that I was entering a "lion's den" when speaking as the lone critic amongst the faithful mindfulness followers at such conferences as Mind & Life Institute's International Symposium for Contemplative Studies and Bangor University's Centre for Mindfulness Practice and Research.

Yet, despite this flack and lack of intellectual hospitality, I perservered, pushing on little by little. Slowly, those sympathetic with my critiques of mindfulness started emailing me. Vigorous exchanges and sharing occurred, and before I knew it, a new "critical mindfulness" network was taking shape. I no longer felt isolated and alone. I made many new friends and colleagues from around the world. They started to visit me in San Francisco. Soon, I realized that it was time to organize a major international conference on mindfulness that would welcome critical perspectives. Without any funds or staff support from the university, I did. To my surprise, some 275 people attended. A year later, my colleagues and I published the *Handbook of Mindfulness: Culture, Context and Social Engagement* (Purser et al. 2016) which included thirty four chapters offering critical perspectives on mindfulness in such domains as philosophy, psychotherapy, business and education. The purpose of such critiques is grounded in the faith that secular mindfulness practices can be reformed and reoriented to enhance the common good. Each author displays courage for going against the mainstream narrative with its self-help rhetoric and psychological-neurospeak explanations that have characterized the benefits of mindfulness. Because mindfulness practices are intended for the relief of human suffering in society, it has taken a considerable amount of courage to question and challenge the dominant narrative that has, perhaps unwittingly, perpetuated an accomodationist orientation to the norms and imperatives of neoliberal capitalism.

Zack Walsh: I undertook formal training in Buddhism and mindfulness during a five-year period of living in Asia and studying at various monasteries and seminaries in Thailand, China and Taiwan. Despite the relative affordances offered by my white privilege, more often than not, I was the Other, and I experienced Occidentalism on a daily basis. What might give me an advantage at home—my whiteness, cisgender, heterosexuality, critical intellect—were all checked at the door of Chinese Buddhist communities. I almost always had to keep my head down, shut up and assimilate—and in the process, I forsook my identity to abide by the norms of my host culture and uphold their standards for social harmony.

But I chose to experience this, and that is in itself a unique white privilege. I liked being other to myself, exposing myself to the contingencies of the moment and to the foreignness of an encounter with otherness. It was at times ecstatic and transcendent, as it forced me outside myself and my comfort zone. It brought me to a better understanding of myself as notself. But at other times, I exposed myself to too much vulnerability and risk, and even lost touch with that most prized of possessions—integrity. I was not always authentic under the social pressure to become other.

My identity was frequently erased both within homogenous Chinese communities and within Chinese Buddhist or secular mindfulness communities in the U.S. Today, I uphold and betray multiple conflicting identities and inheritances which exist only in the interstices of each other. Since I was young, I have felt a migrant, a vagrant, a refugee to myself—alone in one way or another. But isn't that the path that calls many of us to become Buddhists—to be alone together?

I admit, I am not a "good Buddhist". I have taken refuge in the Triple Gem, and I have even received formal Bodhisattva precepts which orient my practice. But, to me, Buddhism is not about taking refuge, since taking refuge is so often predicated on false promises and ideologies—a retreat into the comfort of one's own community and self-absorbed fantasies. Frankly, I am also not interested in mindfulness, which may seem strange coming from a scholar whose last six publications were on the subject. What interests me is bearing truthful witness to my experiences and the multiple conflicting identities and inheritances that I embody. That motivates my promise to #makerefuge for myself and others.

#Makingrefuge is about sharing the responsibility to provide hospitable conditions for living and dying well together. And by dying, I do not only mean when one's heart stops beating, since each moment we are always dying to ourselves and to each other, at the same time that we are renewing the conditions for living and dying, for better or for worse. And let's be honest. #Makingrefuge is a survival strategy. When faced with the precariousness of one's existence, all beings whether human or non-human have sought the conditions for a hospitable co-existence amidst pervasive violence and suffering.

Of course, I say these things at the risk of exposing my perfect Buddhist image to all of my inadequacies and vulnerabilities. You can call me a crank or an unmindful, unhappy, bad Buddhist, and I can accept it, as I am not interested in abiding by the false pretenses of your prescribed path. I am, however, interested in developing people's capacities to contemplate suffering, so that together, we may respond to injustice through informed and compassionate action. That is my promise to #makerefuge.

Notes

1. Parts of this introduction have been adapted and edited from Purser and Loy (2013).
2. Gelles (2015).
3. Lynch (2015).
4. Smail (2005).
5. Carrette and King (2005).
6. Kantor and Streitfeld (2015).
7. Driscoll and Wiebe (2007).
8. Purser and Loy (2013).
9. Goddard (2014).
10. Boyce (2015).
11. Farb (2014).
12. Although see Chapter 3 by Mabey in this volume for a re-interpretation of this heritage.
13. Beausoleil, E. (2016) Embodying an ethics of response-ability. *Borderlands: e-journal*, available from: www.borderlands.net.au/vol14no2_2015/beausoleil_embodying.pdf

Bibliography

Beausoleil, E. (2016) Embodying an ethics of response-ability. *Borderlands: e-journal* [Online]. Available from: www.borderlands.net.au/vol14no2_2015/beausoleil_embodying.pdf (accessed on January 25, 2017).

Boyce, B. (2015) It's not McMindfulness. *Mindful* [Online]. Available from: www.mindful.org/its-not-mcmindfulness/ (accessed on January 25, 2017).

Carrette, J. and King, R. (2005) *Selling Spirituality: The Silent Takeover of Religion.* New York: Routledge.

Driscoll, C. and Wiebe, E. (2007) Technical spirituality at work. *Journal of Management Inquiry* 16(4), pp. 333–348.

Farb, N. (2014) From retreat center to clinic boardroom: Perils and promises of the modern mindfulness movement. *Religions* 5(4), pp. 1062–1086.

Forbes, D. (2012) Occupy mindfulness. *Beams and Struts* [Online]. Available from: http://beamsandstruts.com/articles/item/982-occupy-mindfulness (accessed on January 25, 2017).

Gelles, D. (2015) *Mindful Work*. New York: Eamon Dolan/Houghton Mifflin Harcourt.

Goddard, M. (2014) Critical psychiatry, critical psychology, and the behaviorism of B.F. Skinner. *Review of General Psychology* 18(3), pp. 208–215.

Kantor, J. and Streitfeld, D. (2015) Inside Amazon: Wrestling big ideas in a bruising world. *New York Times* [Online]. Available from: www.nytimes.com/2015/08/16/technology/inside-amazon-wrestling-big-ideas-in-a-bruising-workplace.html?_r=0 (accessed on January 25, 2017).

Lynch, S. (2015) Why your workplace might be killing you. *Insights* [Online]. Stanford Graduate School of Buiness. Available from: www.nytimes.com/2015/08/16/technology/inside-amazon-wrestling-big-ideas-in-a-bruising-workplace.html?_r=0 (accessed on January 25, 2017).

Purser, R. and Loy, D. (2013) Beyond McMindfulness. *Huffington Post* [Online]. Available from: www.huffingtonpost.com/ron-purser/beyond-mcmindfulness_b_3519289.html (accessed on July 2, 2013).

Purser, R., Forbes, D., Burke, A. (2016) *Handbook of Mindfulness: Culture, Context and Social Engagement*, Springer Publishing, NY

Smail, D. (2005) *Power, Interest and Psychology*. Ross-On-Wye: PCCS Books Ltd.

Vignettes

Self-Discovery Through Transcendental Meditation and Spiritual Leadership

Simon Mitchell

My story is one of transformation, both personally and in the organization I led. It is a transformation that brings together two immeasurably influential discoveries in my life: transcendental meditation and spiritual leadership.

As a young adult, I found myself on the wrong side of the tracks. I had rejected the religion I was brought up in and everything that went with it; spirituality, God, ultimate purpose, deeper meaning etc.; I threw it all out with the bathwater. My life became an insatiable and reckless pursuit of happiness through carnal pleasures. There was nothing for me in the present moment; it was all way too boring. In reality, I was racked with fear, anxiety and shame which I tried to hide from the outside world by projecting a carefree, rebellious and wild persona. I was deeply inauthentic which made life incredibly stressful.

In my work life, LinuxIT was on the brink of administration. There was a palpable sense of fear, insecurity and mistrust; key workers were leaving in their droves; and the senior management team were in conflict. It was clear that LinuxIT had no higher purpose beyond profit maximization for shareholder gain. It had been started as an opportunistic, money-making enterprise, and the vacuousness of this approach had left LinuxIT in a similar place to me personally: broken, inauthentic and concerned only with what it could take from the world. Although I was not leading the company at that point, it was clear that my personal imbalance was somehow echoed in the business.

It was only after a particularly distressing episode that my journey of self-discovery began. I went into counseling and started to learn about the psychology behind my dysfunctional behaviors and after a few years found my way to TM [Transcendental Meditation]. Essentially, it is a simple mental technique which is practiced twice daily for 20 minutes while sitting comfortably with your eyes shut. Using a mantra, the mind settles down toward the source of thought, your own inner self. This place is a reservoir of intelligence, creativity and bliss.

I have been practicing TM for almost six years now, and it has utterly transformed my life. I am feeling, relating and behaving better; I feel more hopeful, creative and ambitious. Life appears to be treating me better; I am getting luckier. But perhaps the most profound change for me is how TM has enabled me to spend more time living in the present and with it gain a real sense of fulfilment and joy from simply being. Coming, as I have from such a place of insatiability, it is a truly precious sensation to feel fulfilled.

Having been with LinuxIT since 1999, in 2013, I became CEO. It looked for all intents and purposes as though I had inherited the captaincy just in time to disappear with the ship under the waves. We were in financial and cultural ruin, and it was going to need a miracle. But I hadn't given up hope. If I could turn my personal life around, maybe I could do the same here. My mission was to explore how I might, as leader, help to bring my new found personal balance and meaning to the organization.

Coinciding with this search for meaning was my search for an MBA research dissertation topic. I ultimately ended up writing a paper titled "An exploration of spiritual leadership". It revolved around a real-world, critical incident at LinuxIT where we had to decide whether we were prepared to take on a payday loan company as a managed services customer. On the one hand, we desperately needed the money but on the other we were unable to dismiss our concerns about the unethical nature of their business and felt it would be incongruent with our personal values to support them.

I started by inviting all the key LinuxIT stakeholders to a debate. This was the first time we had brought people together in this way to talk about our individual and group values. What initially emerged was cynicism about our intention and how we would act; a sense of disbelief that anything would trump the pursuit of revenue. Slowly, as I made it clear that I genuinely wanted to consider this incident from the perspective of our values, people started to open up. They explained that they wanted the ability to live an integrated life where work did not conflict with their personal values. Skepticism gave way to a much more trusting approach; one in which we listened to each other more deeply and started to coalesce our values into a shared vision of the future. We were connecting in pursuit of higher ideals in a way I had never before experienced at LinuxIT. We had gained a deeper understanding of ourselves individually and as a group; we had become more aware of our connectedness both within the organisation and beyond; and we were driven by a sense of meaning and purpose, a desire to make a difference.

Although my meditation and exploration of spiritual leadership was explicitly not about a search for a higher power, I began to appreciate an unseen dimension of reality that permeated this incident. Rather than simply gathering all the information possible and then constructing a rationale to act in one way or another, I felt I was gaining inspiration from a deeper source of intelligence. From this place, I derived such a sense of comfort and self-confidence; an unshakable belief that what was happening would be the best possible outcome if I enabled it to emerge.

From this, we learnt to step back and take the time to ask ourselves where are decisions were coming from. Were we acting from fear at the level of the ego, or accessing a deeper reality and acting in line with our deepest values? Spiritual leadership in this case was about providing a safe environment within which my colleagues were encouraged to listen to what life was calling them to do. One that would allow them to connect with their colleagues in a way that inspires the collective to open up to the future that is trying to emerge. It is when we have this freedom that we are able to find true meaning in what we are doing and with inner purpose become so much more creative, productive and committed.

So we set about creating such an environment; one in which our employees could find fulfilment and our customers would gain increasing value. We started by using consultants to evaluate where we were on our spiritual journey both individually and as a culture. As part of this process, we discussed ideas such as spiritual leadership, conscious capitalism, Myers-Briggs, archetypes, spiral dynamics and more. This helped us to see ourselves and the organization in novel ways. We began to value the vertical learning of emotional and spiritual intelligence as well as the horizontal learning associated with our domain knowledge. As a learning organization, we began to share information much more freely with all stakeholders. Mutual trust grew, and decisions began to be made from a place of hope and faith rather than from the default position of distrust and fear. And to retain that trust, we recruited on the basis that we must share values, most other things could be taught. We committed never to make any decisions that would materially affect our colleagues without consulting with them first. We delayered the organizational structure. We brought everyone together on one floor to bring down barriers to communication and flow of information. We introduced a games room and spent more time having fun together. We standardised pay, reduced the differential between top and bottom earners and provided every employee with an interest in the company. From a customer perspective, we re-founded our business model on the principle of co-creation of value rather than purely on profitability. We did this by honestly assessing our ability to deliver value to a prospect and theirs to help us realize our vision before we took them on.

After a couple of years of employing this approach, we became an entirely transformed organization. On a purely financial level, we turned the company around completely with no debt, unprecedented sales and reduced costs. But more importantly, LinuxIT was rich in meaning for the first time in its 16-year history. The conversation metamorphosed from themes of fear, insecurity and mistrust, to belief, optimism and togetherness. We gained a real sense of purpose. We acted with the firm belief that if we did what we believed to be right, even if the outcome from that action appeared to be undesirable, eventually good would come from it; and invariably it did. Our culture buzzed with creativity, commitment, caring, mastery, trust, fun, laughter, ambition and belief. I am very proud of what we built and I believe this outcome would have been entirely inconceivable to me had I not learnt TM and subsequently found my way to spiritual leadership.

Culture Inversion Meets Ethical Leadership

Sara de Marco

This is a story about a return to my hometown, in the north of Italy, due largely to my husband's relocation after a period of 20 years living in the UK, primarily in London. It has presented me with a challenge in grappling with ethical leadership as two cultures collide, and I question certain behaviors in formal leadership positions from my own personal experience of informal leadership in the community; but before I unpack this, I would like to offer a timeline with some background information.

In 1997, I moved to the UK to attend an MA in English Linguistics and discourse analysis; this was the first time I was faced with some critical thinking. After 25 years of spoon-feeding, following rules and not questioning as a well-educated Catholic student from the most entrepreneurial part of northern Italy, I was selected to represent my University abroad and possibly pursue an academic career. I was very proud of my achievement, yet unaware of what was about to happen to me. . . . The MA was attended by young British graduates: only Kyoko from Japan, and myself from Italy were foreign students in the class . . . I still remember the shock we experienced after the first seminar on critical discourse analysis! We both could not get over the fact that a lowly student could be critical of a published article without being judged rude and presumptuous. That MA was for me a year of demanding work and grind, chiseling through the mental granite blocks I had layered up throughout my childhood and adolescence. Nevertheless, it was an authentic experience of liberation and emancipation through education and openness to diversity. Throughout the work experience in the UK I was confronted with cultural bias, stereotyping and a fair bit of discrimination. It was not easy to challenge these in a foreign territory whose values seem so different from those in my native home. Yet, on the way, I met a supportive network of colleagues, who shared similar experiences and quite a few of them were even happy to offer advice on handling difficult relations. These experiences shaped me as a more sceptical and outspoken individual, a rebel with a cause: challenge the oppressive patterns surrounding my existence to hopefully also improve the life of others and redeem myself. They also led me to abandon some strict Catholic practices and embrace a Christian spiritual worldview based on respect for the others and zero tolerance towards the lack of it.

Many years have passed since then. I am now married to a New Zealander, born in Kenya with a childhood in Accra; we have three young daughters, and I recently started to work as a freelancer in youth leadership programmes in the English language. Our recent move back to Italy has been for me the best example of having the courage to grapple with ethical leadership and offer a compelling cause to the rebellious spirit in me. And I am struggling as I go. . . .

What gets in the way?

Obviously, me.

I have a big problem. I have to speak out. I cannot stand witnessing the abuse of authoritative power to those less represented and pretend I have seen nothing . . . I cannot hold on to the *stultifying inertia* and sense of resignation I hear from the people I meet every day at school, in a shop, at a public institution, when discussing an episode of ethical concerns:

> '*E' cosi'*, *That's the way it is* . . .' I am told, 'there is nothing we can do to change it', 'if you say something, something bad will happen to you or your family. I will lose my job'. While I do understand the reason of their reactionless attitude and empathise with their feelings, I deeply burn inside with temper at their effortless resignation. A sense of not belonging to this culture pervades me. Is there something I can do to pursue my purpose?

In trying to understand the cultural issues I am experiencing, I observe two recurrent patterns: on the one hand there seems to be a general less caring eye towards disrespect. Tolerance towards abusive behaviors between people is higher than what I experienced abroad. Children get taught to be "strong" and to put up with mischief. On the other hand, there is a real fear to stand out and blow the whistle. I came across these throughout my children school settling experience in Italy.

Since my arrival back in town, I have reported several cases of oppressive behaviour: bullying at school, discrimination against an immigrant during the Religion lesson and verbal attacks against a vulnerable woman and child in a shop.

My eldest daughter is dyslexic too, which has meant having to challenge a system based on wrote learning, formulaic answering and a lack of anything diverse from the main dictated program. Teachers are the professionals with the authority and the stakeholders (parents and children) having to blindly follow an out-of-date learning system preparing children for jobs that may not exist in the future. In the past five years, automation and offshore manufacturing have had big impacts, creating huge unemployment rates especially in the manufacturing sector in northern Italy. The future is not looking bright for traditional industries in a world that is increasingly automating and experimenting with artificial Intelligence.

A little girl with learning disabilities is bullied at school during the break. They call her "BIG Eyes" because she wears glasses and she has a learning difficulty. My daughter reports this to the teacher who quite reluctantly (she was having her coffee break) addresses the issue. The job is done. No follow up in the classroom, no support to the whistle blower. . . . Up to them to sort these issues out. They are just children after all (I got told later) and therefore not aware of the evil gesture. Consequence: my daughter gets caught by the bullies for reporting the misacts during the break. She manages to confront them and reports the story to us back home. The bullied girl is now even more scared. Nobody reacts. At home, we try hard to discuss these issues and encourage and support our kids for reporting them. Mia, our mid-daughter has done the right/ethical thing. We decide to report the story to the head teacher. His reaction is concerned, yet without immediate action. There are many priorities in his new role. He recently joined the school and having to deal with a long-established teaching staff that is united in resisting any change. Moreover, they are unionized. "We are working very hard to discourage bullies; the teachers take this very seriously. Rest assured the school is dealing with this". That is what we get told. A few other episodes of disrespectful behavior are reported by our child. We discuss and monitor the reaction and talk to other parents. No further actions. It seems to be one singular instance that is not even affecting their own kids, so no reason to act. We realize there is a cultural divergence on matters of respect between us, our daughter and the school. Our threshold is less tolerant than the school and the neighboring community on matters of respect. One day, a similar but more violent episode happens in the classroom. The same vulnerable child gets hit in the stomach by a boy who is known to have difficult family issues. Our daughter is very distressed "The teacher said she did not see anything because she was looking at the board. She has no control of the class!" We decide to report the fact and to remove our daughter from the school. We are not political refugees, nor immigrants in desperate conditions. We have decided to move from Britain, an educated country with a reasonably stable economy (so far), and we have moved our child out of school. This is an alarming signal to the school. The headteacher's reaction has been strong. In an attempt to understand the issues, the class is now being supervised by a team of support teachers and the headteacher. Our letter has been filed as an official complaint. Outside the school environment some rumours have been reported from neighbouring friends". The mother is a snob, the child is not fitting in because of her", some said, while others commented: "they had the courage to do something, but that's because they just moved here. We have a longer established tradition here than them . . . our names, necks will be on the line if we dared to blow the whistle. You have to be careful you know, people know each other well here and they will take it on your child".

The head teacher of the new school is a woman who is firm but sensitive. She hears our story, and—leading five primary and two secondary schools—she offers us a school for our child which has still available spaces. After visiting it, Mia is happy to move in. The class is quite diverse, but the atmosphere is calm, we are told.

Except that . . . one day, the R.E. teacher, whose module is on inclusion and diversity, warns the kids to be watchful of the migrants that recently have come to live in the town: "they come and steal in your houses!" it is a classroom lecture. In the class, there is a Moroccan child that is going through a difficult integration phase. Mia (our daughter) who has so far lived and learnt with children from the world, shows distress and reports it to us. We have a migrant girl from Cameroon that lives and works with the family and this upsets Mia even more. She sees how hard this young woman works and how sad she often looks because she misses her children who are in Africa. Response is fast. After reporting the fact to the headteacher and asking to follow through, she allows Mia to be dismissed from R.E. to follow an enrichment programme. The R.E. teacher receives a warning. She now does not speak to me outside school. She has also been throwing sarcastic comments to Mia inside school, but Mia knows she was right to report this and dismisses the provocations. I learn from her to do the same . . . to pick my battles. This experience has been positive for all of us but what about the Moroccan child in the classroom? Mia is still reporting different behavioral attitudes towards him as the days go by.

Our experience as a family in Italy is overall positive, yet there is an ongoing challenge to understand and claim our identity and our values. It takes courage for a child to change environment, settle in, see, recognize and report. It takes risks for a parent to encourage this behavior. But it is purposeful and fulfilling inside our family unit and in line with our spiritual values. Yet, I am not fitting in and I am Italian, so perhaps I should know how things are done here. But I cannot ignore matters of injustice.

So far, outside my own family unit, I am going against the current on a number of fronts. First, I have not yet been able to build a network of people who share my values and beliefs. Second, I find myself stepping backwards into a more traditional cultural context, very different from London where diversity is handled with more political consciousness and derived from a long established multiracial culture. Third, as a Christian believer, I am encountering the Catholicism of my childhood, which has connotations of repression, guilt and fear of punishment. All this is bringing to the surface deep questions about spirituality and justice.

I am in the front line and am exposing my kids to the decisions I have to make. They laugh a lot about the passionate Italian craziness of their mother. Yet, having attended a British school and embraced Christian values outside the Catholic institutionalized tradition, they can perfectly see and report what and why something does not look/feel right. Disruption is happening for sure within our small circle. . . . My hope is that one day I will find my tribe and make more impact, and, hopefully, I will become a more temperate radical.

Part II

Connection
Where Is Leadership in the Mundane?

In various ways, this section is concerned with recognizing and theorizing the disconnects between who we feel we are as human beings and who we are seemingly expected to be as workplace practitioners, leaders or followers. It is as much a focus on what resides in between the messy, visceral, flawed self and the clean, intellectual self that seems to be in-control of events and circumstances, our cultural and institutional assumptions. Each of the authors address disconnects between the privately experienced self and the publicly presented/expected self: a topic rarely surfaced in conventional leadership discourse.

David Knights challenges the dominant idea of applying individualistic, technical interventions and prescriptions to the problems of leadership. In its place, he advocates a theoretically informed yet practice-driven strategy that takes full account of how leadership is a collective and embodied process of interpersonal and intra-personal relationships the effectiveness of which depends strongly on affective engagement. He seeks to illustrate this through reflecting on some recent highly significant political and sporting events of international importance as also through a vignette outlining some personal experiences. He concludes that its affecting and being affected by joyful and creative productive action best encapsulates leadership.

Leah Tomkins and Peter Simpson highlight parallels between their private experiences of care and their public experiences of leadership. They relate the notion of leading with integrity to a desire for greater wholeness, by reconnecting some of their experiences across the so-called work-life boundary. Using examples from their own family and professional lives, they create a virtuous circle in which the emotional and decision-making dynamics of both care and leadership can be mutually illuminating. They speak honestly and personally about how not only do they learn how to care in the domestic situation from their experience of leading in organizations but also from the inverse of reflecting on their caring responsibilities when pursuing leadership tasks at work.

Hugo Gaggiotti notes that language—and the English language in particular—disconnects us in two ways. First, the lack of understanding that arises between people; in this case, Anglo-Saxon leadership development professionals and students for whom English is not their native language, and for whom "leadership" has odd and difficult resonances. A second disconnect is within the self—this is experienced when we have to engage with a topic that is so "foreignly" constructed that it gets in the way of a heartfelt, ethical and embodied engagement.

Tim Harle invokes the notion of "good enough" in exploring the fallible self and infallible self. His contention is that we often overlook the fact that ethical—and what might be termed great—leadership is actually exercised by ordinary people through a succession of everyday acts in mundane situations.

Another way of seeing this section is that of working with and through difference. When there are disconnections we not only become detached but also estranged from our experiences. So our minds become detached from our bodies, our thinking cuts us off from feelings and emotion, our sense of self loses touch with others on whom it is dependent, our work becomes separated from our lives and leading is in danger of elevating itself above its purpose. The provocation is that much of this goes unnoticed in the mundane and that some re-connections may help restore the ethical wholeness of our leadership as embodied and passionately engaged with life.

In the two vignettes at the end of this section, the contributors give some clues as to what this reconnection looks like in the everyday ordinariness of life. It is unlikely that either felt their "battles" were much to do with personal courage and leading ethically at the time, but, on reflection, both give very personal glimpses on what it means to be disconnected and how this might be dealt with.

Clare Rigg relates a story all too common in organizations . . . a middle manager caught in the crossfire between unreasonable demands of those in charge and the legitimate angst of those below. Despite strong core beliefs and a determination to make a difference, she ultimately decided that the best and ethical thing to do was "to step away rather than be caught up in continuing the dysfunction".

The vignette from Catherine Turner-Perrott starts with a mother confronted by a child uninterested in food, a scenario that could not be further removed from the corporate world of ethics. Yet from these small beginnings unfolds a series of small steps, each incurring some risk and courage, the consequences of which are transforming her into an entrepreneurial leader in developing an organization inspired by ethical care that provides services to restaurants, cafes and canteens, rendering them more efficient and effective.

5   What's More Effective Than Affective Leadership?

Searching for Embodiment in Leadership Research and Practice

David Knights

Key Questions

Why is the body important yet neglected in leadership?

Is affective leadership a way of acknowledging the body in a newly ethical manner?

What blinds us to affective leadership?

Why is embodied engagement ethical?

Is affective leadership effective?

Introduction

A concern with leadership is extensive and has proliferated in the last few years as the pendulum has swung once again away from technology, toward human solutions to organizational problems. Dominated by psychology and prescriptive interventions, the applied science of leadership went through numerous renewals, each believing itself to represent "progress" but none of which offered practitioners the golden bullet. Over recent times, a more critical approach has gained ground where there has been challenge to the individualistic, often heroic and prescriptive, approach of mainstream leadership studies. This has partly taken the path of examining the actual practices of, rather than imposing theoretical ideas on, leadership. However, the topic of this chapter—the body—has tended to be neglected or taken for granted despite everything in human life being embodied, as well as cerebral.[1] This is perhaps not surprising given that even when on death the body is center stage, rituals ensure that it remains concealed or shrouded in social routines of symbolic, rather than material, significance. Yet if we need reminding of the centrality of the body, we may merely reflect on how just as we breathe, we also think, through the body.

As I have intimated, a critical fringe in leadership studies has sought to challenge the separation of mind from body and the domination of cognitive, linguistic and symbolic discourses over concerns with the body and other material relations. Often described as a "new spirituality", post-humanist research traces the neglect of the body to masculine modes of power and offer insights into the ambiguity, doubt and insecurity that befall us when the myth of certainty surrounding "scientific" approaches to leadership is exposed. It also rejects prescriptive rule- and norm-based approaches so as to focus on embodied engagement as part of what it means to practice ethical leadership. It is this recent concern with the body and ethics that is endorsed here as part of an attempt to renew and revitalize leadership matters.

This has resulted in a growing demand to focus more on the body and embodied ways of conducting research, as well as to give attention to other material objects that are significant in human affairs. After several medical investigations, my own attention to the body came about as the result of a very personal and painful experience of finding myself infertile. Despite writing about gender at the time, my masculine ways of thinking made me believe that I had managed the tragedy when actually I had only rationalized it with the effect that subsequently, I suffered depersonalization followed by a nervous breakdown.[2] While negative in many ways, this did force me to experience the inseparability of my bodily from my cognitive experience. It made me realize that our bodies are simultaneously subject and object of one and the same action, and this is what enables and demands our reflexivity about our embodied being.[3] There can be no human activity and least of all any concerned with leadership practice, where the body is absent. Indeed, much of the mainstream in leadership studies and especially those concerned with transformational, distributional and leaderly forms of leadership,[4] have seen charisma, inspiration and empathy as significantly embodied. For as humans, we relate not just verbally or cognitively but also with emotions and feelings expressed through our bodies. Indeed, our first encounter with anyone is embodied, and sexual attraction is through the body usually before mental factors and reasoning come into play. Leadership is corporeal activity in the sense of seeking to inspire and enthuse the corporate body as well as relating to bodies as individual subjects. Paradoxically, it is only when leadership becomes a topic of analysis and investigation that disembodied conceptions of its everyday practice predominate. This is largely because of a subscription to cognitive and mentalist or linguistic and symbolic discourse that eschews the body and soul.

In addition to developing a more embodied understanding, this chapter will also challenge many of the assumptions and presumptions of leadership both in theory and practice around, for example, power and resistance, identity and self, and anxiety and insecurity through returning to the body and embodiment. It will explore alternative approaches and in particular how the notion of affect can be helpful to understanding leadership as an embodied practice. In order to illustrate some of the arguments, I will draw on the recent leadership battles within British politics surrounding the referendum regarding membership of the European Union (EU).

Organized around three themes, I focus first on a discussion of the neglect of the body, embodiment and other material objects. Second I seek to engage with the growing attention being given to the body particularly within studies of leadership. These developments in the literature, however, do not always result in embodied forms of analysis or a concern with ethical leadership. For this, we need to turn to our third thematic—the focus on a theory and practice of affect and its affects and, more importantly, how it might facilitate the development of embodied and ethical leadership. A summary returns to answer the title of the chapter by arguing that nothing is more effective than affective leadership and also seeks to explore both the theoretical and practical implications of these arguments.

Neglecting the Body

There is general agreement that the body has been historically neglected in research and practice in social science and more particularly in leadership studies. It first has to be asked why this is the case and why it is important to reverse this neglect? Before examining reasons for this neglect, I focus on why it needs to be addressed. Broadly, this can be linked to the assumptions and presumptions of leadership theory and practice that revolve around the interlinked notions of power and resistance, identity and the self, and anxiety and insecurity. It can reasonably be argued that effective leadership has to mobilize subjects, whether to reinforce the prevailing power of the leader or in resistance to that power. This can be facilitated through transforming individuals into subjects that find their meaning and sense of identity through engaging in the practices invoked by this leadership.[5] Also in their attempts to transform individuals into subjects sufficiently docile to be led, leaders usually claim, if not even aim, to relieve the anxieties and insecurities of those they wish to enroll into their cause. However, followers are often not so docile and indeed frequently will resist and/or seek alternatives either because the leader(s) fails to confirm the desired sense of self, identity and security or simply due to conventional power struggles that are evident in all organizations.

To provide an empirical illustration of these three conceptual issues, I have focused on a selection of the political events surrounding the EU referendum in the United Kingdom (UK) in 2016, where the fundamental importance of the body in matters of leadership was revealed in a range of struggles around power/resistance, self/identity and anxiety/insecurity. There are, of course, multiple forms through which such struggles become manifest in the body politic, corporate bodies and in the bodies or embodiment of political leaders. While these cannot be easily separated from one another, the analysis here focuses only on the struggles concerning political leadership surrounding the UK referendum about continuing or withdrawing from EU membership. Consequent upon the binary nature of the EU (or any) referendum, leaders from both the leave (Brexit) and remain sides of the campaign were driven to embody their arguments with emotion, feeling and affect. Here we take up the UK referendum events of June 2016, but I invite you to apply a similar kind of analysis to events with which you are particularly familiar. For example, maybe the 2016 US Presidential race for the White House was a more globally important event than the UK leaving the EU. Hillary Clinton was stereotyped as untrustworthy because of making mistakes in sending messages from her personal email that included national security data but at the same time depicted as cold and calculating and thus far from embodied. Donald Trump, on the other hand, was seen as embodied but perhaps out of control insofar as his statements violated anything that could be seen as professional decorum. His embodied attacks on the establishment, however, appealed to large numbers of voters who had felt marginalized by politicians and society at large while also ignored in terms of their sometimes xenophobic nationalist interests, protests about declining standards of living and felt threats from cheaper foreign labor. Parallels were to be found in Brexit, so these can be seen as global political trends.

Because the conservative party had a long history of EU membership being a major fault line of division, the Prime Minister (PM) David Cameron had called the referendum with a belief that the electorate would provide sufficient endorsement to heal this rift in his party and would also prevent defections to the UK Independence Party (UKIP), whose main policy issue was exiting the EU. He therefore led the campaign but had serious leave or Brexit campaigners within his own party and so was grateful to have support from the Labour Party—the official opposition and its leader, Jeremy Corbyn. Moreover, although Cameron led a reasonably engaged campaign for remaining in the EU, Boris Johnson, an embodied and charismatic supporter of the Brexit campaign, upstaged him. Of course, the charismatic and embodied leaders are not one and the same, since the former relates to presentation and personality and the latter more to subjective being as a whole in which the mind is simply an idea of the body and the body an active manifestation of the mind.[6] However, embodied subjects are invariably seen as charismatic in that they project a sense of wellbeing on to anyone with whom they engage although the reverse is not always the case, for charisma is more a performance that can be manufactured at will. Boris who could be seen as more performative than embodied soon began to turn the electorate, especially since UKIP had already secured solid support to leave the EU on the back of issues of national identity—an issue partly sustained by xenophobic concerns to control immigration. Clearly, Brexit was not just a function of engaging the body as well as the brain but also one of resisting the power of the establishment position. The leave campaign appealed to large numbers of the comparatively less well-off parts of the indigenous population whose anxieties and insecurities concerning levels of immigration had been neglected by the two mainstream political parties. In addition, a marginalized population was always likely to feel fragile in their sense of self and identity. Consequently, the appeal to a reclaimed national identity in the form of stricter borders and, the emotional language of let us "take back control" and "we want our country back"[7] found an immediate resonance with the bodily lived experience of those feeling let down by the political establishment. The parallels with the polarized political campaigns of the US presidential elections were uncannily close. Trump demanded strict border controls, empathized with the poor white population and made excessive claims about eradicating crime and terrorism at the same time as upholding the long tradition of every American having a right to possess arms. By contrast, Clinton stuck clearly to rational arguments for liberal tolerance, gun control and claiming to be a safe pair of experienced hands in these troublesome times. In the UK, it was the remaining campaigners that pursued a rational economic set of arguments although they did raise and intensify levels of anxiety and insecurity among the population in an attempt to scare the electorate off from voting to leave the EU. Likewise, in the US, it was Clinton who sought to scare the electorate from voting for Trump on the basis that he was not only inexperienced but also was a loose cannon who was likely to act irresponsibly and could not be trusted to be in command of the country's nuclear arsenal.

The reasons for the neglect of the body in social science are complex but in Western society would seem to be closely associated with the hierarchical elevation of mind over body (Descartes). The consequent binary focus on elevating the intellect and cognition above all other aspects of human life is a practice that tends to reinforce or reproduce masculine hegemony. This binary thinking leads to men and masculinities[8] being privileged over women and femininities, heterosexual (and sometimes homophobic) identities over those that are not Caucasian over other races, and the young and able bodied are elevated over the elderly and impaired.[9] Some of the disadvantaged seek to reverse these binaries as when feminists adopt a standpoint position, claiming that only the oppressed have access to reality since the vested interests of the privileged result in their ideas being ideological or when oppressive regimes are challenged through a politics of identity. Insofar as both these strategies of reversal reproduce the very binaries that critics claim to eradicate, they could be seen as self-defeating. Reversing the hierarchical power and privilege such that black, feminist or other minority identities *dominate* social relations is no more palatable than what this politics attempts to displace. Moreover, seeking to assert identities alternative to the dominant ones could be seen as oxymoronic because it is hardly likely to cultivate a "politics of difference" in which *engaging*, rather than competing with and controlling, the Other[10] is paramount. By contrast, a politics of difference is concerned with respecting and valuing, rather than negating or stigmatizing, those who are different and therefore contributes significantly to removing discrimination at work and elsewhere. As opposed to merely instituting rules aimed at eradicating discrimination or strategies designed to make the business case for diversity, which operate at a distance between leaders and led, engaging with difference involves managers actively relating and thereby developing an understanding and human empathy with their employees. It demands embodied leadership that engages with those whom they are leading not just as functionaries but as human subjects in all their multiplicity and is ethical insofar as it embraces, rather than seeks to classify or stereotype, difference.

The Body, Embodiment and Ethical Leadership

Leadership is often studied quite superficially, exclusively in terms of variables that can be easily observed and measured. For example, leadership effectiveness is regularly associated with physical characteristics such as height, weight, and body type; routinely it is assumed that leaders are able bodied and ostensibly white, Western and male,[11] and many studies have been criticized for a tendency to remain wholly descriptive.[12] Other research, however, has focused on analyzing the body in leadership in terms of gender[13] or has taken a more philosophical approach.[14] Sinclair has analyzed the way that the bodies of men and women leaders are presented to support the myth of men being wholly rational and women more emotional. So, for example, photographic images of male leaders predominantly focus just on the head because this is linked to the mind and cognition, whereas more of the body and of the flesh of women is in view. This simply maps gender onto the mind-body binary discussed above, reflecting and reproducing an image of men and masculinity as in control both physically and metaphorically and women assigned to their uncontrollable, unpredictable and overflowing bodies. No better exemplification of how the gendered body is highly significant can be found than in TV and film media where physical appearance seems to count much more for women than men. As followers more than as leaders, women's bodies are often disciplined in order to render them docile and productive, and as leaders their aging bodies are at a gender disadvantage since the grey elderly man is looked upon as wise and dignified in a way that is not the case for older women.[15] Feminists have sought to reverse this representation by re-imagining women leaders as effective not in spite of their bodies, but because they are more embodied.[16] This disrupts the representation of leadership as being naturally masculine and lacking in eroticism and sensuality. It also acknowledges that embodiment is a necessary condition of ethical engagement since it renders leaders responsible to the other and thereby less preoccupied with themselves or their own identities. For the failure of ethical leadership can be traced to the dominance of individualism, preoccupations with the self and heroism within leadership discourse and practice.

I am able to reflect here on my own limited experience of leadership practice whether through formal positions in university departments or schools, managing quite large numbers of doctoral students or in directing a research center for several years. My way of doing this was always to seek to be engaged in an embodied manner with those for whom I had some responsibility rather than issue instructions from a distance. I tried to be actively engaged and involved in their work and with doctoral students I would write collaboratively so as to help them secure publications before finalizing their PhD. Moreover, in leading the research center, which involved several large financial corporations funding academic research, this engagement generated a loyalty from the members insofar as they followed me to another university when I moved after internal politics had resulted in disruptions that I was no longer prepared to accept.[17]

Through the ESRC seminar series that has generated this book, I have been able to share my experiences but also develop my understandings of how embodied as well as intellectual self-reflection is productive in advancing the theory and practice of leadership. In order to explore further the potential of embodied and ethically engaged leadership, I turn now to how affect is integral to its practice.

Affect and Leadership Ethics

At the time of writing this chapter, as already noted above the UK was passing through one of the more challenging periods of its history and, in particular, in relation to political leadership. We take up the story again:

> *A referendum had resulted in the partly unexpected outcome of leaving the EU and an associated leadership crisis in the political parties as not only the Prime Minister but also several other leaders resigned. Few people in the UK could claim to have been unaffected by these tumultuous events and given that the leave vote was only 4% ahead of the remain vote, throughout the country deep debates, disputes and divisions continued and of a veracity perhaps exceeding the events of the global financial crisis in 2008. Regardless of party political sentiments, when Theresa May was appointed as Prime Minister, there seemed a collective sigh of relief that British politics had returned to some sense of normality—a very embodied sense of salvation in leadership.*
>
> *Although the collective sense of a secure identity took another jolt in the speedy departure of England from the Euro Football Championship, at least Wales exceeded the wildest of expectations in reaching the semi-finals of the competition. Not to be outdone, the Scots and the rest of the UK were able to claim one of the most esteemed tennis prizes when Andy Murray won the men's singles final at Wimbledon and then went on to become the World Number 1 male singles tennis player. Added to this, GB did better at the Rio Olympics in terms of medals (2nd after the US) and Paralympics (2nd after China) than they had done in the record breaking London games and leadership plus major investment was held responsible.*

I have reported in some detail on these somewhat unique events in the contemporary history of the British nation largely because they not only involved affectively engaged bodies affecting other bodies and the material and symbolic lives of a nation's population, they also energized these self-same bodies in ways that enhanced their capacity to be affective. Whether on the winning or losing side of the EU referendum or in celebrating or commiserating national sporting outcomes, not only is there massive bodily energy affecting the process but also the outcome significantly affects us as embodied subjects in all sorts of ways. There has been an increasing use of the term affect to refer to a wide range of embodied experiences from anguish to euphoria, sadness to exhilaration, panic to passion, fear to courage, pessimism to optimism and hatred to love, to mention just a few.

But why refer to *affect* as opposed to feelings or emotions? While affect incorporates feelings and emotions, it has been argued that they are more static, concrete and individualized referring almost always to individual sentient, and usually human, beings. By contrast, affect is dynamic and intercorporeal as well as referring to material objects and not just humans. So, for example, a feeling or emotion is a state of being, or the property, of a sentient subject at a singular moment in time while an affect is always in transition moving from source(s) to destination(s) often in reciprocal fashion, and can just as readily be virtual as real. We affect a vast range of material, animal and human phenomena as they affect us, so affect cannot be seen as the property of a person since it is in a complex web of relations or networks.

By focusing on affect, we are not inventing something new so much as acknowledging the body as simultaneously the subject and object of the same action and how it affects and is affected by other bodies in ways that can enhance or destroy the capacity for reasoned action. As has been argued, traditional thinking about leadership has often been constrained by attributions of it to persons who are deemed to have essential qualities that render them charismatic, heroic, rational and perhaps even magical. While this individualization of the notion of leadership as a property of persons has been restrained in succeeding developments of leadership that emphasize the context, the followers and practice rather than prescriptive ideals, romanticizing the individual remains a legacy that is frequently rekindled. Returning to the examples above:

> it is clear that individuals were often less important than the situation albeit as I argued, the more embodied leaders (e.g,. Boris Johnson) were effective in affecting outcomes in a way that lesser embodied ones (e.g., Jeremy Corbyn) were not. Indeed, Boris's reward for his wholly embodied flamboyance in perhaps being the most popular advocate of Brexit was the highly prestigious position of foreign secretary[18] in the newly reconstituted Conservative Administration. In the end, the Prime Minister emerged partly at least because the chaotic conditions post referendum demanded it.[19] In the Euros, the failure of England and the success of Wales was a function of their differential capacities for collective affect in playing as teams and indeed the winner of the competition— Portugal—played most of the final without their individual superstar Ronaldo. To a large extent, his affect was virtual in the sense that the team were able to demonstrate how they could win without him. Also there is little question that both Andy Murray's and the Olympic/

Paralympic successes were wholly embodied collective achievements. With the exception of England in the Euros, they were also joyous collective affective occasions for the participants and the whole nation.

Summary

By way of conclusion, I return to the title of this chapter—what is more effective than affective leadership? Affect is about making a difference through embodied energy but this energy is as much inter-corporeal as individual and is never static enough to capture in a concrete instance but is forever in transition, as was the case in the political events surrounding the referendum and the sporting events surrounding the Euros and Olympics. In making a difference, leadership enhances the capacity of others to act and also makes a difference so it is infectious but it affects not just other subjects but also the material and symbolic conditions of its practice.

What is distinctive about affective leadership is not that it offers something new so much as it frees the concept of leadership from the belief in techniques or prescriptions to be imposed in interventionist ways on practice (see also Chris Mabey, Chapter 3). Affect does not have to be invented; it just has to be *nurtured* rather than denied or neglected. All leadership is affective but prescriptive and technical interventions invariably distort its effects. Albeit often in the name of the "collective good" and ethical standards, these interventions promote obedience to norms and rules rather than the enhancement of capacities for reasoned action with others. Many leadership theorists and consultants might find this analysis disconcerting because of how it potentially undermines their expertise. However, I believe that affective leadership is capable of generating ethical, spiritually uplifting and joyful modes of collective action and commitment and in so doing, rendering organizations more efficient and effective. But there is a need to abandon the kinds of expert interventions that tend to impose masculine linear rational techniques, which leave subjects devoid of any sense of embodied engagement. Through acknowledging affect as an embodied experience, we can begin to see how leadership is no more than affecting and being affected by our relations in ways that energize us into joyful, creative and productive action. When leaders or their followers speak about the secret of good leadership, they invariably endorse this view. As I completed this sentence, I heard Alan Ayckbourn speak about the film director Steven Spielberg, who, when asked what was his secret, argued that it was just to generate the atmosphere where the actors could cultivate their own creativity. How many famous leaders are more likely to respond in this way rather than to refer to some technique they have acquired from leadership experts?

Finally, I conclude this essay with a brief vignette relating to my experience as an academic and which can be seen to represent the unfolding of my interest in embodied leadership.

Personal Reflection

During my early career, some students and colleagues believed me to be courageous in developing a course called Work, Industry and Society (WIS) in the
management department that was not only different from, but also directly
critical of, many of the other courses. This is because we challenged taken for
granted views of the capitalist social order. As my colleague Hugh Willmott,
who became a tutor on the course after he graduated, described it: "WIS was,
and is, an intellectual and existential *tour de force*—a course that in bringing
together the personal and the political enabled participants to connect their/
our experiences with key ideas in social science".[20] Whereas conventional
teaching would reflect and reproduce the social inequalities of class, gender
and race, this would seek to raise student awareness of these inequities and
promote theoretical and ethical understanding of their genesis and sustenance.
We did this through historically informed discussions of identity, insecurity,
power, inequality and resistance.[21] Through my own and others research, we
also provided empirical examples that enabled students to see that the ideas
articulated resonated with everyday political and workplace life. Perhaps more
important than the content of the course, however, was a student centered-
approach to learning that I deployed some time before it became trendy in the
1980s. This involved asking students questions rather than imposing assertive
knowledge upon them. I would then frame their answers in in relation to
intellectual ideas; theories and empirical or experiential knowledge such that
the students would feel they had been engaged, both in mind and body, in the
collective formation of what might traditionally be called a lecture. While at
this time, I had no theoretical awareness of embodied research or pedagogy,
my practice was clearly anticipating a future set of concerns as represented by
this essay on embodied leadership.

The courage attributed to me was, I believe, misplaced. While my deviance
did raise eyebrows among my more mainstream colleagues, and while speaking out in this way might have resulted in sanctions in lesser liberal institutions,
as long as I could legitimize my arguments academically, I was comparatively
"safe". I was simply expressing my intellectual and ethical beliefs and my courage was merely one of refusing to be the kind of subject that so many exercises
of power have inflicted upon us (Foucault, 1982). In short, I was distancing
myself from the common sense of public opinion in what Foucault describes as
an exercise of truth as difference but "this ethical differentiation is not in fact
the moral quality of a leader" but simply a "position of otherness".[22] So if we
are to take Foucault's conception of courage as developing one's ethical relationship to the other and thereby refuse simply to adapt to normative common
sense, it has little to do with conventional leadership practices other than possibly facilitating the distribution of leadership such that there is collective and
communal engagement. That is to say, only from the perspective of perceiving
it as collective responsibility could it be seen as a characteristic of leadership,
although there is now a movement leading (excuse the pun) in this direction.
Leaderful practice involves everyone in an organization exercising leadership
concurrently, collectively, collaboratively and compassionately and it is possible to argue that any commitment to such change is courageous.

Perhaps what was more courageous was developing a range of activities with private sector funding. While this was financially beneficial to the university, it seemed to attract the disdain of many of my colleagues on the basis that this was seen as "selling out" to the big corporations. Either directly or indirectly, the activities with large financial services corporations raised several million pounds but the opposition of some colleagues and a heavy phase of organization politics resulted in my moving to another university. I organized for the activities to be transferred, although clandestinely since this was during the period of serving my notice. A degree of courage was involved: firstly, in originally setting up this industry-academic collaboration and, secondly, in feeding back to these companies quite critical analyses of their business.

Another potential courageous aspect of my work was, as a man, to establish and edit the journal *Gender, Work and Organization* especially while working in a management school since this journal sought to undermine the masculine managerial norms within such institutions. It also meant working primarily with feminist women who sometimes implicitly if not explicitly would see this as a further example of men invading and appropriating their territory. Of course, this account could be perceived as masculine paranoia rather than courageous leadership because many of my colleagues saw me as a pro-feminist male ally rather than an imposter. However, probably one of the more courageous forms of leadership has been for me to encourage students of management to consider doctorates in, and more advanced researchers to pursue, critical studies of management and organization. In doing this, I had to steer them away from their desires or anticipations of advancing a career of big earnings and high social status that would ordinarily follow from pursuing a more mainstream trajectory either in academia or the world of management practice.

Finally, I should reflect on how I have come full circle since in the early part of my career I felt that leadership was just another myth through which class, gender, race and other forms of inequality were legitimized and reproduced. I have now come to realize that, while this is still often the case, it is possible to generate opportunities where leadership as traditionally understood can undermine itself in its very practice and thereby help to transform us all into leaders of ourselves and one another. I am writing this on the day (21st May 2017) of the pop concert bombing tragedy in my hometown Manchester where there appears to be precisely this sense of collective/self-leadership building some momentum against terrorism around the city and, of course, the world.

Notes

1. Certain colleagues have argued that the term embodied could be seen as obscure, but I would suggest that this is precisely a reflection of its neglect due to the continual elevation of mind over matter.
2. Although traumatic, fortunately, it only lasted seven weeks; for more detail, see Knights (2006).
3. Merleau-Ponty (1962).
4. Raelin (2010).
5. Knights (2002).

6. See Spinoza (1677/1833).
7. EU Referendum: The people v the elites? *BBC News Website*, available from: www.bbc.co.uk/news/uk-politics-eu-referendum-36458369 (accessed on June 26, 2016).
8. The term masculinity is used to describe both gender and sexual identities and practices ordinarily but not exclusively associated with men and tend to render practices disembodied or narrowly manly. While there are multiple expressions of masculinity (e.g., gay, transvestite, bisexual), a dominant if not hegemonic form prevails in contemporary society wherein there is a preoccupation with individualistic competition, conquest and control (Knights and Kerfoot, 2004).
9. It may not seem obvious why the elevation of mind over body reflects but also reproduces the dominance of men over women and heterosexuality over homosexuality, but this is largely because of the association of masculine discourses with linear rational cognitive thinking and action. Masculine rationality disavows what it sees as the overflowing viscosity of bodies that are then linked to the subordinated Other—women, sexual minorities and the impaired.
10. The capital O in other reflects the sense in which this encompasses not just other humans but also non-human sentient beings and even nature itself.
11. Pullen and Vachhani (2013, p. 315).
12. Ladkin (2013).
13. Trethewey (1999), Sinclair (2011), Pullen and Vachhani (2013).
14. Kupers (2013), Ladkin (2013).
15. Trethewey (1999), Knights and Morgan (1992), Knights and Willmott (1992).
16. Bell and Sinclair (2016).
17. See Kerfoot and Knights (1998).
18. Given his history of numerous diplomatic gaffes and insults of foreign dignitaries, this was a shock appointment to many.
19. Of course, the postscript to this was that in a shock June general election called by the UK Prime Minister in the belief that opinion polls predicted a landslide win for her, the situation was reversed, as Teresa May had a disembodied and lackluster campaign and Jeremy Corbyn the opposite, thus almost inverting the political situation.
20. Willmott (2017).
21. I developed the course over a period of 25 years, but it still continues to be taught by my successors in an even more radical fashion although under a more mainstream title. Eventually the course was written up in the form of a pedagogic text (see Knights and Willmott, 1999/2004).
22. Foucault (2011, loc. 7434).

Bibliography

Bell, E. and Sinclair, A. (2016) Re-envisaging leadership through the feminine imaginary in film and television. In Beyes, T., Parker, M. and Steyaert, C. (eds.) *Routledge Companion to the Humanities and Social Sciences in Management Education*. London: Routledge.

Foucault, M. (1982) Afterword: The subject and power. In Dreyfus, H.F. and Rainbow, P. (eds.) *Michel Foucault: Beyond Structuralism and Hermeneutics*. Brighton, UK: Harvester Press, pp. 208–226.

Foucault, M. (2011) *The Courage of Truth: Lectures at the College de France 1983–4*, Kindle Edition. Basingstoke: Palgrave Macmillan.

Kerfoot, D. and Knights, D. (1998) Man/management: Ironies of modern management in a post-modern era. In Whitehead, S. and Moodley, R. (eds.) *Masculinity in the Public Sector*. London: Taylor and Francis, pp. 200–213.

Knights, D. (2002) Writing organization analysis into Foucault. *Organization* 9, pp. 575–593, reprinted in S. Linstead (ed.) (2004) *Organizations and Postmodern Thought*. London: Sage Publications, pp. 14–33.

Knights, D. (2006) Authority at work: Reflections and recollections. *Organization Studies: Vita Contemplativa Section* 27(5), pp. 723–744.

Knights, D. and Morgan, G. (1992) Leadership as corporate strategy: Towards a critical analysis. *Leadership Quarterly* 3(3), pp. 171–190.

Knights, D. and Willmott, H. (1992) Conceptualising leadership processes: A study of senior managers in a financial services company. *Journal of Management Studies* 29(6), pp. 761–782.

Knights, D. and Willmott, H. (1999/2004) *Management Lives!: Power and Identity in Work Organisations*. London: Sage Publications.

Kupers, W. (2013) Embodied inter-practices of leadership—Phenomenological perspectives on relational and responsive leading and following. *Leadership* 9(3), pp. 335–357.

Ladkin, D. (2013) From perception to flesh: A phenomenological account of the felt experience of leadership. *Leadership* 9(3), pp. 320–334.

Merleau-Ponty, M. (1962) *The Phenomenology of Perception*. London: Routledge Kegan Paul.

Pullen, A. and Vachhani, S. (2013) The materiality of leadership. *Leadership* 9(3), pp. 315–319.

Raelin, J. (2010) *The Leaderful Fieldbook: Strategies and Activities for Developing Leadership in Everyone*. Boston: Nicholas Brealey.

Sinclair, A. (2011) Leading with body. In Jeanes, E., Knights, D. and Yancey Martin, P. (eds.) *Handbook on Gender, Work & Organization*. London and New York: Routledge, pp. 117–130.

Spinoza, B. (1677/1883) *The Ethics*, trans. R.H.M. Elwes. A Public Domain Book, Kindle.

Trethewey, A. (1999) Disciplined bodies: Women's embodied identities at work. *Organization Studies* 20(3), pp. 423–450.

Willmott, H. (2017) Reminiscences in *This Is Your Life*. Privately published book and Seminar University of Lancaster, 31 March.

6 An Ethic of Care
Reconnecting the Private and the Public

Leah Tomkins and Peter Simpson

Key Questions

Can we draw on our private lives, rather than textbook models and methodologies, for leadership development?

Can we challenge the assumption that so-called "soft" skills of care have no role to play in business and leadership?

What do caring relationships and leader-follower relationships have in common? What might we learn from these commonalities?

Our Perspective

This chapter draws on the authors' own personal and professional experiences more than most conventional leadership textbooks. We interweave ideas about familial care and organizational leadership based on our own first-hand experiences of both. We are amongst the growing number of people who juggle full-time professional careers with extensive duties of care for a family member. We have an intimate understanding of how difficult it can be when a relative's needs take our attention away from work abruptly and unpredictably and of the stigma of unreliability in the workplace that accompanies this. Whenever we talk to students, colleagues and friends who similarly juggle work and care, we are struck by the way that carers' anxieties are molded by a powerful sense that work and life are two separate domains, whose boundaries must be managed to avoid the unreliability of domestic care spilling over into the reliable world of work. This chapter is therefore born from a desire to expose and critique this binary thinking, because it stops us seeing the similarities and complementarities between relationships of care and relationships of leadership. In our own lives, we are discovering that reflecting on our relationships of care can help us to understand the dynamics of our relationships with colleagues and subordinates and vice versa, that reflecting on how we interact with others in the workplace can shed light on our instincts and interactions within the family. Since one of the most notoriously difficult challenges for leaders is to build and sustain effective interpersonal relationships, we believe that experiences of care can be an invaluable source of insight for leadership.

Common Sense Understandings of Care

What images are conjured up when we hear that someone is caring? We tend to associate care with kindness, gentleness and compassion. Perhaps we also think that caring involves putting another person's concerns ahead of our own, at least for the period in which care is most acutely needed, such as during a crisis. We probably relate care to feelings and emotions, too. A caring person is assumed to be in touch with, but able to control, his or her own emotions and to have enough empathy to connect with the emotions of the person for whom he or she is caring. In this way, care invokes notions of protection and nurturing of others less able or experienced to care for themselves.

In contemporary society, care has strong, often unconscious, associations with gender. Feminist scholars have elaborated an ethic of care to differentiate between feminine moral development, which is grounded in relational attachments, and masculine moral development, which draws on rules-based, abstract justice.[1] Psychoanalytic scholars have highlighted the ways in which care evokes the archetype of the mother and thereby speaks to our fantasies of maternal love and our primeval need for comfort, security and unconditional acceptance.[2] Through these filters, we see that care has deep associations with relationship—both in a positive sense of empathy and connection and in a potentially more negative sense of dependency and neediness.[3]

Care and the Work-Life Boundary

The enduring popularity of the notion of work-life balance sustains the idea that our lives are divided into two spheres—the public and the private. The public is the space for social identity, performance and achievement, whereas the private is the space for personal identity, relationship and belonging. We invest considerable energy in preserving our sense of a work-life boundary, because we recognize the risks of letting work encroach too much on our private time. We can probably all think of examples of people who routinely allow work to spill over onto the life side of the boundary, enabled by increasingly sophisticated technology, and often at tremendous cost to their health and well-being. But we want to highlight the way the boundary seems stronger when approached from the opposite direction, i.e., that we go to even greater lengths to stop life spilling over into work.[4] Despite knowing that our leaders, colleagues and subordinates are as human as we are, and that they, too, will have things happening in their private lives which variously enhance and compromise their workplace performance, we try to prevent the messiness of our private lives from encroaching into our work-spaces. Perhaps we worry that talking about the challenges of our private lives will trigger associations of unprofessionalism or unreliability.

The boundary between private and public has a particular relevance for care and leadership. Care has such powerful associations with gender and domesticity that it is usually associated with the private rather than the public sphere. Care does not fit easily into our everyday understandings of work because, in the corporate world especially, work is where we show-case our tough, rational, independent selves; where we get things done; where we deploy our technical skills of managing, prioritizing, monitoring and so on. The so-called softer skills of relationship can often be ignored in favor of business strategy and performance; or, if not ignored, they are outsourced to the people functions such as Human Resources rather than seen as core to business, management or leadership. Because it concerns relationships and emotions, care easily gets denigrated as something "pink and fluffy" or "touchy feely" and therefore irrelevant or even inimical to leadership.

If business leadership is associated with masculine performance, and care is associated with feminine relationships, this creates a considerable chal-lenge for those who advocate an ethic of care as a guiding principle in orga-nizational life. It is so easy to relegate care to the domain of the private—the stuff of intimate, trusting relationships rather than successful leadership of strategy or change. And yet, if we return to the notion that care involves putting other people's interests and concerns ahead of our own, and perhaps "going the extra mile" for one's supporters and subordinates, then think how many of our most commonly invoked exemplars of leadership seem to be specifically *caring* leaders. As Yiannis Gabriel suggests, care lies at the heart of many of our archetypes of good leadership, such as Nelson Man-dela, Jesus Christ or the Dalai Lama:

> I would go as far as to say that caring outweighs any other consider-ation regarding the moral obligations of leaders in the eyes of their followers—a leader may be strong, may be legitimate, may be com-petent but, if she is seen as 'not caring', she is likely to be viewed as a failing leader.[5]

We find this view of the moral obligations of leadership a persuasive argu-ment for the importance of *leaders who care*—and for notions of care to therefore make it over the "work-life boundary" to inform our under-standing and practices of leadership. In this chapter, we build on this argu-ment by looking at a group of people whose experiences of care involve a particularly complex negotiation between private and public. These are the growing numbers who combine paid work with some form of unpaid care, usually—but, of course, not always—for an elderly relative. In the UK, people in this position are known as "working carers", although we do not always choose this label for ourselves.[6]

Our approach is unusual in leadership studies, because it values personal experience as primary data for our understandings of organizational life. We are arguing that what happens on the life side of any work-life boundary we construct is more valuable for our work performances than has traditionally been assumed. We are not suggesting that there should be *no* separation between the private and the public; our image of people on holiday incapable of switching off is enough to remind us why some separation between domains might be healthy. But we are suggesting that we might look to our private experiences of care to understand and enhance our public experiences of leadership.

The Intertwining of Care and Leadership

In arguing that experiences of care offer valuable insight into the challenges of leadership, we go beyond the suggestion that juggling work and care makes us better at multi-tasking, planning and prioritizing. This is probably true but almost too obvious. We also go beyond the argument that, with the demographic time-bomb of an aging population, we are simply going to have to find better ways of accommodating the increasing numbers of working carers at all levels of our organizations. Instead, we hope to show how, despite initial impressions of being on opposite sides of the boundary, the experiences of the relationships of both care and leadership are intimately interrelated.

Emotional Undercurrents and Projections

Care is fundamentally concerned with relationships of inequality—whether of skill, capability, stature or experience. As such, care relationships are a blueprint for the relationships between leaders and followers, which are similarly—and some would argue, inherently—grounded in inequality or asymmetry of skill, capability, stature or experience. Thus, the things we experience as caregivers to an elderly parent, say, challenge us in a very similar way to the things we experience as leaders.

These inequalities of skill or capacity are difficult, because being aware of one's need for help often triggers feelings of resentment on the part of the care-recipient. It is, therefore, not uncommon as a carer to find oneself on the receiving end of emotional projections, which can be hostile, painful and unreasonable. Carers can often feel a bit of a scapegoat or whipping boy for the emotional outbursts directed their way, and one of the core skills of care is thus an ability to self-care, that is, to protect oneself from taking such emotional scapegoating too much to heart.

Being on the receiving end of unreasonable emotional projections is also a core feature of the leadership experience. If care triggers archetypal associations with maternal love, and leadership echoes these early childhood fantasies, then leaders need to expect to be the targets of primitive emotions amongst their followers. These are often flattering, such as when a subordinate is hero-worshipping us. But they can also be more hostile, such as when leaders are blamed for organizational failures that could not possibly be their fault. Either way, the exaggerated reactions towards leaders are grounded in fantasy more than reality. A core leadership capability must surely therefore be to acknowledge this and learn to cope with it. Otherwise, if we remain in the domain of fantasy, we may start to believe in our own hype, and take excessive risks; or we might collapse under the weight of projection and unrealistic expectation. In this way, our discussion of care intersects with contemporary debates in leadership ethics, and the argument that leaders should be given neither all the credit for organizational success nor all the blame for organizational failure.[7]

Care—with its primitive expectations, fears and hopes—evokes powerful feelings and emotions. So, being able and willing to deal with the experiences and implications of care must surely help us in our efforts at leadership, or indeed, any of our organizational or institutional relationships which involve difference in status or power. Psychotherapists know they need to contain the often hostile feelings experienced by their clients in the dynamics of transference and counter-transference. Teachers and educators know that they are sometimes the recipient of projections from students, both flattering crushes and less flattering instances of blame and displaced anger. And people in caring relationships need to cope with the complex and often hostile emotional torrents experienced by and between care givers and care receivers. But the theory and rhetoric of leadership have been relatively slow to acknowledge that leaders, too, have a role to play in both triggering and containing the emotional undercurrents of organizational life. The experiences of care—with their inherent relational asymmetry—give us invaluable resources with which to tackle this challenge.

The Politics of Engagement

One of the things that carers understand very well is the need for sensitivity and tact when deciding whether and how to intervene on behalf of the person for whom we are caring. Because care is a relationship of inequality and asymmetry, there will be many occasions when a carer is better qualified or more capable of carrying out a task than the person in their care. Indeed, difference in capability or capacity is arguably central to a definition of a relationship as one of care rather than, say, love or friendship.

For instance, when your elderly father struggles with a simple task, do you step in to do it for him, or do you muster the patience to try to encourage him to do it for himself? If you do it yourself, the task will be done quickly and properly, but you risk infantilizing him, making him feel even more useless and helpless than before. If you stand back and try to encourage him to do it for himself, you risk it not getting done at all or getting done in some crazy, shambolic way, and your father might feel unsupported and frightened. These are difficult decisions to make in a caring relationship, not least because it can be so disconcerting to have to watch a once proud and capable parent now struggle and fail to accomplish things for himself.

Not only are these difficult decisions to make in our private lives; they are also difficult in our professional experiences of leadership, too. Working out whether, when and how to intervene in caring relationships is not dissimilar to the decisions that leaders make in their relationships with followers. And as the vignette below suggests, one of the challenges of both care and leadership is how *not* to intervene. It can be difficult to rein oneself back—as a leader or a carer—if one is used to making things happen. We are so used to being proactive in our lives that it can be uncomfortable to stand back and let things happen in their own time and their own way.

Vignette: Learning to Wait for a Fall

The following is an excerpt from the transcript of a leadership workshop that Peter facilitated. The excerpt is taken from part-way through a conversation, and one of the participants has just made a point about the frustration of working for a leader who was not very proactive, describing him as someone who 'made waiting an art form'. This was followed by some discussion about whether such apparent passivity could constitute good leadership. This triggered a memory for Steven.

Steven: "You saying that reminds me of my previous training [in Social Work]. Often you would see a situation in a private home where they clearly needed to move on to a residential nursing home or a mental health hospital, but they weren't ready to do that. I won't say it was always easy, but on the whole it was easy to walk back to Social Services and just write on the file, 'Waiting for this person to fall'. Whether it was emotional or physical, because eventually that happened. 98% of the time it happened and then you would get a 'phone call either from them or from a relative to say, 'actually I need to do it'. Whereas if I had gone in and said you need to do this, that and the other it probably would have failed. Sometimes that can take 18 months, but it happened eventually".

Ian: "From what you are saying, that whole leadership thing is a fine line between abdicating and delegating. It's standing back and waiting for it to happen, and it will happen because other people will make it happen, and you are then abdicating that responsibility completely".

Patricia: "It's incredibly difficult to do if you are someone who is used to making things happen".

In short, the power dynamics of leadership interventions contain strong echoes of the power dynamics of care interventions. Indeed, it is striking how strongly the tension in care relations between intervening to *fix* things versus empowering others to work things out for themselves is mirrored in many of the most famous models of leadership, change management and organizational decision-making—not least the enduring distinction between "management" and "leadership".

Take, for instance, the well-known distinction between transactional and transformational leadership that appears in many of the core management texts. Without wanting to simplify to the point of distortion, the former fixes things, while the latter enables others to work on things for themselves. Transactional leadership emphasizes direction, control and achieving pre-formulated objectives and results. Transformational leadership, in contrast, emphasizes the importance of leaders empowering, inspiring and enabling their followers. And there are many other models of leadership and change in the management consulting world which invoke a similar dynamic, whether this is framed as supply versus demand, push versus pull, direction versus enablement, hard versus soft. In our view, these all reflect the core dynamic of the care experience, clothed in the language of leadership, OD and change management.[8]

Vignette: Having the Courage Not to Pick Up the Pen

The following is an excerpt from an interview conducted by Leah as part of a research project on the challenges of leadership in government. At the time of this interview, senior UK government officials had just completed a program of leadership development based on the theory of transformational leadership, which emphasized empowerment as a core leadership capability. The interviewee, Susie, is a management consultant, on secondment from the private sector to the government department in question.

Susie: "*I understand the theory of letting things happen at their own pace; and not always jumping up to take over. I do appreciate that my demonstrating my competence or my willingness to assume responsibility can be disempowering for others—and actually, quite irritatingly goody-goody. What I can't do so easily is reconcile this with the pressures I face from, kind of, professional expectations. I mean, my job means that every single encounter seems to require that I demonstrate my qualifications or my expertise. It's that whole idea of adding value all the time. People judge me on how much value I add. Why else would you bring a consultant in?! Adding value seems to be the complete opposite of all the rhetoric about creating the space for others to work things out for themselves. How can others tell you are adding value if you are not saying or doing anything?! What is the difference between being 'transformational' and just being lazy?!*

If I think about the person [identity hidden] who seems to be the absolute embodiment of this transformational leadership thing, she is the last person I would want to model myself on, because nobody has any respect for her whatsoever. She doesn't seem to have any skill, other than the skill to deflect difficult questions onto other people. And because she does that pretty much all the time, people question whether she can actually do anything herself. She is the type of consultant who justifies that joke that a consultant will take your watch and then use it to tell you the time!

When I had my last meeting with my coach, she talked about the challenges of transformational leadership by using the idea of a pen waiting to be used on a flip-chart. You know, when you are in a meeting and everyone is brainstorming, there comes a moment when someone just has to pick up the marker pen to start writing on the flip-chart. So, the pen is sitting waiting on the table for someone to take ownership of the ideas, or the process, or whatever. And whoever does pick up the pen kind of assumes the leadership role. But at the same time, that person is letting everyone else off the hook a bit. And ever since [Susie's coach] talked about that idea, I have been much more conscious of who picks up the pen—kind of literally as well as metaphorically—and what that means for everyone else in the room. So, I wonder whether transformational leadership means having the courage not to pick up the pen, and trying not to worry about other people thinking you are lazy or don't know the content enough to shape the bullet points yourself".

This dynamic of care can also be traced in one of the catchiest ideas in our organizational conversations, the notion of tame versus wicked problems. Tame problems may be extremely complicated, difficult and time-consuming, but they are always fixable if we intervene with the right skills, resources and techniques. When we tame a situation, we are operating on the assumption that there is a best way of approaching it and a best solution, based on theory or data from past experience. Wicked problems, on the other hand, are essentially unique. Each situation requires a new diagnosis for which there is no rule-book or example from best practice. With wicked problems, fixing the situation may not be possible, and it may be that no solution is ever found. Sometimes the leadership role in wicked problems is about just being there; it involves presence, relationship, containment and understanding.[9]

We see the tame versus wicked dynamic as having its blueprint in our experiences of care, specifically in relation to decisions about styles of engagement. Making these connections is invaluable for leadership development, because discussions of tame and wicked problems emphasize that we *choose* how we interpret a situation as tame or wicked, i.e., whether we approach it as one requiring intervention or enablement—fixing or understanding. Our reading of the situation informs how, when, why and whether to intervene. It influences our approach to stakeholder communication and engagement, that is, whether to *tell* or to *sell*. And it will affect how we deal with ambiguity and complexity in our leadership roles, because tensions and inconsistencies are removed or resolved in tame problems; but they are an inextricable part of the experience of dealing with wicked ones.

From this perspective, our ethical challenge as leaders involves what we are calling the politics of engagement. Based both on theory and our own experiences, we see this question of engagement as central to the experience of both care and leadership. The way we respond to asymmetrical responsibilities, seniorities, capabilities and potentialities in our organizational lives takes up much of the time and space in leadership development programs and management textbooks. These asymmetries have their prototype in the engagements and interventions of care.

How to Rethink This Space? What Might It Mean to Act Differently?

As we suggested earlier, our approach in this chapter is unusual in leadership studies, because it values personal experience as data for our understandings of organizational life. We really do believe that care can illuminate the challenges of leadership, and vice versa, that analyzing what we do as leaders can sensitize us to our presence and behavior as carers. The reason we can advocate for this "virtuous circle" is that we are drawing on our own experiences to make this claim. For both of us, thinking about the commonalities between our private experiences of care and our public experiences of leadership has helped to shed light on the challenges and choices in both domains.

Personal Reflection: Leah's Story

From my corporate career in management consulting, I was steeped in the concepts of transactional versus transformational leadership, and directive versus empowering change. Through years of performance management, I was aware of my tendencies towards some styles of leadership over others, specifically, my instinct to take responsibility for, i.e., tame, a situation rather than empowering others to work things out for themselves. In my leadership roles, I was known as a "safe pair of hands", and this was an important aspect of my professional persona. The downside of this was, of course, that sometimes I could leave my subordinates feeling a little disempowered, perhaps disenfranchised. In my more open and trusting discussions with mentors and colleagues, I became aware that the more I "led from the front", the more I risked making my subordinates feel they could not live up to the standards I set.

As I worked on the notion of an ethic of care in leadership, I also reflected on what this might mean for my relationship with my mother as she drew close to death, and needed increasingly heavy-duty (but open-ended) care from me. I found myself using the models I had developed and deployed professionally to frame the way I related to her. For instance, how often did I step in to do the talking and explaining for her, especially when we were dealing with the large number of medical professionals and social care staff who needed a quick summary of what was happening in her world? I knew that my version would be quicker and more to the point. The professionals needed the executive summary, not a long drawn out narrative, or so I thought in my construction of the situation as requiring taming and managing. But I also came to realize that letting my mother explain things in her own way and her own time served a purpose beyond the criterion of efficiency. It made the situation more wicked for me to bear, but it helped her to keep some semblance of dignity and control in an increasingly frightening world. So, if I could try to suspend my desire to tame things, I might be better able to provide the kind of care she truly needed . . . not always, but sometimes.

Personal Reflection: Peter's Story

I have also spent the last several years increasingly involved in caring for my aging mother. Since the death of my father six years ago, Mum has developed dementia. As she was living alone, my three siblings and I became concerned about Mum's erratic behavior and found ourselves in what I will describe below as a challenging sense-making process. We also found ourselves in a complex political process of wicked problem solving.

We reluctantly, and unthinkingly, became a care team. But from the start we were split down the middle. Two factions, sibling pairs, formed with significantly differing views on what form of care was required. The eldest sibling and I, who both lived about two hours away and typically visited every month or so, felt that Mum was becoming a danger to herself and that we needed to intervene. The other siblings, who lived approximately ten minutes away and visited regularly, were convinced that Mum needed to be encouraged to maintain her independence. What was believed by the distant pair to be "serious mental and physical deterioration" was interpreted by those close at hand as "deliberate and manipulative behavior" designed to get more attention. The proposed remedy for the former was increased levels of intervention; for the latter, challenging Mum to be less reliant on others and to take better care of herself. All of us "cared"—this really mattered—but the complexity of the situation, with such divergent interpretations, created a context where it seemed that others clearly did not care "enough" or "as much". Arguments erupted, voices raised, tears shed. Pairings became primary alliances. Conversations that excluded the other pair became prevalent.

Two difficult years later, negotiated solutions included the employment of in-home care-workers, cleaners, delivery of meals, increased frequency and duration of visits by the distant siblings and, finally, a move into a care home. After a period of illness leading to hospitalisation, Mum could no longer walk and had to be moved to a new care home for those with advanced dementia.

Four months after moving in, I was sitting with Mum when a care-worker I didn't recognise stopped to chat about their mutual love of cats. She asked Mum, "Do you want to take your son to your room?" When I intervened and said that Mum wasn't able to walk, the carer said with a mischievous grin, "Oh, you'll walk with me, won't you Jean?!" Taking hold of the carer's hand, Mum promptly stood up and walked at speed out of the lounge and up the corridor. Following quickly behind, I looked on in surprise, as did several other members of staff.

We are sharing these stories because, for both of us, reflecting on the dynamics of projection and intervention has helped to re-frame our understandings of both care and leadership. It has enabled us to trace parallels between the things we instinctively do in our private relationships and the approaches we tend to deploy in leadership situations. We are not suggesting that this cross-fertilization of ideas from normally separate domains has necessarily made us better carers, or a better son or daughter, or even better leaders. But it has sensitized us to the choices that are available to us in *all* our relationships and to what might be at stake in the decisions we make.

Learning from these experiences, we both try to bring some of this thinking back into the workplace, that is, to create a kind of virtuous circle between our experiences with our mothers and our experiences with colleagues and subordinates. It is all too easy to speak for—or over—others in meetings and discussions, especially if one has more experience and/ or expertise in the topic in question. We would both say that we do this with the best intentions, that is, we are trying to get to a good outcome as quickly and efficiently as possible. Surely, that is part of what leadership is all about?! However, sometimes it is more important to engage in the process of relationship and confidence-building than to race to the right outcome or output. The textbooks have been telling us for decades that, as leaders, we should empower and enable at least as much as direct and steer. Being able to tap into what empowering and enabling look and feel like with our mothers—and why they are both so important and so difficult—helps to bring the textbooks to life.

In one of the vignettes in this chapter, we used the word "courage". In that particular example, it was the courage *not* to take charge too overtly or powerfully; but on other occasions, an ethic of care will involve having the courage to step forward and take control of a situation more proactively. Our proposition is not that we should always refrain from intervening in the affairs of others, whether at work or at home; but rather, that we should try to develop the sensitivity and judgment to balance different kinds of intervention/non-intervention and be more mindful of the effects of these decisions on other people. Ethics is thus woven into the fabric of our moment-by-moment dealings with issues, choices, emotional reactions and relationships with others; it is not reserved for the "Big-Ticket" items that are flagged a-priori as "Ethical Dilemmas". Ethics is the stuff of our everyday encounters.[10]

Concluding Thoughts

In this chapter, we have made a case for paying greater attention to care in our organizational lives. We do not want to down-play the challenges of either caring or leading or to present some simplistic new leadership recipe. Rather, we have argued that there can be a mutually illuminating relationship between the things we do in our organizational encounters and the things we do in our domestic worlds. Based on our personal reflections as well as our engagement with theory and philosophy, we believe the experiences of care—with their joys and rewards as well as their frustrations and compromises—are an important framing for many of the other relationships in our lives.

In summary, leadership which is grounded in the personal experiences of care involves:

- Reconnecting our experiences across the so-called work-life boundary.
- Challenging the notion that care is purely a domestic issue, or something "pink and fluffy".
- Acknowledging the emotional undercurrents of both workplace and private relationships.
- Acknowledging the complexities of decision-making, especially in relation to the question of intervention.
- Learning to value the evidence of our own experience, rather than always reaching for evidence in the shape of facts and figures.
- Developing a sense of ethics as embedded in our everyday encounters, involving empathy, attentiveness and humility.

Notes

1. For classic scholarship on an ethic of care as the feminine counterpoint to a masculine ethic of justice, see Gilligan (1982), Tronto (1993) and Noddings (2003).
2. Gabriel (2015) discusses fantasies of maternal care in relation to leadership.
3. For problematic associations between care and dependency, see Fine and Glendinning (2005).
4. Frone et al. (1992) is a classic paper on the idea that the work-life boundary is "asymmetrically permeable", i.e. harder to breach from one direction than the other.
5. Gabriel (2015, p. 322).
6. For the fear of being exposed or "outed" as a carer, see Tomkins and Eatough (2014).
7. See Tourish (2013) and Gabriel (2013).
8. See Tomkins and Simpson (2015) for a philosophical version of our argument that the challenges of leadership revolve around this core question of intervention.
9. Grint (2005) elaborates tame and wicked problems in leadership decision-making.
10. See Edward and Willmott (2015) for an ethics of decision-making in intersubjective encounters, framed around the experience of friendship. See also Crevani et al. (2010, p. 84) for a similar view of an ethics of the everyday; as they suggest, there is "leadership potential" in every social situation.

Bibliography

Crevani, L., Lindgren, M. and Packendorff, J. (2010) Leadership, not leaders: On the study of leadership as practices and interactions. *Scandinavian Journal of Management* 26(1), 77–86.

Edward, P. and Willmott, H. (2015) Between reason and the ethico-political moment. In Pullen, A. and Rhodes, C. (eds.) *The Routledge Companion to Ethics, Politics and Organizations*. Abingdon: Routledge, pp. 198–215.

Fine, M. and Glendinning, C. (2005) Dependence, independence or interdependence? Revisiting the concepts of 'care' and 'dependency'. *Ageing & Society* 25(4), 601–621.

Frone, M.R., Russell, M. and Cooper, M.L. (1992) Prevalence of work-family conflict: Are work and family boundaries asymmetrically permeable? *Journal of Organizational Behavior* 13(7), 723–729.

Gabriel, Y. (2013) Book review: The dark side of transformational leadership: A critical perspective. *Organization Studies* 34(9), pp. 1407–1410.

Gabriel, Y. (2015) The caring leader: What followers expect of their leaders and why? *Leadership* 11(3), pp. 316–334.

Gilligan, C. (1982) *In a Different Voice: Psychological Theory and Women's Development*. Cambridge, MA: Harvard University Press.

Grint, K. (2005) Problems, problems, problems: The social construction of 'leadership'. *Human Relations* 58(11), pp. 1467–1494.

Noddings, N. (2003) *Caring: A Feminine Approach to Ethics and Moral Education*. Berkeley: University of California Press.

Tomkins, L. and Eatough, V. (2014) Stop 'helping' me! Identity, recognition and agency in the nexus of work and care. *Organization* 21(1), pp. 3–21.

Tomkins, L. and Simpson, P. (2015) Caring leadership: A Heideggerian perspective. *Organization Studies* 36(8), pp. 1013–1031.

Tourish, D. (2013) *The Dark Side of Transformational Leadership: A Critical Perspective*. London: Routledge.

Tronto, J.C. (1993) *Moral Boundaries: A Political Argument for an Ethic of Care*. New York: Routledge.

7 Leading When Using Other Words

Reconnecting Leadership to Language

Hugo Gaggiotti

> **Key Questions**
>
> Have you ever used a foreign word without being sure about its mean-
> ing but couldn't find a better alternative?
>
> The English word *leader* has been introduced in other languages and
> is used to displace other words. Is this the reason why some people
> use the word leader reluctantly?
>
> Is it ethical to ignore the significance to others of using the word
> leader?
>
> How might use of the word leader potentially produce negative
> resonances?

Introduction

The Italian adage *traduttore, traditore* (a translator is a traitor) makes profit
of the similar resonance of these two words to suggest the inevitable change
of meaning that occurs in translation; when using words from a language
that is not ours, we are not representing our world with our own words,
but we create a sort of replica, we disconnect ourselves from the world; in
short, we commit putative *treason*. We are leaders, who want to understand
leadership better and want some pointers on how to think and behave differently and lead ethically. Consequently, we are at some point imposing
our world on theirs. This *linguistic* imposition of a foreign language is limiting, disciplining and ultimately unethical because it prevents us and others
from experiencing an embodied engagement with leading. In this chapter, I
explore the negative consequences of ignoring language differences and why
is this so important for everyday leadership. Language—and this particular
language—could distance us from others.

It is assumed that borrowing words from another language is due to the
fact that the phenomenon or the object under consideration does not exist in
the local context, or has no adequate name in the local language. In the chapter

I describe cases where borrowing provokes negative *semantic resonances*. The example is the use of the English word leader in Italian and Spanish.

The vernacular words for leader (*duce, caudillo*[1]) are never used, neither in Italian and Spanish texts on leadership nor in every day organizing. The native speakers use an English word, *leader* (pronunciation '*lider* in Italian and *líder* in Spanish). I am a native Italian who has lived most of my life in Spanish speaking countries; I have conducted most of my teaching in the multilingual world of British and European universities and my research in the polyglot spaces of Italo-Latinamerican corporations and the border-lands between USA and Mexico and British. I never met a student or a manager who claimed we should start using *duce* and *caudillo*. To the contrary, the use of leader (in different forms) proliferates and is taken for granted.

However, I have met with denial, reluctance, or apologetic clarification when Italians or Spanish speakers use the term. Sometimes they explained it to me (*Hugo, sorry, I want to be very clear in what sense I am saying what I am saying . . .*), and some other times, they said they preferred to use other words, like *capo* or *jefe*. The impression is that we were discon-necting because of how different the word we used were resonating to us. I had the feeling I was even disconnecting from myself, engaging with a topic constructed with foreign words.

Indeed, I recognize that I do something similar quite often. I have a mix of feelings and thoughts that *leader* is a word that needs to be used with extreme care in multilingual contexts. I almost never use *leader* to refer to anyone who is managing or directing something, the way in English the terms *team leader, project leader, module leader, course leader, program leader* etc. are used. Obviously, the selection of the right word depends also on my audience, the organizational experiences of my Italian or Spanish interlocutors and the political context in which the organizing under scru-tiny is being carried out.

Our interest could be the obvious domination of the English language in descriptions of leadership practices—what some authors described as the colonizing power of English.[2] However, what I think is more interesting is to explore why people use this English word in multilingual contexts, even if they are not sure of using it the way the native speakers do, and, in addition, how negative resonances of the word prevent to engage with the issue of leadership. In other words, could language operate as a barrier to heartfelt engagement, and if this is the case, how ethical is to ignore it?

Is it just because of potential misunderstandings or the loss of cultural richness/heritage, maybe resulting in discrimination or misuses of power? However, another way of querying the issue is from the point of view of how the words resonate, a perspective that is popular in linguistics and linguistic anthropology.[3] The notion of semantic resonances suggests that the meaning of a term in a given language is defined not only by its ety-mology and literal sense, but the way it resonates with other words in that language. Indeed, there is a classification usually used to understand how words resonate: *verbal* (the word sounds like another word, or has been used as a metaphor), *experiential* (the meaning depends on the history of use—individual or national) or *intertextual* (when the term alludes to some specific meaning known from literature or popular culture).[4] In my experience, this is what happen when Italians and Spanish speakers use *leader*: it resonates negatively for all these reasons.

Indeed, used in a particular cultural Italian organizational context, leader could resonate to *duce* and, in a Spanish context, to *caudillo*. Are we aware of that? Why we should we be aware? Anthropologists have tried to understand cultural practices when people represent and construct their world with their own words.[5] Geertz is usually referred to as one of the anthropologists who reflected on the complex relation between words and their capacity to organize our world but also the world of others.[6] Indeed, words like *country, state* and *nation*, whose resonances and meanings are culturally, in the words of Geertz, "highly localized", have been used "as general paradigms for political development overall and everywhere" (p. 235). The use of the same word operates as a self-evidence that the resonances and meanings are necessary the same in any cultural settings, but they aren't. At some point, we are always imposing our world when we ask someone to use our words to represent her/his world. But also, defining words and meanings is itself an exercise of power and so can never be innocent. The following lines discuss how this happen in the complicated context of using different languages and in particular when using words borrowed from other languages, like *leader*. To be aware that a word resonates differently, even if it is the same and it is used in different languages, is crucial in our practices of leading and be lead. Our relation with others could change dramatically; a better understanding of what we are trying to say in the context of humility and openness to positive or negative resonances could benefit our organizations, open up the possibilities of working better and, at some point, became closer and tolerant to other points of view, conducting ultimately to a more sophisticated way of dealing with organizational issues.

Business Schools: A Place to Observe How the Words Are Used

The material analyzed here comes from the log of fieldnotes I produced conducting participant observation when teaching and supervising Italian and Spanish postgraduate students in Business Schools across Europe, Eurasia and Latin America (most of them MBAs with managerial roles in multinational or international organizations). The log is a collection of accounts I have produced in the last 26 years of teaching, research and administrative experiences in Business Schools. In its current form it contains 346.345 words, 2.321 pictures and 256 video clips. The original intention was to demonstrate how Business Schools constitute themselves as distinctive academic groups on the model of ethnic groups. My interest was due to the fact that I joined the faculty of Business School with previous experience in social anthropology, a truly different academic culture if there is one. The Business School's world seemed truly exotic to me; my log became a space of self-reflection and observation.

For the purpose of this chapter, I first extracted from this log references to leader/ship by doing a simple search of the words leader, leadership, leading, conducting, directing etc. (in different languages) that were a part of my reflections of my work with students, generally when doing tutorials, supervision or fieldtrips. My teaching was predominantly at postgraduate level and a great majority of postgraduates, in particular MBA students, made references to their organizational and working experiences when using the words for leader/ship. I then proceeded to select the notes I produced when I was working with native Italian and Spanish speaking students. This allows me to show how by avoiding, clarifying or deciding when and how to use *leader*, Spanish or Italian managers (formally, business students) who use English every day tried to avoid semantic resonances of the local words for leader and leadership, which they clearly consider controversial. This discussion of the reasons and ways in which non-native speakers use or avoid to use words borrowed from other languages has not just a cultural, but also an ethical dimension, which we all as leaders ignore at our peril. There is more to it than just simple *colonization*.

Feelings and Resonances When Using the English Term *Leader*

It is impossible for Italian and Spanish speakers from my generation to use the local terms *duce* and *caudillo*, for the obvious negative resonance that history equipped them with. We all use the terms *leader* and *leadership*, but we remain insecure of that use. Of course, I don't think of the etymology of the word every time I use it, but as a non-native English speaker, I often ask myself: Is this word really fitting what I want to describe? Younger people may have similar doubts, though perhaps for other reasons. Let me try to illustrate my point with some excerpts from my log.

Recently, one of my postgraduate Italian students who is finishing his dissertation (in English) emailed me in Italian (my translation):

> Dear Hugo. Attached is chapter 4 where, as you asked, I produced a thick description of what engineer X did when he was leading the takeover. I decided to use *capo* instead of leader. *Leader* for me associates with *guide*.

I asked him how he would translate *capo* into English if not as *leader*. He replied:

> Dear Hugo. I am not sure. I will prefer to use *Director* as leader could suggest someone who is imposing his power on others.

I wrote in my diary:

> Why imposing? From which of our discussions has the idea of leaders as people imposing their ideas emerged? It seems we are speaking in a different language.

The feeling that leadership vocabulary was helping people to be disconnected instead of connected was evidenced during my fieldwork. In the following excerpt from my fieldnotes I described my impressions from a discussion of the meaning of leadership with Mexican Business School students:

> I am here writing in English from the borderlands between Mexico and the United States, where I am working with Business Students from UMAC University [name fictitious]. In this space of multilingual, Spanish/English encounters, conflicts and creativity, to use the English word 'leader' epitomizes violence that I don't want to be part of, suggesting an imposition of a monolingual space disconnected with the world of the borderlands that is being taken for granted. I remember Steyaert and Janssens's (2013) paper on how new changing perspectives on leadership studies have so far taken place within an assumed monolingual space. I ask to myself [in Italian]: do I need to start a debate about this? Why do we need to reflect on this? Are we really losing something by not giving the multilingualism dimension on leading some attention? AC, a Mexican-American student addresses the audience (American students from Texas, Mexican-Americans from Juárez, one bilingual Tex-Mex engineer from a MNC and myself) and gives a speech of what a '*maquila, líder de línea*' does: 'she has to be smart, work hard. If she doesn't demonstrate knowledge, her *liderazgo* (leadership) will be soon dissolved. It is better not to call her *líder*. She never has to impose her power in the production line; the *maquila líder* has never been associated with a *caudillo*, but the contrary, she needs to be the first in everything, by knowing everything, by managing all very professionally. She has to lead by managing. She has to be more than a *líder*; she has to be a real *jefe*'.

This avoidance of the use of the word leader is something I have experienced in other non-Italian or non-Spanish contexts as well. A colleague from the university with Serbian origins explained to me once that in Belgrade they *try not to use the word leader; it associates with Tito*. I wrote in my diary:

> Then I asked her which other words they use instead of leader. She replied by saying they preferred to use several words, not one. 'It depends of what I am doing or I have done and I need to explain, not to apply a category, a single word', she said.

The avoidance, or preference for, certain words because of their resonances has been associated with stereotyping and the preference of using neutral vocabularies. The linguistic anthropologist Cliff Goddard pointed out that the use of English words is intended to appear *more technical* and to impose an objective, culture-free, analytical framework.[7] In this context, Pavlenko spoke of the mono-multilingual paradox.[8] A good illustration of this paradox is the famous quote from Derrida who said (in French, not in English) that: "We only ever speak one language . . . (yes, but), we never speak only one language".[9] When my students and I said "leader" while speaking Italian or Spanish, we were speaking three languages and their multiple semantics condensed in the use of one word. The emotional resonances of the word leader become multiple; we became speakers of English but non-English native speakers, using an English word that resonates with various English, Italian and Spanish images.

The repercussions of the monolingual imposition of a singular meaning to a one word became clear to me in a note I wrote during the fieldwork, when I was teaching "Leadership and change" in a top-ranked Business School in Barcelona.

> I asked students to give examples from their experiences at work that could illustrate the theories of leadership we have discussed. They said they have examples, but that they are not illustrative and feel they're too simplistic when explaining in their own language (Spanish). They ask if they can give examples from *the English world*. Suddenly I see my grandmother before me, as she tended to switch from Italian to Piedmontese when she tried to explain something complex, (usually through metaphors). 'We need to respect others' worlds', she always said.

The need to use only one word or several to express our understanding of leadership is still an underexplored area of research, even after some attempts to study them at the beginning of this century.[10] The following is an example from my log describing my impressions when talking about the distinction between leaders and managers with Italian Business School students:

> Then FS (an interviewee) asked why the leaders should be different from the managers. FS said he understood they were two different words in English and therefore must have different meanings, but he said that in Italian it is very difficult to think in this way. The '*capo* could also be a *guida* and a *capitano*' he said, even if the words are different. They are leaders and managers at the same time. He said that sometimes they do call neither one thing nor the other, but instead an *engineer*. We discussed that in fact in Italian films from the 60s, the engineer was the *direttore*, because to be a *direttore* they needed to be engineers. We went for coffee after the tutorial and we talked about football: AC Milan. He

then re-engaged with the discussion, explaining that leader sounds *parla Americano* (to speak American English) and sometimes sounds *duce* to him, a fascist. A guy who commands because he has power, but he knows nothing, a perfect *stronzo* (asshole). He acknowledged that if he has to use it because it is part of the company jargon, then he will use it.

Similar associations between leader and power were suggested by Mexican students of CEHLIDER, an association of youngsters who live in Ciudad Juarez, Mexico. Here are my fieldnotes:

> She asked me what leaders we were talking about and began to explain that to be a leader in the borderlands it all depends on the power; if the power shifts, you are no longer a leader she said; you are a leader only if you have the right connections. She remarked several times that it is better not to be called a leader of . . . (political, group, etc.), because for a lot of people it sounds synonymous with corruption, a character of a wealthy *capanga* (henchman), essentially someone with enough contacts to stay there. It is better to use *director* (manager), which sounds more professional; someone who knows how to do things professionally.

Another Italian student was much more explicit about her feelings when using the word "leader". I wrote:

> She sounds upset. At one point of the conversation she came to me saying, 'Hugo, all of this discussion of being a leader and leadership *mi fa schifo* (it is disgusting) . . . what does it mean? It is like being a messiah who everybody is following with closed eyes'. She explained to me later that for her, leader relates to evangelical pastors of American TV shows and the people crying amongst them. I said that there is a module of the programme that is called 'Leadership and Change'. She said that in the Faculty it's referred to as something different, that we study leadership as it is defined for North American managers in the context of business, but for 'normal' people it resonates more with TV shows.

After working in Argentina with MBA students of SM University, I comment in my log about a conversation I have with one of my students:

> He emphatically explained to me that he talks about leadership, leader, motivation, etc. if he works for a North American company and when he attends the business school. Nobody thinks about leading when working because it sounds authoritarian, something from a political movement or party, like the *peronists* and Peron. Peron was indeed named something like *el gran líder*, like the *Furher* o the *duce*. I made a comment saying that Peron was never called *Fuhrer, duce* or *caudillo*. He vehemently responded that it was the same with other words, that

it sounded and resonated the same, as he was called '*el primer traba-jador*' (the first worker) and the '*gran conductor*', the great conductor. He started to sing the Peronist anthem to show me the parts when Peron was named '*Peron . . . gran conductor . . . que supo conquistar la masa del pueblo. . . .*' (Peron . . . great conductor . . . who knew how to con-quer the great masses of the People . . .).

What Consequences Does the Practice of Imposing the Word Leader on Other Vocabularies Have?

I was not convinced when working with Italian and Spanish students that the adoption of the English word leader was limiting, disciplining and ulti-mately wrong. I argued quite the opposite: that the use of the English terms allows Spaniards and Italians to refer to leadership in an alternative way, out of the constraints of the negative resonances of *duce* and *caudillo*.

Yet both the students and I had to admit that the use of the English term felt at times limiting or at least disciplining. Saying *leader* in English did not seem to resonate with the meanings that are open to native English speakers—namely, leadership that is pluralistic, democratic, participative, etc. The positive resonance in English seemed to be combatting in our use with the negative resonance of local terms. After all, when speaking another language, we do translate into our native language, if subconsciously.

The fascinating variation of the "mono-multilingual paradox" consists in the fact that the word *leader* is defined in English by using words from non-English vocabularies, like Italian and Spanish, precisely languages whose contemporary speakers have intentionally excluded their vernacular words for leader from their vocabularies.

> **Leader:** Old English lædere 'one who leads, one first or most prominent, "agent noun from lædan" to guide, conduct' (see lead (v.)). Cognate with Old Frisian ledera, Dutch *leider*, Old High German *leitari*, German *Leiter*.
>
> *As a title for the head of an authoritarian state, from 1918 (translating Führer, Duce, caudillo, etc.).*[11]

Even if dictionaries are rarely the best place to turn for meaningful usage of words in everyday conversations, non-native speakers still use them, in particular those online. Indeed, I found a large number of articles (academic and non-academic) that quote literally the above definition when explaining the meaning of leadership. An article stated that "by 1918, in Europe and the United States, the title of leader became synonymous with words such as, *führer* (German), *Duce* (Italian), *caudillo* (Spain), and so forth".[12] Are English dictionaries suggesting that in English, leader resonates the same ways as *führer, duce* and *caudillo*? In Italian and Spanish contexts, the contrary is the case; the English term is used to refer to the opposite of the local equivalents: leader is someone who should not be associated with authoritarianism. The practice of using *leader* in other languages than English is not only the result of the global dissemination of the English vocabulary.

Cliff Goddard claimed that the imposition of "highly localized conceptual categories on the world at large is typical of today's increasingly 'globalized' thought, transmitted around the world through the first ever global *lingua franca*, English". Yet the use of the English term leader by Italian and Spanish speakers suggests that this concept acquires quite specific meaning—by combining some global with some local resonances. This sounds like an enriching effect of *lingua* franca (which, by the way, means French language), and indeed it is so. Yet when inserted back into an English text, the local enrichment is lost.

One could argue that it is not lost in dictionaries, and, as I pointed out before, they are being used, especially online. Yet the definition I quoted suggests that the authoritarian version of the phenomenon of leadership had place only in certain places, as the examples *Fürher, duce* or *caudillo* suggest. There is not a single example in English dictionaries of British, American, Canadian, New Zealand, Australian or any other English-speaking country's authoritarian leader used to illustrate the meaning of the word. However, we do not conclude that leaders in such places are never authoritarian, and that the negative resonance of local translations is the local error.

The main conclusion is that leadership languages and their resonances have indeed the potential to disconnect between as well as within selves: between selves—the lack of understanding between Anglo-Saxon leadership development professionals and students for whom English is not their native language, and for whom "leadership" has odd and difficult resonances. This gets in the way of conversation, understanding and relationship; within the self—i.e. that having to engage with a topic that is so "foreignly" constructed prevents a heart-felt, experiential, embodied engagement. How to deal with this emotional disengagement and disconnection? I close this chapter whit an experience from the fieldwork:

Personal Reflection

After years of living in the UK and working in Business Schools, I have gained courage and lost my fear of using words from the business and management vocabulary—despite their negative resonances—such as the word *líder*. I am no longer afraid of being misunderstood. It is true that often I prefer, as Ducrot (1993) explained, to communicate by not saying. I know that when I say *leader/líder* (leader) or *liderazgo* (leadership) in front of my Italian- or Spanish-speaking students, a sort of distance, a disconnection can occur. It is inevitable to feel that I am using terms which exist in my vocabulary but that

I do not fully understand: words that do not always communicate an easily definable meaning when interpreted by others. Their use forces me to explain and clarify exactly what I am trying to say. However, sometimes I encourage myself to use these words intentionally. Indeed, I aim to avoid the security of not saying, to take the risk and potentially provoke a reaction from the students. I recall once giving a lecture at a Latin American university famous for its strong anti-American ideology. I lectured on research I had conducted on engineers who oversaw takeovers and mergers, a specific role assumed by international managers when assigned the task of expanding operations of a multinational. I knew that using *líder* to describe this role would spark some kind of debate and maybe some reaction. Indeed, a student reacted at once and explained that when one describes a person as *líder*, the feeling is that of describing Che (Guevara) or Fidel (Castro). Hence, the student said, *líder* should not be used in vain. I assumed that by using the word there would be some kind of ideological or partisan connotation and felt that the student was moving away from me. Later, I found myself with another student who apologetically tried to clarify what his classmate had explained, saying that what I had suggested was that Guevara and Castro were "unique" people, "exceptional" individuals who could be called *líderes* because of their ethical standing. That night I had dinner with some of the students who were at my lecture. In a more familiar and less academic environment, another student explained to me that she never used the word *líder*, as it reminded her of Latin American military dictators, evil religious leaders, corrupt politicians and executives from greedy and soulless multinational corporations. I have always thought that it is the right of my audience, mostly academic, to give meaning to my words. However, I continue to exercise the right of not saying, not using certain words from the managerial vocabulary, to at some point be a coward, when I suspect my words will distance me from my students.

Notes

1. The same can be noticed in German texts, where the authors avoid using the term *führer*. In what follows, however, I limit my discussions to languages of which I am a native speaker. *Duce* was applied to Benito Mussolini as head ofbItalian state. General Franco assumed the title of *caudillo*. Both ruled as dictators of fascist regimes.
2. See the essential works of Bhabha (1990, 1994).
3. See, for example, Goddard (1991).
4. Hanks (2013).
5. See Ottenheimer (2006).
6. Geertz (2000, p. 234).
7. See Goddard (1991).
8. See Pavlenko (2005).
9. Derrida (1998, p. 10).
10. See, for example, Charles and Marschan-Piekkari (2002) and Fredriksson et al. (2006).
11. www.etymonline.com/index.php?term=leader (accessed on May 24, 2016). Emphasis added.
12. Reed (2014, p. 2).

Bibliography

Bhabha, H. (ed.) (1990) *Nation and Narration*. London: Routledge.

Bhabha, H. (1994) *The Location of Culture*. London: Routledge.

Charles, M. and Marschan-Piekkari, R. (2002) Language training for enhanced horizontal communication: A challenge for MNCs. *Business Communication Quarterly* 65(2), pp. 9–29.

Derrida, J. (1998) *Monolingualism of the Other*, trans. P. Mensah. Stanford, CA: Stanford University Press. Originally published as Derrida, J. (1996) *Le Monolinguisme de l'Autre*. Paris: Galilée.

Ducrot, O. (1984) *Le dire et le dit*. Paris: Minuit.

Fredriksson, R., Barner-Rasmussen, W. and Piekkari, R. (2006) The multinational corporation as a multilingual organisation: The notion of a common corporate language. *Corporate Communications: An International Journal* 11(4), pp. 406–423.

Geertz, C. (2000) *Available Light: Anthropological Reflections on Philosophical Topics*. Princeton, NJ: Princeton University Press.

Goddard, C. (1991) Anger in the Western Desert: A case study in the cross-cultural semantics of emotion. *Man*, New Series 26(2), pp. 265–279.

Hanks, P. (2013) *Lexical Analysis: Norms and Exploitations*. Cambridge, MA: MIT Press.

Ottenheimer, H. (2006) *The Anthropology of Language: An Introduction to Linguistic Anthropology*. Belmont, Canada: Wadsworth.

Pavlenko, A. (2005) *Emotions and Multilingualism*. Cambridge: Cambridge University Press.

Reed, M.A. (2014) *Leadership Throughout the Ages*. Available from: http://reedership.com/Articles/Leadership/LeadershipThroughout.pdf (accessed on October 9, 2016).

Steyaert, C. and Janssens, M. (2013) Multilingual scholarship and the paradox of translation and language in management and organization studies. *Organization* 20, pp. 131–142.

8 From Great to Good Enough

Reconnecting Leadership to the Ordinary[1]

Tim Harle

Key Questions

What constitutes greatness in your life?
Is your leadership seen on the big stage or in everyday encounters?
How can you connect experiences in your life at work and beyond?

One of the best-selling leadership books leadership in the 21st century is Jim Collins's *Good to Great*.[2] In it, Collins explores what contributes to sustained success over a period of time in companies by comparing the merely "good" with the "great". Collins describes a hierarchy of leaders from highly capable "Level 1" individuals to "Level 5" leaders, who "[build] enduring greatness through a paradoxical blend of personal humility and professional will". Collins's work has been highly influential in the leadership field.

There is an irony in the popularity of *Good to Great*: leadership scholars had consigned the Great Man theory of leadership to the dustcart of history, yet the language of greatness has reappeared. The personal humility identified by Collins is often lost in images of greatness—the dominant discourse for many continues to be a fantasized, mythical leader. Yet leadership scholars have encouraged us to think in terms of authenticity, relationships, servanthood and other concepts.

Not So Great?

Significant criticisms have been made of Collins's work.[3] Areas of criticism include:

- **Subsequent performance.** Several of the great companies identified by Collins have subsequently disappeared, through bankruptcy (Circuit City Stores) or takeover (Gillette), or have needed government rescue (Fannie Mae).

- **Data collection and analysis.** Researchers question the rigor of data collection: despite large volumes, this tends towards the self-selecting and anecdotal. When analyzing the data, the key question is whether the association of greatness with Collins's principles implies causation.
- **CEO agency.** Dennis Tourish notes the tendency "to over-attribute either success of failure in business, politics, sport and elsewhere to the role of those who hold a handful of top positions", adding that, "In business, this error is particularly pronounced in the influential work of Jim Collins".[4]

From time to time, additions are made to the litany of apparently successful leaders who demonstrate the pride and self-confidence, hubris, that precedes a fall. The 2008 financial tsunami gave us Dick Fuld at Lehman Brothers and Fred Goodwin at RBS, among others. More recently, John Stumpf of Wells Fargo—one of Collins's great companies—has joined the roll call of former CEOs as business practices were exposed that can hardly be described as "great". In such cases, I find it sobering to consider the impact on loyal company workers at all levels. Their disenchantment is understandable.

However, rather than pursuing these criticisms, I want in this chapter to explore a potentially negative and disempowering side-effect of Collins's work. If all should aspire to the greatness of "Level 5" leadership, what of the large numbers of managers who feel excluded, unable to achieve such heights? Indeed, does the perceived impossibility of achieving the ideal have a negative impact on individuals and the organizations they seek to lead? To explore this question, I wish to introduce insights from a practice where perceived failure to reach impossible ideals has been examined and applied for some time: parenting.

Good Enough Parenting

The concept of "good enough" parenting was developed by the British pediatrician and child psychiatrist Donald Winnicott (1896–1971).[5] In a blog written in the run up to the card industry's annual Mother's Day bonanza of idealizing and idolizing mothers, Jennifer Kunst summarizes what a good enough parent looks like:

> Winnicott's good enough mother is sincerely preoccupied with being a mother. She pays attention to her baby. She provides a holding environment. She offers both physical and emotional care. She provides security. When she fails, she tries again. She weathers painful feelings. She makes sacrifices. Winnicott's good enough mother is not so much a goddess; she is a gardener. She tends her baby with love, patience, effort, and care.[6]

Kunst goes on to say how a mother feels under pressure and strain. She is ambivalent, being both selfless and self-interested, turning both toward and away from her child. Mothers (I would add, parents and carers) are capable of great dedication yet are prone to resentment. As Leah Saunders and Peter Simpson show in their chapter in this book, powerful emotions surround parent-child and caring relationships, which can surface in unexpected ways. Kunst highlights how Winnicott even dared to say that a good enough mother loves their child, but also has room to hate them. Mothers are real. Should leaders be any less real?

In the same way that Winnicott reassured parents that they were doing a fine job in bringing up their children when things seemed less than ideal, I wish to explore whether similar comments be applied to leaders who see their efforts as falling short of a fantasized ideal. Before exploring the "good enough"' concept in relation to leadership, we can note that it has been applied to a number of fields beyond Winnicott's original conception of motherhood and parenting (Box 8.1).

Box 8.1   Examples of Good Enough Approaches

- **Politics**. Marc Howard Ross applied Winnicott's work to the fraught area of ethnic conflict management. Exploring questions of success, identity, empowerment and relationships, he suggests that "good-enough conflict management" recognizes inherent tensions, but encourages a developmental, transformative process. Andrew Samuels recognized that political leaders are often perceived through extremes of idealization or denigration. He identifies the possibility of failure as a key insight from the good enough vocabulary, and suggests that bottom-up, networked, collaborative organisational models may be more appropriate than top-down hierarchies.[7]

- **Education**. Keith Swanwick explores the educational and social contexts in which teachers and students work, aiming to draw up criteria to identify the "good-enough" teacher. Such teachers are seen in more ill-defined roles than those expected by the conventional teacher. The blog from a "good enough teacher" is right in Winnicott territory—"granting permission to let go of perfection"—but makes no explicit reference to the originator of the good enough concept.[8]

- **Healthcare**. Noting that the idea of being "good enough" in medicine has been explored, but not gained acceptance in the general medical community, Savithiri Ratnapalan and Helen Batty call for a path to excellence through being "good enough":

  > We should not confuse good enough with merely good . . . Good enough is not mediocrity. It has to do with rational choices as opposed to compulsive behaviour. The good enough approach is a way to drive ongoing improvement and achieve excellence by progressively meeting, challenging, and raising our standards as opposed to driving toward an illusion of perfection.[9]

- **Pastoral practice**. Writing autobiographically from her experience as a mother and priest, Emma Percy asks if "the concept of being good enough [could] provide a more honest understanding and evaluation of the role of parish clergy".[10] Topics identified in Percy's concluding chapter—guilt, confusing success and failure, using inappropriate measurements, dealing with growth, and especially a holistic view of being and doing—appear to have a wider resonance when considering leadership more generally.

Good Enough Leadership

So, might we posit a concept of Good Enough Leadership? I have seen leaders who struggle to maintain an aura of perfection, and find myself wanting to encourage them to relax and be more realistic. Those who come from a counselling or therapeutic background can help us here: in discussing narcissistic leaders, Manfred Kets de Vries and Danny Miller draw attention to the importance of understanding the difference between the ideal of perfection and just being "good enough". Writing from a similar psychoanalytic background, Robert French draws a parallel between a child's development in physical, emotional, mental and spiritual terms and a "good enough" mother and the demands of change, which require "good enough" managerial and leadership capabilities.[11]

In preparing this chapter, I encountered a research project, inspired by Winnicott's approach, which is especially relevant. Aaron Nurick mused about the application of the good enough framework to management, and developed a survey to explore the possibilities. Analysing the results, he identified three key elements demonstrated by "good enough managers":

- serving as mentors, teachers and supporters to their employees,
- building effective relationships on a foundation of trust,
- managing with high levels of integrity.[12]

Nurick's first point squares with my own experience: I identify "always learning" as a key aspect of good enough leadership (see Box8. 3). While also recognizing the second and third points, I would want to add a further question: how do we develop trust and integrity? They cannot be imposed: as I explain later, I believe the need for *consistency*—in word and deed, in great and small actions—is crucial here.

Another important aspect of both parenting and leadership is the need to offer *security*. Such a challenge may be fine in theory, but how do we achieve it in practice? This knowing-doing dynamic is something that is explored, using Winnicott's good enough thinking, by Jacob Storch and John Shotter. They highlight such questions as relationships and finding security in the bodily environment (see also David Knights's Chapter 5 in this book). Storch and Shotter highlight the dynamic, developmental role of leadership and make explicit links with Winnicott around such issues as unrealistic ideals and the need for sensitivity and responsiveness in interactions. Drawing attention to the importance of knowledge, they conclude a thoughtful article thus:

> rather than laying out explicit but de-contextualized plans or "recipes" ahead of time for others to follow—no matter how well-intentioned or well-fashioned—the task of "imperfect or good enough leaders (or consultants)" is to help to create the *occasions* or *circumstances* in a company within which (and through which) employees can develop *their own ways* of orienting or relating themselves to the situations within which they must work.[13]

They add, "However, we see contemporary leadership and consultancy practices outlined in the mainstream literature doing the exact opposite".[14]

Storch and Shotter's work is aimed at practitioner-consultants, and it is from that field that some of the most sustained writing advocating good enough leadership comes (Box 8.2).

Box 8.2   YSC Consultancy and Good Enough Leadership

Gurnek Bains and colleagues, from their experience in the YSC consultancy, describe how the good enough mindset is good enough. They offer an example of a parallel between a good enough parent's ability to tolerate destructive impulses and a good enough leader's ability to process multiple conflicting agendas. Another suggestive parallel is between a parent promoting learning by holding up a mirror to a child and a manager offering feedback and coaching. Parallels in likely outcomes include children with a realistic sense of their own power matched against co-workers who are neither meek nor arrogant, and children in touch with their own selves, reflected in authentic workers whose professional and personal lives are aligned.[15]

I find it particularly interesting that YSC operates across a number of national cultures, suggesting that good enough parenting—and leadership—transcend cultural norms and expectations.

How helpful is the concept of good enough leadership? When seeking talent, can we envision world leading institutions advertising for "good enough" candidates to join their "great" organizations? Or will expensive company leadership development programs aim to produce "good enough" leaders? Perhaps not. But there is one particular aspect of Winnicott's work on good enough parenting to which I should like to draw attention. It is noticeable that, although the language of "good enough" is widely used, Winnicott chose a rather different phrase when addressing parents through a series of BBC radio talks—the ordinary.

The Ordinary in Leadership

Winnicott continually refers to "the ordinary", a phrase applied to practicing leaders in a research project led by George Binney, Gerhard Wilke and Colin Williams. Indeed, Binney and colleagues conclude their summary thus, "A child thrives on 'good enough' parenting. A group will, we believe, thrive on 'good enough' leadership".[16]

Two representative quotes from Winnicott about being ordinary provide further links to leadership:

1. "In the ordinary things you do you are quite naturally doing very important things". This echoes the work of Mats Alvesson and Stefan Sveningsson, who doubt the very concept of leadership, drawing attention instead to managers, who engage in the "extra-ordinarization of the mundane".[17]
2. "The ordinary good mother and father do not want to be worshipped by their children".[18] Studies of narcissistic leaders and critical approaches to charismatic or transformational leaders often use language that is close to that of worship.

My own career has, from one perspective, covered a range of circumstances, from geopolitical maneuvering to mundane transactions in a call center, from multi-billion-dollar merger and acquisition negotiations to ensuring people have clean drinking water. Yet, from another perspective, I have been struck how the approach of good—and bad—leaders produce similar patterns in different parts of their organizations. Consistency in a leader's actions from everyday occurrences to strategic announcements produces repeating patterns, fractals, at different levels in an organization.[19] Might this link between small and grand be where good enough meets great, and where group leadership meets corporate leadership? In Box 8.3, I reflect on the connection between apparently mundane actions and courage.

In the next section, I wish to explore how the consistency of small and large actions observed above promotes a sense of psychological security. Here we encounter two further insights from the work of Winnicott and his colleagues: the holding environment and the secure base.

Box 8.3   The Courage to Fail

Discussions about ethical challenges in our working lives may evoke images of confronting questionable behavior at a corporate or individual level. However, when I was invited to reflect on facing up to ethical issues, I was drawn to incidents from my managerial life that I had not previously thought of as involving ethical choices. At the same time, I found myself thinking more deeply about courage and its source.

I recently stayed at a 4* hotel (not belonging to the group I refer to in this chapter). The abiding memory I took away had nothing to do with common aspects of room, food or view. It was the precious reserved car park spaces on either side of the hotel entrance. On one side were spaces rightly reserved for what society refers to as the disabled. But it was the spaces on the other side I remember—they were reserved for "Management". I was outraged. Mere customers like me had to take our place further away (I wasn't directly impacted as we arrived by public transport). I couldn't help but think of a biblical saying: "the last shall be first, and the first last" (which I have subsequently tracked down to the Gospel of Matthew, chapter 20, verse 16).

In the course of this book's development, I have had the privilege of meeting fellow authors on more than one occasion. I have been struck by the commitment many show to a faith or spiritual tradition. Some share the Christian inheritance in which I was nurtured; others follow a Buddhist path; others would eschew a label allied to any organised religion. But they have challenged and encouraged me by their example to reflect on my own story. In particular, I have been drawn to two apparently unconnected incidents—one very public, one reasonably private—that I hope provide real-life vignettes into the ethical choices that a good enough leader is called to make.

If there was phrase that linked the two occasions, I would say it is the *courage to fail*. In neither case did I feel particularly courageous at the time, and I certainly had no idea I was making ethical choices. I simply acted from a deep instinct: in the first case, I had a few hours to prepare; in the second case, it was a spontaneous reaction.

> I was standing on a Town Hall stage in front of 200 members of the project team I led. A meeting of project managers the previous day had identified major risks to our high profile program. Failure would cause considerable damage to our company, and come at a very high personal and professional cost for many in that room. I have no memory of what I said. I felt vulnerable and exposed, but I now look back at this occasion and realize the ethical dilemma I faced. Stark alternatives from "this is a mess—we're all doomed" at one extreme to "steady as you go—this will be fine" at the other seemed less than honest. I remember the terrible responsibility of having to offer some stability, even as our plans were in disarray and the future looked uncertain.

We kept going and, after long months of hell, emerged into a period of modest success. By several measures, corporate performance was transformed, and colleagues won a national award from their peers. It was during the emergence from the gloom that the second incident occurred.

> Huge administrative backlogs had grown, which directly impacted customers. Staff had to work constant weekend overtime to address these. One Saturday morning, I had a stark—even hostile—encounter with one of them. But I sensed a passion. So when, a few months later, we needed a special team to tackle a business-critical task, I suggested this individual should be part of the team. No, I was told; they were "difficult". One

person's passion is another person's difficulty. I quietly insisted, and the team succeeded (I still have the tee-shirt I was given during subsequent celebrations).

This second vignette may simply be a case of my being stubborn. But I hope it says something about seeing the good, the potential, in all. Of recognising that passion goes with an underlying commitment. Yes, it was risky, but it illustrates the potential achievements of ordinary people.

It was only as I came to write down these reflections that I realised they might illustrate another concept I discuss in this chapter: fractal leadership. The exposed position on a Town Hall stage, the fierce debate with a junior member of staff. In each case, things might have gone wrong. Was I stubborn, reckless or courageous?

Which brings me to a key question. What was the source of my courage? Although I would have found it hard to articulate at the time, I think it has something to do with the Christian heritage I mentioned earlier. The last shall be first, and the first last. It certainly provided me with a radically counter-cultural perspective. And a perspective that there can be more to life than external measures.

I finish this reflection with another example of the teachings of Jesus. Matthew's gospel includes a parable of a king who was questioned about feeding the hungry and clothing the naked. The listeners had no recollection of such actions. 'And the king will answer them, "truly I tell you, just as you did it to one of the least of these who are members of my family, you did it to me"' (Matthew, chapter 25, verse 40). Is not this the epitome of fractal leadership, of consistency between the large and the small? Lest any accuse religions of otherworldliness, note the everyday nature of these actions. But, like many contemporary insights we may describe as discoveries, this is hardly new. Our spiritual traditions offer enduring wisdom that can be a source of courage in the practicalities of business life.

Aspects of the Ordinary

The Holding Environment

I have long been interested in what leadership can learn from music, and have been especially attracted to what we can learn from jazz, as opposed to the classical disciplines of an orchestra. Frank Barrett, writing as a management professor and jazz musician, draws attention to another aspect of Winnicott's legacy: the holding environment. "Jazz players look for and notice instability, disorder, novelty, emergence, and self-organization for their innovative potential rather than as something to be avoided, eliminated or controlled".[20] Barrett's language is suffused with complexity theory: indeed, echoing Dee Hock's pioneering work, he sees jazz bands as "chaordic systems". But Barrett laments that, "We have been socialized in the other direction: to assume that systems need hierarchy to organize and have some stable order. Mechanistic forms of organizing feed the belief that the individual leader is the most important factor in keeping an organization on track". He identifies Jim Collins's "mega-bestseller" *Good to Great* as a prime culprit in this trend.

Barrett notes that the holding environment relies on the group, rather than an individual: "A healthy group creates a good holding environment for all members, a space in which they can experiment with the awareness that they will receive empathy, understanding, support, and also challenge. In such holding environments, adults are better able to advance in learning and development".[21] This raises two points for me. First, it reinforces the role of learning, that we have already identified. Secondly, it challenges my thinking about the role of a conductor and an orchestra. I have traditionally seen the former as top-down controllers, so not a helpful model for leadership. But what if conductors promote a safe holding environment in which members of the orchestra can flourish? Here is another link between individuals and group leadership.

We also encounter Winnicott's holding environment in a group context in Ralph Stacey's work: "we might think of a good-enough holding environment as enabling groups of people to operate as a transitional group, a group in a state of not knowing what its task is yet, a group that must therefore employ creative imagination, fantasy, and play".[22] Given Barrett's references to complexity theory, it is notable that Stacey has been at the forefront of applying complexity thinking to organisations in the UK. Stacey notes the emerging state of the group not yet knowing what its task is. In his work referred to earlier, Robert French also highlights the importance of "not knowing": French's work, along with his colleague Peter Simpson, is noted in Nurick's study of good enough managers.[23]

The Secure Base

If music helped me to think more deeply about the holding environment, my own experience of leadership in tough situations has helped me to understand—if only in retrospect—the role of secure bases in times of uncertainty and change. Once again, I make some brief observations in Box 8.3. For now, we can explore the impact of charismatic leaders in groups through Irene Harwood's research, which links Winnicott's work with that of his colleague, John Bowlby (1907–90).[24] In particular, Harwood draws attention to insights from attachment theory. Here we encounter once again a key aspect of the ordinary in parenting and leadership: the importance of *consistency* of actions. Bowlby and his colleague Mary Ainsworth (1913–99), developed the idea of the *secure base* through observations ranging across the fields of psychology and anthropology. A secure base allows change to be embraced and innovation to be encouraged. George Kohlrieser and colleagues have applied this concept to leadership, defining a secure base as

> a person, place, goal or object that provides a sense of protection, safety and caring and offers a source of inspiration and energy for daring, exploration, risk taking and seeking challenge.[25]

The Dutch management ecologist Peter Robertson first drew attention to how attachment need not be restricted to people, coining the term "matter" for such attachment.[26] Kohlrieser and colleagues note something similar: "In an organization, a secure base may be a boss, peers, colleagues, the corporation itself, the work or even the product". In my own work, I have observed several examples of secure matter attachment: these range from a beloved old mainframe computer system, through a strong sense of professional identity (actuaries and town planners), to fierce loyalty to a startup company (I found it hard to untangle attachments to the founder, the product, and the company brand). Given the use of complexity theory made by Barrett and Stacey, it is worth noting that Robertson is also strong on this perspective. The need to find some form of security in a turbulent world is something that parents and caregivers will also recognise.

Before moving on, we can note that both the holding environment and the secure base have affinities with "zones of psychological safety" identified by Amy Edmondson in her work on teams.[27] Several of the features identified by Edmondson resonate with what we have been considering, e.g., learning and risk-taking. Could we add playing together to this list?

Good Enough in Action

So, what might good enough leadership look like in action? At the urging of the editors, I have reflected on episodes from my working life, which may provide examples of the good enough in action (Box 8.4). It is for others—especially my co-workers and clients—to judge how effective this was. And this is written in retrospect. If someone had mentioned to me in the depths of struggling with hellish company challenges that I was acting as a secure base, I might well have despatched them back to their consulting room or ivory tower with a well-placed right hook.

Some of the examples may appear almost trivial: my reason for including them is to illustrate my point about consistency and fractal leadership. Having worked in the private, public and third sectors, I am struck how some people (co-workers, customers, external partners) are treated in a way which contradicts espoused corporate values. The trigger for my thinking around fractals was the juxtaposition of hearing the Chair of a global hotel group speaking at the INSEAD business school in France and an everyday experience at a hotel front desk in a drab UK city. The hotel belonged to the group I had heard about at INSEAD. The responsibilities of Group Chair and Reception clerk were clearly different, but I recognised a similar pattern of behavior. In the box below note some particular examples from my experience.

Box 8.4 Examples of Good Enough Leadership in Action

- **Listening to the environment.** I was asked to engage in a local community setting, with a history of social and racial tensions. I risked being seen as an outsider who had been imposed on the group. This viewpoint was hardly helped by my introduction at the first meeting: "This is Tim, he's come to tell us what to do". I replied immediately that I was indeed called Tim, but I had come to listen. After some months of hard work together, we achieved a solution to which everyone was committed.

- **Promoting teamwork, avoiding silos.** In a large open plan office, I noticed how often phones went unanswered, even if there was someone working at a neighboring desk. As the senior manager responsible for the operation, I found myself picking up such phones as I walked around. I noticed two things: first, how many queries I could resolve, even though I had no specialist knowledge. And more importantly, how phones gradually began to be answered by co-workers. A quiet cultural change of helping each other had begun to take place without edicts or company memos.

- **Always learning.** After a 25-year business career, I volunteered to serve as a board member for a local elementary school. Having been used to hold my own under tough questioning from investors, broadcasters or politicians, I remember the feeling of utter vulnerability when confronted with the unexpected questions of young children. This showed me how we must be always learning, and how acknowledging our own vulnerabilities can be a powerful part of this process.

- **Being in it together.** When I took on an advisory role in a non-profit, I found myself drawn not just to fellow board members, but to front line employees serving visitors in the cafeteria. I discovered that the organization hadn't given them email addresses. This made me wonder not just about communications, but about the overall sense of belonging to what proclaimed itself as a community. Another example: twice in my life, I have worked in high rise buildings with dedicated elevators to executive floors. I used one once during some perceived emergency, but I normally waited in line with co-workers for the ordinary elevators. To my regret, I never challenged this practice with other corporate executives.

- **Saying thank you.** I hesitate to include this as being too trivial, but I remember the impact a new Executive Vice-President had when she suggested to me and other senior managers that we should get a stack of Thank You cards. Some years after leaving that company, I met a former member of staff who had kept such a card, and remembered it—and the manager who gave it—with pride and fondness.

- **Consistency.** It seems strange to have to mention the importance of absolute confidentiality. When I am told things in strict confidence, whether for business or personal reasons, I keep things to myself. (There is a difference if questions of safeguarding or criminality arise.) I was once shocked when a HR consultancy casually mentioned that they could breach a privacy wall to find something out about me. I am reminded of the Dutch proverb that, "Trust arrives on foot, but leaves on horseback".

- **Being real, not perfect.** This last point relates to the community project mentioned in the first point. A key published document was to include input from local people. My instinct was to correct the spelling and grammar of those who had either been failed by the school system or did not have English as a first language. But we left things as they had been written: the result was an authentic document that drew people to the reality of the situation.

To finish this autobiographical sketch, I reflect on what I now see as the toughest ethical challenge of my working life. A major corporate initiative, for which I was responsible, was at risk becoming a financial and reputation disaster. The external environment was highly charged, and internal technical problems seemed insurmountable. My challenge was somehow to provide security for those who worked with me, and the wider business, while being realistic about the scarily unknown future. How honest could I be publicly? I was dogged and determined through the dark days, and ultimately became part of a team which enjoyed real success. A bit like parenting? My children, who were then teenagers, tell me how much easier I was to live with then (despite the exhaustion and 4am phone calls) than when I was subsequently offered a quieter, office-based job!

Where Good Enough Is Great

A blog which appeared while this chapter was at a formative stage provides a good example of how language and expectations intersect. I must confess that the Collins-esque title, *Strive for Greatness*, hardly enthused me. But I was surprised:

> The secret to greatness lies in the small actions we each take every day.[28]

So we conclude where we began. Collins's "Level 5" leaders may well display a paradoxical blend of personal humility and professional will. But such humble determination may also be displayed in everyday ways in mundane situations by ordinary people for whom the epithet "good enough" may be liberating.

Notes

1. The key elements of this chapter were developed for a conference before the publication of Howard Stein and Seth Allcorn's article (2014). Some of their observations—about trust, mutual respect, and being decisive without resorting to command-and-control—echo observations here. I found their suggestions about creating a playful space especially helpful.
2. Collins (2001). The "enduring greatness" quote is from p. 20.
3. Rosenzweig (2014).
4. Tourish (2013, p. 10f).

5. Winnicott (1991 [1957]).
6. Kunst (2012).
7. Ross (2000), Samuels (2001, p. 82).
8. Swanwick (2008); Krystal (n.d.).
9. Ratnapalan and Batty (2009, p. 240).
10. Percy (2014, p. 30).
11. Kets de Vries and Miller (1985), French (2001).
12. Nurick (2012, p. 25).
13. Storch and Shotter (2013, p. 15), italics original.
14. Ibid.
15. Bains et al. (2007), Bains (2007).
16. Binney et al. (2005, p. 244).
17. Winnicott (1991 [1957], p. 15), cf Alvesson and Sveningsson (2003).
18. Winnicott (1991 [1957], p. 84).
19. Harle (2011).
20. Barrett (2012, p. 68). The Collins quote is from note 1, p. 187.
21. Barrett (2012, p. 131).
22. Stacey (2001, p. 103).
23. French (2001), Nurick (2012, p. 92). Simpson co-authored two chapters in this book.
24. Harwood (2003).
25. Kohlrieser et al. (2012, p. 8). It is important to flag a limitation of this work. In a footnote, the authors state, "We recognise that there may be negative secure bases . . . For the purposes of this book, we are focusing on the secure bases that influence us to achieve positive things in our lives" (n5, p. 287). They are referring to the Jonestown massacre (a case considered in Tourish (2013)): I believe the danger of inappropriate attachment should form an integral part of introducing the power of secure bases.
26. Robertson (2005). The Kohlrieser et al. quote is from p. xix.
27. Edmondson (2012).
28. Stoner (2014).

References

Alvesson, M. and Sveningsson, S. (2003) Managers doing leadership: The extraordinarization of the Mundane. *Human Relations* 56(12), pp. 1435–1459.

Bains, G. (2007) Good enough leadership. *Business Strategy Review*, Winter, pp. 67–68.

Bains, G. (2007) *Meaning Inc.: The Blueprint for Business Success in the 21st Century*. London: Profile Books.

Barrett, F.J. (2012) *Yes to the Mess: Surprising Leadership Lessons From Jazz*. Boston, MA: Harvard Business Review Press.

Binney, G., Wilke, G. and Williams, C. (2005) *Living Leadership: A Practical Guide for Ordinary Heroes*. Harlow: FT Prentice Hall.

Collins, J. (2001) *Good to Great: Why Some Companies Make the Leap . . . and Others Don't*. London: Random House.

Edmondson, A. (2012) *Teaming: How Organizations Learn, Innovate, and Compete in the Knowledge Economy*. San Francisco, CA: Jossey-Bass.

French, R. (2001) 'Negative capability': Managing the confusing uncertainties of change. *Journal of Organizational Change Management* 14(5), pp. 480–492.

Harle, T. (2011) Fractal leadership: Emerging patterns for transformation. In Barbour, J.D. and Hickman, G.R. (eds.) *Leadership for Transformation*. San Francisco, CA: Jossey-Bass, pp. 33–49.

Harwood, I. (2003) Distinguishing between the facilitating and the self-serving charismatic group leader. *Group* 27(2/3), pp. 121–129.

Kets de Vries, M.F.R. and Danny, M. (1985) Narcissism and leadership: An object relations perspective. *Human Relations* 38(6), pp. 583–601.

Kohlrieser, G., Goldsworthy, S. and Coombe, D. (2012) *Care to Dare: Unleashing Astonishing Potential Through Secure Base Leadership*. San Francisco, CA: Jossey-Bass.

Nurick, A.J. (2012) *The Good Enough Manager: The Making of a GEM*. New York, NY: Routledge.

Percy, E. (2014) *What Clergy Do: Especially When It Looks Like Nothing*. London: SPCK.

Ratnapalan, S. and Batty, H. (2009) To be good enough. *Canadian Family Physician* 55(3), pp. 239–240.

Robertson, P.P. (2005) *Always Change a Winning Team: Why Reinvention and Change Are Prerequisites for Business Success*. Singapore: Marshall Cavendish Business.

Rosenzweig, P. (2014) *The Halo Effect: How Managers Let Themselves Be Deceived*, Revised Edition. London: Simon and Schuster.

Ross, M.H. (2000) Good-enough isn't so bad: Thinking about success and failure in ethnic conflict management. *Peace and Conflict: Journal of Peace Psychology* 6(1), pp. 27–47.

Samuels, A. (2001) *Politics on the Couch: Citizenship and the Internal Life*. London: Profile Books.

Stacey, R. (2001) Complexity at the 'Edge' of the basic-assumption group. In Gould, L., Stapley, L.F. and Stein, M. (eds.) *The Systems Psychodynamics of Organizations*. London: Karnac, pp. 91–114.

Stein, H. and Allcorn, S. (2014) Good enough leadership: A model of leadership. *Organisational and Social Dynamics* 14(2), pp. 342–366.

Storch, J. and Shotter, J. (2013) 'Good enough', 'imperfect', or situated leadership: Developing and sustaining poised resourcefulness within an organization of practitioner-consultants. *International Journal of Collaborative Practice* 4(1), pp. 1–19.

Swanwick, K. (2008) The 'Good-enough' music teacher. *British Journal of Music Education* 25(1), pp. 9–22.

Tourish, D. (2013) *The Dark Side of Transformational Leadership: A Critical Perspective*. Hove: Routledge.

Winnicott, D.W. (1991 [1957]) *The Child, the Family and the Outside World*. London: Penguin.

Online Sources

Krystal. (n.d.) *Good Enough Teacher: Granting Permission to Let Go of Perfection*. Available from: http://goodenoughteacher.blogspot.co.uk/ (accessed on January 10, 2017).

Kunst, J. (2012) *In Search of the 'Good Enough' Mother: How to Honor the Complexity of Motherhood*. Available from: www.psychologytoday.com/blog/headshrinkers-guide-the-galaxy/201205/in-search-the-good-enough-mother (accessed on January 22, 2017).

Stoner, J.L. (2014) *Strive for Greatness*. Available from: http://seapointcenter.com/strive-for-greatness/ (accessed on January 22, 2017).

Vignettes

"You Don't Think You Can Make a Difference, Do You?"

Keeping Integrity as a Middle Manager

Clare Rigg

I opened my mouth to make a retort, defensively, to the woman who had stormed late into the departmental meeting and scathingly challenged me to explain the method I was attempting to use to make a decision on resource allocation. No matter that I had pre-circulated an agenda and documentation, had consulted on the proposed method, and believed I had an open door policy for anyone to come and discuss things. She felt justified in her contemptuous, indignant behavior. And where she started, others followed. In the moment of catching the words that were forming on my lips, and the anger behind them, I sensed myself about to, as I saw it, sink to the same level of disrespectful, unkind and bullying disdain which prevailed in inter-actions between department members, and most particularly towards "The Management". I checked myself and thought, "This is not who I am; this is not how I want to be relating to people; I have to do better than this". I also knew I was not going to alter anything in that dysfunctional ethos of communication if I got drawn into the same ways of inter-relating. This incident concerned ethical leadership, because for me this was a question of my core values and integrity. Recognising a connection between the threat to my self-control and holding true in how I responded, I found Kathryn Goldman Schuyler's ideas of integrity very helpful, in the sense of "the capacity to hold one's shape" despite high levels of stress (2010, p. 26).

The context for this vignette is a public sector organization where a little while ago, I took on the role of head of section. The position had a history of frequent turnover for various reasons and was regarded as a problematic and difficult section to lead. When I was considering the role, a wise colleague confronted me with the question that forms the title of this contri-bution. Nevertheless, I took on the role, propelled by my ego and my sense that I could perhaps be a better leader/more mature/better listener . . . [more fool me]

As a middle manager, you accept that, as principal-agent theory tells us, you are the agent expected to implement senior management decisions. And you anticipate a degree of antipathy. But in my public sector organization context, where austerity prevailed, where staff was accustomed to having little influence and where fear of closure, particularly in my section, was rife, following years of decline, middle managers were the accessible repository of staff angst and anger, while senior managers kept aloof.

As an agent of the principal (Director), some of the decisions such as, for example, closing down particular services were ones that I would have sought to avoid. But even when deemed to be short sighted, issues of this kind are not the prerogative of middle management to decide. In the forum of departmental meetings, some of these decisions became the lightning rod for combat. They became an opportunity to release anger and discharge emotion. I drew solace from my understanding of psychodynamic literature (Vince, 2011) remembering that the ways people sub-consciously deal with their emotions lie at the heart of organization practices. This helped me see the emotions people displayed, not as a personal attack, but as a product of their anxiety, projections or dependency. I sought to accept myself as a "container" and interact in such a way that might aid a shift, allay anxiety or, at least, not reinforce dependency.

Then I read Vince and Mazen's (2014) work on violent innocence. I recognised in myself the idea that in one's naivety one can end up allowing violence to be done. I identified how my own coping mechanism of constantly looking for the positive, always seeking out the possibilities in preference to the barriers, could perpetuate harm. I saw too late how the power dynamics throughout this organization rendered perfectly capable, articulate people silent in meetings and kept some awake in trepidation of the next encounter. I came to understand that the combative pattern of interactions had become entrenched and affected not just me, as the manager, but other organization members who might want to voice dissenting views.

As one example, the Director informed me, just as one Christmas holiday period began, that he was taking a key staff member off my team for the next six months, after repeatedly assuring me previously that this would not happen. In the austerity climate that severely restricted public sector recruitment of replacements, and yet with an obligation to deliver service to clients in the New Year, I found myself coercing other colleagues to plug the gap. Critical management steers you to ask where the power lies? But I found it necessary also to ask how are you being played? With this example I felt myself to be put in a position of perpetuating harm. Just as the senior manager acted without sufficient care or consideration of my situation, I was passing this on to my colleagues.

There is a lot about middle management that can be uncomfortable. The role is sandwiched between senior management and frontline staff. You expect to be asked to communicate, cajole and direct staff to implement decisions that you might not necessarily agree with yourself. I was good at using phrases like "this will be so good for your CV", "there isn't anyone else with the strengths to do this. ". in my attempts to persuade a colleague to take on an extra task. But when is this unreasonably calculative and excessively manipulative? And as you live with this sense of continuous compromise and discomfort, how do you stop yourself becoming acclimatized to being so calculating. What is the trade-off? For me, I took on the role and I stayed for the period I did because there were things I felt I could affect in the service we delivered for clients. This was pre-eminent for me and for many of the people I worked with. This priority enabled us to work together, and after 18 months, I felt there was an improvement in trust, there were some achievements amongst staff to be proud of and a gradual warming in the departmental interactions. However, into this fragile rapprochement, the senior management board threw yet another grenade. They presented a restructuring of the organization, and in this, my department was demoted. Like a match to dry tinder, this was enough to re-ignite the scarcely dormant fears in staff of closure of our particular service, and there was uproar. During this period, the Director refused to make himself available to meet staff or even to respond to messages. In this vacuum, the obvious recipient/target for staff angst, anger and anxiety was the departmental manager, me.

As I've said, as a middle manager you expect and accept a degree of being the instrument through which senior managers seek to work. But when you hear boasts of the desire to leave a legacy in history, and you see little respect or compassion for clients or colleagues in their actions, that was the moment at which I realized that to stay would be to further perpetuate violence, and no longer in innocence. When I realized I could not (as my wise colleague had counseled) make a difference for the better within the particular dynamics of my organization, I chose to leave. For me, I felt the "right" thing (the best ethical thing) to do was to step away rather than be caught up in continuing the dysfunction.

Bibliography

Goldman Schuyler, K. (2010) Increasing leadership integrity through mind training and embodied learning. *Consulting Psychology* 62(1), pp. 21–38.

Vince, R. (2011) The spatial psychodynamics of management learning. *Management Learning* 42(3), pp. 333–347.

Vince, R. and Mazen, A. (2014) Violent innocence: A contradiction at the heart of leadership. *Organization Studies* 35(2), pp. 189–207.

Dotty's Kitchin

Catherine Turner-Perrott

From the day my daughter was born, she had no interest in food. I remember having to feed her milk in her sleep or with a blanket over her eyes when she was a baby. As she grew up my husband and I, who both love food, began to dread mealtime, as they'd consist of hours of coaxing, bribing and nagging. I was terrified that she'd have such negative memories of food that she'd develop an eating disorder when she was older.

I remember clearly, after one particularly stressful mealtime I sat down beside her on the naughty step and held her defiant little body close to mine. I had already started to research child psychologists but I was still wondering what I could do better? As most mothers would, I very much felt the weight of responsibility lay with me. If I took her to a child psychologist, I was concerned that it would become a "thing", and she'd still have negative memories of being made to eat as a child. I just wanted her to love food and have happy memories of it. That's when it hit me like a light bulb moment that in hindsight I believe was an answer to prayer: I would cook *with* her!

We started simply by doing things like buttering toast, peeling vegetables or whisking eggs and gradually progressed from there. Almost immediately, I noticed our relationship change. The arguments and dread around mealtimes were replaced by excitement about what we were going to cook. I loved spending time with her, seeing the pride on her face and watching her confidence grow. The turning point arrived when she came home upset from school one-day because her friends didn't believe that she was a chef! I thought, "bingo!" I don't need to worry about her having negative memories of being made to eat as a child or having a dangerously limited repertoire of foods that she'll actually eat!

I decided that if this process could work for my daughter, then maybe it would help other parents, so I set up a social media site called *Dotty's Kitchin* to share our recipes and tips. Some time later, I got the opportunity to change the children's menu at a local gastropub so that it was healthy yet appealing to fussy eaters.

I've now just finished their summer menu, which will hopefully be rolled out to the group. Other restaurants and groups have also approached me to write their children's menus, plus I've received numerous speaking requests.

As well as working with eating establishments I'm now creating an online chef qualification for children, with all the tools a parent needs to cook with their child and encourage a love of good food.

Editorial Comment

At first sight, this largely domestic story may appear to have little to do with leadership and ethics in a business arena. However, a number of resonances with the themes and particularly Section 2 of this book struck us as editors as having implications for entrepreneurial leadership that is ethically inspired. First is the reference to the "mundane" setting of the home and the kitchen table; heartfelt decisions made in this apparently ordinary domain turn out to have positive and extraordinary consequences (see Harle's chapter). Second, there is a link with Tomkins and Simpson's chapter, who invoke care for elderly relatives as a valuable resource and bridge into the world of work. In Catherin's vignette, we have a child playing a part in formative leadership, with the dynamic being played out with the mother and daughter alternating in leading and following. Third, this unfolding discovery and enjoyment of healthy food—which expands from kitchen to classroom to restaurant chains—also illustrates the way affect is about making a difference through embodied energy, while recognizing that this energy is shared and never static enough to be captured in a concrete instance but is forever in transition (see the chapter by Knights in this section). In short, we have here a story of the way affective leadership is capable of generating ethical, spiritually uplifting and joyful modes of collective action and commitment.

Part III

Meaning

Has Leadership Lost Its Soul?

There appears to be a growing interest in the spiritual dimension of the work-space and a desire to see our daily labor in transcendent, rather than just material and economic, terms. It was the sociologist Max Weber who described mid-twentieth-century bureaucracy as a "ratio-instrumental cage". He was expressing disenchantment with an overly instrumental society based on what Oscar Wilde described as the measurement of everything and the value of nothing; weights and measures and consumer choice were displacing ideas of depth and belonging. If anything, this lament has gathered more acuity in the current age. We are witnessing strong resistance to the idea that we can exist without community, without meaningful relationships and the rich experiences which actually make life worthwhile. Whether or not we are conventionally "religious" and believers in God (as a person somewhere "out there"), we all value things that we cannot put a price on, or even properly define. How do we explain, in the realm of work for instance, self-sacrificial compassion, going the extra mile, philanthropy and love itself? So a book on leadership would seem to be incomplete without consideration of what we might call "soul".

For **Andrew Henley**, to view the individual in purely materialist and productive terms is ultimately de-humanizing. He makes a case for regarding created persons as having intrinsic value beyond mere physical or intellectual capability. From a theological standpoint, he calls for a quality of leadership which implicitly values the led as being created in the image of the divine.

Karen Blakeley turns our attention to power, pointing out that unless this is balanced by a high responsibility orientation, powerful organizations will tend to attract and promote leaders with high social dominance exhibiting all the signs of bad leadership, namely unethical, narcissistic and excessively risky behaviour. Unless individuals and groups resist such collusion, an organization is in danger of losing its soul.

Finally, **Merv Conroy** explores this challenge of what it takes to recover the soul of professional practice and cultivate ethical decision-making. Drawing upon action research among medical staff, the author begins to trace the kind of thinking and practical wisdom required for leaders seeking to navigate a chaotic world of practice, rife with competing demands and complex relationships.

Phil Jackman attended most of the ESRC seminars on Ethical Leadership upon which this book is based. Inspired by these debates, he and a colleague devised a training course to raise spiritual self-awareness among the individuals participating (a mix of business and educational professionals, some with faith and most with none) and to explore how this might translate into enhanced resilience and integrity in their respective organizations. Now mid-way through the course, this very personal account provides some insight into the collective efforts of delegates and tutors to discuss matters of beliefs and values, to identify the basis of moral courage and—in a word—to re-discover soul in the workplace.

9 Reclaiming Our Organizations Through Collective Responsible Leadership

Karen Blakeley

> Never doubt that a small group of thoughtful, committed citizens can change the world; indeed, it's the only thing that ever has.
>
> *Margaret Mead*

Key Questions

Why is it relatively rare to find people in senior positions who consistently role model ethical, responsible and humane leadership?

What part can you play, wherever you are in the system, in cultivating organizations that are responsible and ethical in their dealings in the world?

Introduction

Of the top ten trends identified by respondents to the World Economic Forum global survey of 2015, a lack of leadership was number three on the list with 86% strongly agreeing that the world is facing a leadership crisis (Gergen, 2015). Two years later, the World Economic Forum issued a worldwide plea for more responsive and responsible leadership (Schwab, 2017 [Online]).

It is somewhat ironic that after over 100 years of formal academic research into leadership effectiveness, here we are, at the beginning of the 21st century, facing a leadership crisis. This is not due to a lack of theory on the subject; while academic debate continues, we do have a relatively clear sense of what good leadership looks like, as well as key features of best practice in leadership development. In fact, leadership development is a multi-billion-dollar business, with estimates of spending in the area ranging from \$10–\$50 billion a year.[1] Despite this, we continue to experience extremely high levels of unhappiness and disengagement in our organizations. Research by Gallup shows employee engagement in the US ranges from 30% engaged, 52% not engaged and 18% actively disengaged; for the

UK, the figures are particularly poor with 13% engaged, 57% not engaged and 26% actively disengaged[2] (Gallup, 2013). It would appear that a lot of effort is being invested in leadership research and development to very little effect.

Every reader will have their own theory of the contributing causes behind this state of affairs but this chapter will argue that the current crisis of leadership in part reflects the fact that, for a number of reasons, our most powerful organizations, in both the public and private sectors, tend to promote leaders high in "social dominance orientation" (SDO). Those high in SDO are more likely to manifest irresponsible leadership and to espouse and enact values inimical to the long-term wellbeing of stakeholders in their organizations and of society as a whole. They are not receptive to normative pressures to adopt ethical or even "effective" leadership practices as they do not regard leadership in the same manner as those perpetrating research and best practice in the field—to social dominants, leadership is a reward for out-maneuvering the competition.

While acknowledging the power of the social, cultural and systemic drivers that underpin these organizational dynamics, I argue that change can only come about when we personally and collectively recognize and confront our own roles in the subterranean processes that often confer power on those least likely to wield it with fairness, justice and wisdom. This implies that change involves us all engaging in the long hard process of becoming responsible leaders, wherever we are placed in the system. Social dominants thrive within systems and communities that reward, fear and collude with them. As Professor David Gergen put it in his report on global leadership and governance to the World Economic Forum,

> we must remember the old adage that we get the leadership we deserve . . . Globally, we the people have been hesitant to speak up when it matters most, when we are facing the toughest of crises—from climate change to poverty to fiscal stability, and so on.[3]

I will argue that responsible leadership is not only for those at the peak of power; it is a calling that demands a response from us all. But behaving responsibly and acting with integrity, according to the most recent studies in social and moral psychology, is not easy. Researchers operating in these fields are revealing new insights into moral behavior that take us beyond the normative and functionalist bias in leadership studies. Moral psychology reveals the underlying psycho-social and neurological dynamics that actually drive our moral behavior, demonstrating the complexity and difficulties we face as embodied human beings in trying to enact our espoused values and beliefs. Authors such as Jonathan Haidt and Dan Ariely argue that our moral responses are pre-conscious and the explanations we provide for our behavior are simply post-rationalizations for what are instinctive and often "irrational" decisions. This is where the world's spiritual traditions and practices have a lot to contribute in restoring a sense of personal agency to the situation. We cannot be responsible unless we can exercise some degree of choice and learn to moderate our instinctive responses. This is precisely what spiritual practices such as meditation and contemplative prayer set out to achieve. Hence, this chapter seeks to show how responsible leadership is most effective when it is aligned with spiritual practice; if responsible leadership guides us as to the what of leadership, spiritual practice show how we can live out our espoused values and beliefs with integrity. If more people embrace this challenge, wherever they are in the system, we have a powerful combination that could help to restore trust in leadership as a mechanism for addressing the global challenges we face today.

Why Do We Get Irresponsible Leaders at the Very Top of Our Organizations?

Research and practice in the 1980s and 1990s led to a pre-occupation with heroic leadership focused on cultivating transformational leaders who could motivate their followers to rise above their self-interest in service of organization goals. Subsequent events reflecting increasing awareness of high levels of corruption, abuse of power, personal greed and incompetence at the top, has led to a disillusionment in "heroic" leadership paradigms and an increasing interest in the role that power, and the desire for power, plays in relation to ethical leadership behavior.

Perhaps the person most known for his research in this field is David McClelland, an organizational psychologist whose voluminous work spanned four decades. McClelland was interested in three interactive characteristics of both people and organizations that appeared to predict leadership success: personal psychological motives (inner states that drive and direct behavior), role incentives (intrinsic or extrinsic rewards that interact with motives to select behavior) and activity inhibition (the tendency to modify and restrain motive-driven behavior). McClelland's work investigated the pattern of motives that appeared to predict success in rising to the most senior levels of leadership in hierarchical organizations. His work revealed that the motivational profile which best predicted promotion into senior positions of leadership consisted of a high need for power, a medium need for achievement and a low need for affiliation.[4] His research showed that those with a high concern for power fell into one of two groups. Some sought power for personal gain (personalized power) and were found to demonstrate behaviors such as bullying, intimidation and excessive risk-taking. A second group were those who sought power in order to contribute to the organization's success (socialized power); here, power motivation predicted *responsible* leadership. These leaders manifested high needs for power but also exhibited high "activity inhibition" and were able to restrain egotistical behaviors in a manner that those high in needs for power but low in activity inhibition could not.

More recent research led by Professor Jim Sidanius at Harvard University supports McClelland's findings. Sidanius and his colleagues present extensive evidence to show that the people who often get to the top of our largest and most powerful organizations are high in SDO,[5] a construct that is similar to McClelland's need for personalized power. Sidanius shows how some of our most powerful organizations have senior management teams comprising high social dominants whose main motivation is to retain power and maximise their personal remuneration which may be at the expense of focusing on long-term performance and meeting the needs of a range of stakeholders. SDO is part of social dominance theory, which draws on McClelland's work but takes a broader, more systemic perspective regarding the distribution of power in society.

Social Dominance Theory

According to social dominance theory (SDT), all human communities organise themselves as group-based social hierarchies where powerful groups dominate others. These hierarchies always include the subordination of children and women, but there is a third category. This is known as an *arbitrary set*, where various groups may be defined as being inferior to others based on, for example, ethnicity, social class, religion or nationality.

These hierarchies are sustained through a number of mechanisms. At the societal and cultural level for example, there are *hierarchy legitimizing myths* which people throughout society will tend to believe and support—an example of this might be: *high pay for CEOs is necessary to attract the greatest talent*. This is widely believed in society and yet there is extensive evidence that high CEO pay is not correlated to outstanding business performance.[6]

At the organizational level, there are *hierarchy-enhancing* organizations, which include profit-making corporations and banks, which promote and sustain inequality by allocating disproportionately more resources, status and influence (through processes such as recruitment, promotion and reward) to dominant groups than to subordinate groups.

At the individual level, people differ in terms of how much they discriminate against others who they consider in some way "inferior". This is known as SDO.

Social Dominance Orientation

People high in SDO see the world as a zero-sum game where groups compete for access to desirable resources such as financial wealth, education, health services, status and influence. Those high in SDO, see certain groups as naturally superior to others, therefore deserving of greater access to resources than those lower in the hierarchy. High social dominants are more competitive, less empathetic, colder, more narcissistic, hubristic and ruthless than those low in SDO and regard those low in SDO as inferior.[7]

Research has shown that hierarchy-enhancing institutions, such as banks and multinational corporations, attract people who are high in SDO.[8] Once inside corporations and banks, social dominants are far more likely to reach the highest levels of seniority than those who are more competent or more effective leaders.[9] They then use the institutions they control to concentrate even more wealth and power into their hands and see this as entirely legitimate and natural. They typically use fear of punishment and the enticement of rewards to control others. They are attracted to others high in SDO and hence will promote other social dominants at the expense of women (lower in SDO than men) and other groups viewed as lower status.[10] They are not attracted to egalitarian ideals and practices and are far more likely to be climate change deniers and to avoid putting into place meaningful corporate responsibility programmes.[11] It is important to note that high social dominants are motivated predominantly by the defending of their power bases hence, they expect complete obedience and loyalty and are highly susceptible to flattery and deference. Once performance targets are met, they expect a disproportionate share of the rewards.

The research shows unequivocally that the characteristics of social dominance are associated with irresponsible and unethical leadership. Most corporate scandals have involved organizations led by people known to display these characteristics such as Bernie Ebbers of WorldCom, Tony Haywood at BP, Didier Lombard of French Telecom, Bob Diamond at Barclays and Ferdinand Piëch of Volkswagen, who, according to a Fortune article on the emissions scandal, was "a brilliant engineer and a ruthless, terrifying manager who dominated VW for more than two decades".[12]

How Social Dominants Affect Our Own Moral Compasses

When those driven by personal power gain positions of leadership it matters. Once in place high SDOs magnify the worst elements of the system and affect the ethical climate of the organization.[13] This is important because most people will adapt to the cultures within which they find themselves. We are pragmatists and will tune in to "what works around here". Once we find out what works, we will demonstrate the behaviors that help us to achieve our goals. This is why we get the leaders we deserve; we are all complicit in the system.

Social psychologists have effectively demonstrated that most of us are neither highly ethical nor highly unethical.[14] Let's imagine, as part of a thought experiment, a normal distribution curve depicting human ethicality, which we will define at one end as pure psychopathy (think Hitler) and at the other end as pure altruism (think Mother Teresa). Most of us are, by definition, in the middle—we will balance pursuing our self-interest with our willingness to help others. Dan Ariely, a leading expert in the field of moral psychology, shows how we balance our needs to be seen by others as ethical with a drive to pursue our own selfish interests. He shows how we cheat only to the extent that we can still retain our self-image as reasonably honest individuals. If we can cheat and get away with it, most of us will.

However, this is not an argument of despair. Of course, the social dominants will always be with us but we can temper their behaviour and influence. What we are seeing in the current leadership crisis is a skewed distribution curve—skewed towards the social dominant end of the scale, because in some way, many of us are buying into the social dominant narrative and colluding in their power. This is partly because, particularly in the business world, there does not appear to be many other credible narratives around and partly because we are inculcated with social dominant narratives so effectively that it is very difficult to see the world from any other perspective.

Personal Reflection

As a management development consultant, I once found myself working for a social dominant. He ran a new country office in Eastern Europe which was part of a professional services firm that had hired me to help with the training and development of the consultants in that country. Following the training, we moved into the coaching phase and as we did so, one by one, the individual consultants told me of the bullying and intimidating behavior of their boss, which ultimately undermined everything we were trying to achieve via the training. As the evidence of his extremely aggressive behavior became overwhelming, I had to decide what to do, as there was no one overseeing his behavior, and clearly, people were suffering. I had been coaching one or two consultants on how to question the inappropriate behavior, but clearly, this was not working. Now, I decided, it was my turn to exhibit moral courage. Before I left to catch my plane, I asked to see the boss. Gently, I tried to explore the kinds of bullying behaviors commonly raised by the consultants which seriously discouraged any experimentation or change. As soon as the individual sensed that I was "challenging" him, he exploded with anger, hurling abuse at me and telling me to get out of the building. That, I thought, was the end of my contract. I informed my client in the UK (who was more junior than the social dominant boss), letting him know what had occurred and took full responsibility for my behavior. I did not hear anything for some months and then I was informed that the incident had been raised with a more senior partner. This partner broached the topic with the social dominant, only to have him explode with rage in front of his eyes. The problem had been recognized: the social dominant was sent to anger management training and his behavior, along with the morale in the office, subsequently closely monitored.

Responding to the Crisis of Leadership

I find the image of the normal distribution curve quite useful; it reminds me that most of us are not really bad or good—we want to pursue our self-interest and we want to help others. The problem seems to lie when our institutions are controlled by social dominants who, through their power and influence, skew the distribution curve towards the sociopathic end of the curve. But the image of the distribution curve also reminds us that we can skew it back towards the more altruistic end—one behavior at a time.

In order to do this, we could all start to think of ourselves as responsible leaders, embracing an alternative vision for the leadership of our organizations and playing our own role in perpetrating the responsible leadership narrative through our words and actions. And it is important to remember that responsible leaders do get to the top of powerful organizations. The systems and cultures of social domination do not have to be as they are, for with responsible leaders at the top and throughout our organizations we can change things. Examples of responsible leaders include. Paul Polman, the CEO of Unilever and a global leader in making the argument for business to play a pivotal role in achieving the UN sustainable development goals; Yvon Chouinard of Patagonia; Ray Anderson formerly of Interface; Anita Roddick formerly of Body Shop; Blake Mycoskie of Toms; and Jochen Zeitz of Kering and Puma. These people are all known for their humanistic and responsible leadership styles and can act as an inspiration for our own responsible leadership wherever we are in the system.

What Is Responsible Leadership?

Responsible leaders act as "agents of world benefit"[15] to bring about a fairer, more inclusive and sustainable world. They build coalitions committed to the flourishing of all stakeholders in society by developing relationships of trust, empowering others to facilitate change, cultivating a shared sense of meaning and purpose and by exhibiting personal integrity and ongoing development of character.

Responsible leadership draws on three important theoretical traditions: 1. corporate responsibility and stakeholder theory; 2. Leadership theory and 3. business ethics.

Corporate responsibility is underpinned by stakeholder theory and is based on the premise that corporate leaders have a responsibility to a broader range of stakeholders than normally included in mainstream leadership theory. These stakeholders comprise people throughout the supply chain, non-governmental organizations, employees, customers, governments, and future generations all of whom are affected by the organization's activities.

Leadership theory emphasises the importance of cultivating an inspiring purpose (or vision), influencing and empowering others to bring about change, building relationships of mutual trust and remaining authentic to one's personal values and principles.

Finally, business ethics and ethical theory stresses the significance of self-awareness, clarifying clear personal values, understanding how and why we fail to live up to our values and how to develop the character (or virtues) to maintain our integrity during times of pressure and stress (moral courage).

Responsible leadership can clearly be accused of "romanticism" promulgating an "ideal-type", a fantasy that is impossible to live up to. It implies the conquering of the ego and embracing of socialized power for the benefit and love of others—even those that are not yet born. For me personally, this is where I feel my faith helps, for I see the core elements of responsible leadership as essentially part of a spiritual journey. I am not a responsible leader, nor could I ever be. But I am more of a responsible leader today than I was yesterday and even more so than I was ten years ago. Similarly, I am not a perfect Christian, as I do not love my neighbor as myself (impossible), nor do I love God with all my heart, soul, strength and mind. However, I hope I am on the journey towards being a slightly more robust Christian today than I was yesterday or last year (although my journey has its ups and downs). Like the two love commandments at the core of Christianity, or the achievement of Aristotle's eudaimonia, responsible leadership manifests in a set of practices that help us grow into the part. It is not there to act as a sword of Damocles dangling over our heads, ready to come down on us whenever we (regularly) fail to live up to its precepts but rather to act as an inspiration in our everyday lives and to provide us with hope whenever we see someone else living according more or less according to its values.

There are multiple practices that support the development of responsible leadership and these can be found in many of the world's spiritual traditions. I have extracted six practices, two from each theoretical tradition, although they very much overlap. From leadership theory, I have focused on the importance of working for a higher purpose and, in the light of the discussion above, the importance of embracing power well. From stakeholder theory, I have emphasized the importance of cultivating a love of humanity and acting out a sense of service to others. From ethics, I have stressed the importance of connecting to conscience and cultivating our awareness of ethical issues.

A Higher Purpose

At the core of responsible leadership lies purpose—what are we exercising leadership for? Somehow our business leaders seem to have got their priorities skewed. The WWF Living Planet Report of 2015 reminds us: "Ecosystems sustain societies that create economies. It does not work any other way round". It is difficult in the day to day to remind ourselves of this fact, but to be rooted in a spiritual view of life is to be connected to a sense of awe and transcendence. Responsible leaders look up to the heavens and see a lonely and beautiful planet despoiled and endangered; they look through time and see the wonders of human development and achievement and then they look at the present and see how little these wonders have been shared with the people who inhabit our planet. Of course, senior executives have to build sustainable and profitable businesses, but is this their life's purpose? Very few business leaders go down in history but many of those that do seem to be either animated by a higher purpose (Anita Roddick is a great example) or to be renowned for their greed and abuse of power. It is unfortunate that we have forgotten that business can be a higher calling, and particularly in a time when business leaders are as powerful as the world's greatest political leaders, it is important that we expect our business lives to be dedicated to something meaningful that takes us beyond our self-interest and connects us to higher purpose. The first practice of responsible leadership is to work towards identifying a higher purpose that lies at the core of one's leadership.

Embracing Power

This practice may be surprising. It encourages us to embrace power rather than cynicism, hopelessness, despair or collusion. It is intentionally reminiscent of Martin Luther King's great words:

> Power properly understood is nothing but the ability to achieve purpose. It is the strength required to bring about social, political, and economic change. . . . And one of the great problems of history is that the concepts of love and power have usually been contrasted as opposites—polar opposites—so that love is identified with the resignation of power, and power with the denial of love. Now we've got to get this thing right. What [we need to realize is] that power without love is reckless and abusive, and love without power is sentimental and anaemic. . . . It is precisely this collision of immoral power with powerless morality which constitutes the major crisis of our time.

The embracing of power as responsible leaders in the context of conscience, good purpose, love, awareness and service is one of the most important ways we can address the crisis of leadership in our own time. How we embrace power is a challenging question. For those to whom power feels natural and attractive, this practice may be about developing greater humility and seeking honest feedback from others. For those who balk at taking power, the practice may involve learning to recognize and utilize power for a higher purpose.

Love of Humanity

Responsible leaders learn to love. A recent piece of research showed that love enables us to expand our circle of concern in a way that other emotions cannot. When shown pictures that evoked compassion, participants in the research experiment decided to donate to charities that cared for people closest to home—in the local community or nationally. However, when shown pictures that evoked love, participants expanded their circle of concern to donate to causes that helped people who were less familiar and less like themselves. Paul Bloom, leading neuro-ethicist, argues that empathy can be a source of racism or prejudice towards those who are least like us. Love appears to be the only faculty that expands our circle of concern and evokes altruism towards those most different to and distant from ourselves. If responsible leaders are to embrace the needs and interests of stakeholders in distant lands, love is the means by which they will be able to do this. Love, in this sense of "love of humanity", can be learned. Mother Teresa reminds us, "we can do no great things; only small things with great love".

Service to Others

Stakeholder theory suggests that as business leaders (and leaders in other spheres of life) we need to take account of the needs of those affected by our decisions. Service to others is also evocative of the leadership theory closest to that of responsible leadership, that is, "servant leadership". Service to others is also part of the Christian spiritual tradition and acknowledges that the hardest of all journeys involves letting go of our own ego and placing the needs of others high in our list of priorities. This is the opposite of social dominance. The world's great spiritual traditions have dedicated millennia to understanding how this process can be embraced and needless to say, it is the very few, and the greatest of us, that come closest to it. These are often the people we hold in most esteem—Nelson Mandela, Mother Teresa, Martin Luther King and, more recently, Malala and Paul Polman of Unilever. These are not perfect human beings, but they are inspirational examples of life as an embodiment of service. Their examples can help us in our ongoing spiritual journeys to overcome the egotism that is the root of much personal, as well as societal, unhappiness.

Connecting to Conscience

Conscience is a complex and troubling faculty which needs more space to explore than we have in this chapter. However, we do know that someone without connection to their conscience cannot be a responsible leader; psychopaths, for example, are often defined by the absence of conscience. Conscience is a reflection of both an inborn sense of right and wrong (a sense that is seen in experiments with pre-verbal children preferring puppets that behave kindly over those who behave aggressively) and a "container" of social norms and expectations. And this is where it can be troubling. When does our conscience call us to stand up against social norms and when is it right to listen to the social norms as they gently prod us to examine ourselves and our motives? Is that inner voice that pricks us the source of good or is it a voice of rationalisation and self-justification? With conscience comes guilt and all the words associated with it—tormented, haunted, worried, infected. It is no wonder that we can easily find ourselves switching our conscience off, not paying attention to it. Excessive guilt not only torments, it disempowers and drains us of energy; it undermines our self-confidence and robs us of the ability to act. For me personally, engaging with my conscience in the context of a faith, enables me to weigh any guilt with a sense that I am loved and lovable and that being fallible is part of what it is to be human. From a spiritual perspective, conscience is a "faculty" that connects us with the divine or transcendent and guides our behavior through a balance of love and guilt, compassion and remorse, forgiveness and, in a Christian worldview, redemption.

Personal Reflection

I remember vividly the moment I decided to cut myself off from my conscience. It was a time when I did not have a faith and was trying to do everything in my own strength. I was involved in various campaigning organizations such as Amnesty International, Nicaragua Solidarity Campaign, War on Want. I also subscribed to "Ethical Consumer" when it was not fashionable and used to spend much of Saturday searching out ethical goods to purchase instead of the normal, compromised fare. Not only was this exhausting, it was impossible. The turning point was watching a film called *Salvador*, which described American intervention in El Salvador and its consequences for the extremely poor, downtrodden people of that country. I felt overwhelmed to such an extent that I felt a switch flick in my brain. Enough was enough. I gave up my quest to make a difference in the world and embraced materialism—I wanted to have some fun. I cannot say that I did not have some fun, but ultimately it became nihilistic, empty and banally stupid. Not caring about matters of equity and social justice left me not caring about anything very much. It was only when I found a faith that I found I could care without feeling overwhelmed. Of course, this was just a normal journey to maturity, but I have found a difference between a conscience rooted in taking personal responsibility for the problems of the world and a conscience rooted in a transcendent spirituality of love and forgiveness.

Ethical Awareness

One of the things that most shocked me on entering academia was my complete ignorance of issues of sustainability, corporate governance and the complicity of business in some of the most shocking examples of social injustice I had encountered—from the draining of wells in India in order to produce fizzy drinks, to the mining of coltan for our phones in the Democratic Republic of Congo and the shocking conditions of the Chinese Foxconn workers, 11 of whom committed suicide. I had been aware of general matters of injustice but not the specifics nor the extent. Like conscience, it is easy to steer attention away from these issues. In my previous work my attention had been possessed by matters of performance and effectiveness with no room, nor appetite for, detailed matters of social justice in the business context. Attention is a multi-billion-dollar business and marketers research the latest findings in neuroscience in order to find the best ways to possess our attention. It works. I feel I have to battle to stay in control of my attention and as many of the authors in this book point out, meditation is a crucial part of this ongoing battle.

Embracing Responsible Leadership

I have argued that unless everyone embraces responsible leadership in some way, we are highly susceptible to be ruled by social dominants who abuse the organizations and social institutions they run. If we do not embody responsible leadership in our own lives, we collude with the social dominants we consistently encounter in our organizations and in our lives and in this way our systems become skewed towards social dominance. We collude when we go along with values that suggest that some people (the wealthy, powerful, educated, successful) are in some way "better" than others; when we idolize or mimic these people in our goals, ambitions, behaviors and words; when we allow them to take power from us by colluding with the ways they behave or make sense of the world; when we cut ourselves off from our conscience or when we tacitly agree not to rock the boat in return for job security or promotion. When we collude with social dominants we get the leaders we deserve but, as we have seen, it is not easy to resist—we all have these Darwinian, competitive drives within us and we all have deep-rooted needs for security, success or a sense that we occupy a senior position in the social hierarchy. My own feeling is that resistance is ultimately a spiritual path of recognizing, confronting and overcoming the social dominant inside us all.

While it is difficult to stand one's ground in an indifferent or hostile environment, it has been suggested that we can all embrace the call to responsible leadership. While this is difficult and uncharted territory the risk is worth the prize. We are living in uncertain times, where the scale of the issues confronting us is unprecedented. The cost of failure could involve the "perfect storm" of rising populations, unsustainable demands for energy, water and food, mass migrations, internecine conflict and global war. Perhaps we are damned if we do and damned if we don't. The question is simply what kind of world do we want to co-create because whatever we do and whatever we don't do, we are co-creating a world regardless; hopefully, it will be one of which we can be proud.

Notes

1. See: Schyns et al. (2012).
2. Gallup (2013).
3. (Gergen, 2015, [Online]).
4. McClellend and Burnham (1976).
5. Sidanius and Pratto (1999).

6. According to the UK Government's Department for Business Innovation and Skills, CEOs of FTSE100 companies received average increases of 13.6% per annum between 1999 and 2010. This compares with just 1.7% annual increase in the FTSE index during the same period. They conclude that the FTSE index appears "to have had no impact on the level of remuneration awarded" (Department of Business Innovation and Skills, 2011, p. 11).
7. Sidanius et al. (2013).
8. Pratto et al. (2006).
9. Anderson and Brown (2010).
10. Sidanius et al. (2013).
11. Jylha and Akrami (2015).
12. Smith and Parloff (2016, p. 103).
13. Schminke et al. (2005).
14. Bazerman and Gino (2012).
15. Pless and Maak (2009, p. 60).

Bibiography

Anderson, C. and Brown, C.E. (2010) The functions and dysfunctions of hierarchy. *Research in Organizational Behavior* 30, pp. 55–89.

Bazerman, M.H. and Gino, F. (2012) *Blind Spots—Why We Fail to Do What's Right and What to Do About It.* Princeton, NJ: Princeton University Press.

Department of Business Innovation and Skills. (2011) *Executive Remuneration: Discussion Paper.* Available from: www.gov.uk/government/uploads/system/uploads/attachment_data/file/31660/11-1287-executive-remuneration-discussion-paper.pdf (accessed on Auguest 23, 2014).

Gallup. (2013) *State of the Global Workplace—Employee Engagement Insights for Business Leaders Worldwide* [Online]. Available from: www.gallup.com/poll/165269/worldwide-employees-engaged-work.aspx (accessed on April 29, 2016).

Gergen, D. (2015) *A Call to Lead: The Essential Qualities for Stronger Leadership* [Online]. Available from: http://reports.weforum.org/outlook-global-agenda-2015/global-leadership-and-governance/the-call-to-lead/ (accessed on April 8, 2015).

Jylha, K.M. and Akrami, N. (2015) Social dominance orientation and climate change denial: The role of dominance and system justification. *Personality and Individual Differences* 86, pp. 108–111.

McClelland, D. C. and Burnham, D.H. (1976) Power is the Great Motivator, *Harvard Business Review*, 54(2), 100–110.

McClelland, D.C. and Burnham, D.H. (1995) Power is the great motivator. *Harvard Business Review* 73(1), pp. 126–139.

Pless, N. and Maak, T. (2009) Responsible leaders as agents of world benefit: Learnings from 'Project Ulysses'. *Journal of Business Ethics* 85(Supplement 1): 14th Annual Vinventian International Conference on Justice for the Poor: A Global Business Ethics, pp. 59–71.

Pratto, F., Sidanius, J. and Levin, S. (2006) Social dominance theory and the dynamics of intergroup relations: Taking stock and looking forward. *European Review of Social Psychology* 17(8), pp. 271–320.

Schminke, M., Ambrose, M.L. and Neubaum, D.O. (2005) The effect of leader moral development on ethical climate and employee attitudes. *Organizational Behavior and Human Processes* 97, pp. 135–151.

Schwab, K. (2017) *A Call for Responsive and Responsible Leadership* [Online]. Available from: www.weforum.org/agenda/2017/01/a-call-for-responsive-and-responsible-leadership/ (accessed on April 20, 2017).

Schyns, B., Tyman, A., Kiefer, T. and Kerschreiter, R. (2012) New ways to leadership development: A picture paints a thousand words. *Management Learning* 44(1), pp. 11–24.

Sidanius, J., Ketily, N., Sheehy-Skeffington, J., Ho, A.K., Sibley, C. and Duriez, B. (2013) You're inferior and not worth our concern: The interface between empathy and social dominance orientation. *Journal of Personality* 81(3), pp. 313–323.

Sidanius, J. and Pratto, F. (1999) *Social Dominance*. Cambridge: Cambridge University Press.

Smith, G. and Parloff, R. (2016) Hoaxwagen. *Fortune*, 15 March, 173(4), pp. 98–115.

10 Creating Value

Andrew Henley

Key Questions

Is "good" leadership too often focused solely on private benefit for the organization, or should good leaders focus first and foremost on public value?

What approaches to understanding and acquiring knowledge about value have you been exposed to as a leader?

How might Christian ethical thought and spiritual reflection help leaders to gain insight and understanding of value?

Introduction

Contemporary leaders want to lead well, but are often unclear or conflicted about whether their leadership practice is creating something of value. Indeed, the word value itself can be both controversial and yet interpreted so widely as to be almost devoid of meaning. Value can be whatever one wants it to be. Nevertheless, well-intentioned leaders will often say that they want their efforts to be recognized as valuable. For many leaders and organizations value is framed in terms of economic or financial performance, or consumer satisfaction. However, a wider, non-material understanding of value might include human flourishing and fulfilment. In this chapter, I explore these issues, and their implications for a more reflective perspective on leadership. This is a perspective that will encompass a wider sense of value beyond "objective" conceptions of material gain, to address the important questions of leadership for what purpose and for whom.

As James McGregor Burns observes, leadership is one of the most misunderstood concepts in the language.[1] While research may seek to identify the character and charismatic qualities of successful leaders, practice often becomes harnessed to the transformation of the fortunes of a particular organization, set in a particular economic or social context, rather than in transformation for the wider common good. There is something of a parallel here with the myth, central to traditional economics, of an invisible hand guiding markets towards the greatest good for the greatest number. Why should we assume that, if individual business leaders pursue narrow self-interested private objectives, then the greatest common good will follow? And yet there is a taken-for-granted assumption in much that is said and written about leadership that economic value takes primacy. Consequently, when things do go wrong such as they did in the 2008 global financial crisis,[2] attention turns to what leaders and managers have been taught about value on business school programs.[3]

Therefore, the experience for many in leadership is fraught with a level of nagging insecurity. When we look under the surface of leadership experience, particularly in smaller entrepreneurial organizations, we often find a lack of clarity and consistency about objectives and intentions, a preoccupation with process and compliance, and a potentially unhealthy level of self-doubt. There is also a struggle for space to reflect on these concerns about purpose and whether it is legitimate to expect that purpose to be shared. Is the idea of leading to achieve value an illusion? Or is it possible for a leader to find settled leadership with a sense of self-ease that one is genuinely achieving something of value? For many leaders, one route towards this place of personal equilibrium is through the application of spiritual practice.

The lens here through which I frame this spiritual context is one informed by Christian theology. This is the perspective that has informed and supported my own experience, as both an academic, a facilitator of leadership development and as a leader myself. The Christian biblical accounts comprise a narrative through which humankind are able to understand at a deep level that a selfish, ego-driven perspective is at odds with divine value and purpose, expressed in the person of Christ. This is often expressed in the Christian tradition through the notion of the common good. However, I am not seeking to exclude the relevance of the argument here for those who prefer to follow other religious or philosophical approaches.

The Taken-for-Grantedness That Economic Value Is Supreme

To state that leadership should have purpose or an over-arching teleology (to use the philosophical term) might seem obvious, especially in the world of for-profit business activity. However, it is worth considering the dominant narratives on what organizations are for, beyond simplistic notions of economic value. Business organizations can of course differ in the purpose for which they were established and that purpose may adapt and change over time. Economists and others have debated for many years whether shareholder-owned businesses in fact do pursue the highest possible returns for those shareholders. And taking the view that economic value is all that matters is not the same as subscribing to a neo-liberal view of economic policy; economic value may be adopted as the primary objective[4] for businesses even by those who still believe that there is a legitimate role for the state and other regulatory institutions. But discussion amonst economists has not fundamentally challenged the materialist conception of human activity and value inherited from the origins of modern economics in 17th- and 18th-century Enlightenment thinking, and which still finds moral expression and refinement in the utilitarian paradigm of 19th-century neoclassical economic methods.[5]

Nevertheless, deeper critiques from a moral or theological perspective are emerging of the perceived supremacy of economic conceptions of value. Eve Poole highlights a list of questionable taken-for-granted assumptions underpinning materialist economic analysis that have arguably lasted beyond their usefulness.[6] These include, for example, the universal virtue of competition, the usefulness of utilitarianism (that is the philosophical idea of pursuing "the greatest good for the greatest number") and the efficacy of the invisible hand which is alleged to make markets work.

I want to highlight two assumptions in particular. The first is that the *relentless pursuit of shareholder value* is a good thing. This focuses on ownership interests that in modern financial markets last on average for only a few seconds. Poole argues that shareholder value is a convenient device conveniently embodied in company law and promulgated by business leaders to align the activities of internal stakeholders, particularly employees and lower level managers. This links to the second assumption that *agency theory* functions as a useful device for realigning the incentives of employees with owners. The importance of agency follows from the separation between ownership and control which began to emerge in the 19th century with the growth of limited liability companies. It implies a taken-for granted assumption that realignment can be achieved through narrow individualistic approaches to human resource management focused on financial performance, reinforced by a range of financial instruments. Ultimately agency theory suggests, I would argue, a very pessimistic view of human nature and, implicitly, a functionalist view of leadership which confirms that pessimism.

Why does this have spiritual relevance? Because it sees the individual in purely materialist, productive and ultimately de-humanizing terms, rather than as a created person with intrinsic value beyond mere physical or intellectual capability. Leadership which values the led as anything less than fully human stands in stark contrast to the Christian position that all are created in the image of the divine. Of course this critique of economic value is not in any sense unique to a Christian perspective; we also find it, for example, in the work of an author such as E.F. Schumacher.[7]

Exploring a Wider Sense of *Telos*

Public Value and Common Good

As a leader is it possible to escape from the clutches of a materialist *telos*? The pursuit of financial performance, dressed up in a range of indicators depending on organizational context, seems to be all-pervasive. Some would argue that economic performance is so hollow that it would be more honest to abandon any sense of *telos* altogether, and reject what is seen as a "myth of certainty".[8] Coordinated methods at the level of society as a whole, such as regulatory institutions or corporate social responsibility initiatives, might aim to constrain individual expressions of materialist ego. But these are often unlikely to lead to more moral outcomes. Religious expressions of individual morality, as prominent American theologian and social ethicist Reinhold Neibuhr argues, may even lead to individual otherworldliness and disinterest in wider society.[9] Those who worry about the moral purpose of the business world sometimes prefer to withdraw from it altogether. Each of these positions seems unduly pessimistic, even though there is a strong tradition in Christian thought and practice which advocates monastic seclusion.

I would like to highlight the recent attention paid by social science researchers to the idea of public value proposed by John Brewer.[10] He draws, in particular, on Michael Burawoy's work on conceptualizing different forms of knowledge.[11] This highlights a key distinction between the value of merely instrumental knowledge and the value of knowledge that is reflexive. While instrumental knowledge will tell us about means (how to achieve a particular stated objective), reflexive knowledge is knowledge applied in a critical fashion to the question of ends (what the objective ought to be). Reflexivity implies dialogue and reciprocity, or, in Habermas's terminology, communicative action.[12] In pursuit of the instrumental, organizations find themselves pressured to harness a wide range of managerialist tactics, often thinly veiled as expressions of the leader's own ego. These forms of management for material gain have the potential to co-opt not just physical resource, but also psychological and even spiritual resource dimensions.[13] Leading on the basis of such instrumental knowledge, with a given objective in view, may seem uncontroversial. But once logically developed, these forms of leadership have huge potential to become narrow and stultifying, precisely because they treat the led simply as human resource[14]—as means towards end.

Knowledge in support of public value needs to be normative, in the sense that it will require us to give careful consideration to ethical, moral and even spiritual dimensions. This has direct relevance for thinking about leadership because it focuses attention towards the question of what we might need to know as leaders in order to engage in a reflective, critical evaluation in search of reflexive understanding of those objectives we have chosen to achieve. By reflexive I mean that we gain an understanding that any objective or purpose is actively shaped by our experience and dialogue with others rather than taken for granted.[15] That process of evaluation might lead us to a conclusion that the leadership task be focused on far more than a set of narrow indicators of economic or material value. There is a further dimension here. Most leaders lead from a position where objectives are proposed, implicitly or explicitly, by others. Those goals may be derived from one's position in a hierarchical management structure. They may be determined by agency relationships, or may arise from how, as individual leaders, we perceive external economic and societal demands; pressures which might be difficult to challenge or confront.

Reflexive Knowledge

Brewer directs our attention away from instrumental knowledge for inward self-referential purposes towards reflexive knowledge for the public arena. For example:

- The idea of public value asks important questions concerning purpose and direction. It requires me to reflect on why am I engaged in a given course of action, and the value of this for others (considered as ends rather than means).
- This, then, prompts me to find out and understand how to support others in the achievement of a shared or public sense of value or common good.
- This approach leads naturally to public conversation both within and beyond the formal boundaries of the organization in question, to determine what kind of leadership is desirable (for example, emotionally connected, morally aware, even spiritually centered) and to what end (to pursue normative value rather than a narrative of instrumental, economic teleology).

Business history provides many examples of the latter. For example, leadership decisions to withdraw profitable investment from locations in order to accelerate political and social change, such as in apartheid South Africa, or where 19th-century Quaker business leaders in Britain preferred to divert funds into social projects such as improved housing rather than into private business investment[16] (see also Box 10.1).

Box 10.1

The industrial base of the UK economy remains populated by significant numbers of medium-sized family owned companies (what in German would be termed "mittelstand"). Despite the challenges faced by family-owner companies, as that capital base becomes more and more diffused across second and later generation leaders, many of these companies have inherited a strong values base derived from the religious (often Christian non-conformist) faith of their 19th- and early 20th-century founders. Modern competitive pressures (as well as equal opportunities principles) often require such family owners to recruit the best available professional executive leadership regardless of strong commitment to the original faith positions of their founders. Re-intrepretation of these values for a less paternalist, multicultural or secular society in the early 21st century has required a reflexive process to align "good" professional leadership values and virtues with that faith legacy. So, for example, a common theme has been the re-examination of contemporary commitment to environmental sustainability as mere regulatory compliance into one that reflects a Christian faith-based perspective of "good stewardship".

Any discussion about leadership, once it extends into the public arena, has to be reinvigorated with an open conversation about spirituality, virtue and morality. A Christian perspective has to turn its attention to the moral, as well as physical order embodied in the created world and to the hope that Christians place in the future physical and moral restoration of the universe.[17] This creates a sense of development, which is expressed in Christian thought in the idea of the "kingdom of God"—moral and spiritual authority instituted in the model of Jesus Christ and yet at the same time to be fulfilled in the future when he returns. Moral order is directed teleologically towards leadership for the purpose of establishing justice in the present for people as ends in themselves, as well as furthering progression towards the belief in the possibility of an ultimately fully just future.

In my experience some leaders, when embarking on leadership development activity, appear to place significance in explaining their religious or philosophical frameworks to their peers.[18] This suggests that normative moral and spiritual frameworks, and the opportunity that these provide for acquiring reflexive knowledge about their leadership position and activity, are also very important.[19] However, for others, an important aspect of leadership development work is in the opportunity it provides to acquire a more reflexive understanding. This understanding can help us to acquire clarity about meaning and purpose. When thinking about public value and common good, spiritual reflection and practice encompass both the private personal world and the shared public world in which, as leaders, we engage. This also means that what is valuable extends beyond our private spiritual formation as individual leaders towards the well-being and flourishing of those we lead.

The Uncertain Contributions of Business Ethics, Institutions and Spirituality at Work

Proposed solutions to the problem of value that we find within the mainstream management curriculum are ones based around ideas of socially responsible leadership and ethical discourse. Studying business ethics or corporate social responsibility allows us to become familiar with management practices such as the use of codes of conduct, programmes for raising ethical awareness, policy statements which set out corporate values, and training frameworks for ethical reporting such as the triple bottom line approach. Their intended purpose is to direct our attention as leaders, or perhaps as members of another group of business stakeholders, towards the achievement of ethical outcomes or the acquisition of economic value through the pursuit of ethical strategies. But do companies use these tools to reframe their corporate objectives, or to support and strengthen existing economic value objectives by using them instrumentally to make the organization appear more attractive to stakeholders? Undoubtedly many companies take corporate social responsibility seriously for its own sake, but for others it may merely be a means to an end.

These approaches may also identify the significance of compliance with institutional demands or norms. Institutions can be both formal and informal. In his influential work on new institutional theory Richard Scott observes that the impact of institutions on human behavior extends well beyond the merely economic function of regulating or restricting behavior.[20] Their impact extends into the realms of the normative and social-cognitive, since the social function of institutions, particularly informal ones, is to articulate and clarify taken for granted assumptions about appropriate behavior. Sometimes, but not always, it might be possible for social institutions to fix what is wrong with the taken-for-grantedness of individualistic ideas of economic value. These social institutions may help leaders to appreciate and realize the benefits for wider common good to be derived from social organization and interaction.[21] But pessimistically, we might conclude that social institutions often merely reinforce the *status quo*.

The growing level of interest in what has come to be termed "spirituality at work" (SaW) or "spiritual leadership theory" (SLT) is also relevant here.[22] Many organizations, including a number of prominent global businesses, have sought to leverage the interests of employees and managers in spiritual practice in order to pursue a less ego-centric leadership approach for the benefit of the organization, or seek to stimulate new interests because of the perceived benefits for employees. There is no doubt that many leaders find the ideas here and the practices that proponents espouse as helpful. It is hard, however, to know whether SaW and SLT practices are able to equip leaders to challenge the dominant narrative of value, or whether they have become tools through which organizations engage in the appropriation of the spiritual in an instrumental fashion, as as well as the intellectual and emotional resources of their employees. SaW and SLT activity thus risk becoming a functional part of the internal institutional landscape, or a social technology within the organization,[23] that supports rather than challenges dominant narratives about value.

Christian Spirituality in Support of Creating Value

The approach I have taken to understanding value has focused on the nature of the knowledge that underpins how value is framed and understood; knowledge that can be merely instrumental and therefore focused on objective questions, or knowledge that is reflexive and therefore normative. If we want to acquire reflexive knowledge, then we will need to engage in reflective practice. Such practice need not be predominantly spiritual or religious in nature, but it can be. We acquire knowledge and learn in a variety of different ways, depending on our personality, cognitive characteristics and learning style. However, we might, as others do, conclude that spiritual reflection is helpful in supporting and enriching a leader's understanding of purpose and value.

My aim in this final section is to explore briefly how a Christian perspective of intentional spiritual practice has the potential to reconnect the leader to an appropriate *telos*. At this point, agnostic or non-theist readers may come to a halt, but I would encourage you to persist, because it is important to be able to appreciate the breadth and range of spirituality you may encounter in others. Spiritual practice for leaders ought to be directed towards a particular end, but normative in that it challenges the dominance of economic value, rather than harnessing spirituality for the taken-for-granted purposes of the organization.

Christian belief has much to say about the nature of knowledge. Christian epistemology[24] emphasizes the idea that knowledge is as much revealed as discovered through intellectual endeavor. This kind of knowledge emerges as our relationship with Jesus Christ develops, often in surprising and unanticipated ways and often not immediately apparent. Spiritual reality encompasses but extends beyond physical reality, and therefore has the capacity to impart knowledge beyond that which we can deduct from physical observation and experience. However, such knowledge can never be complete—it may be (in the words of the writer of the Book of Job) "too wonderful for me", or it may be obscured by the human ego. For Christians knowledge is embodied in the person and teaching Jesus Christ[25] and, in the Jewish (Old Testament) scriptures, is personified in the form of wisdom. This is both a challenge and an encouragement because it shows that we may not find engagement with reflexive knowledge easy. Trying to grasp a fully public- as distinct from private-centered understanding of what is valuable, will require personal reflection and introspection. We will need to clear out of the way our own ego-driven goals. It is an encouragement because the Christian faith emphasizes the role of the third person of the Godhead, the Holy Spirit, at work to support us through life. Fulfilment is not just in the achievement of ends, but in each moment of life itself. The form this fulfilment takes is in an appreciation that as leaders we have the opportunity to further the advancement of a more just world.

Christian spiritual practice encompasses a huge range of perspectives and approaches, developed and refined over two millennia. It is hardly possible in a few sentences to do this justice. Indeed, it is precisely the absence of formulaic patterns and the diversity of practice to be found in Christian heritage which makes this heritage so attractive. Thus, the Christian tradition actively avoids slavish adherence to a codified approach to good behavior. As American Franciscan writer, Richard Rohr, explains, there is a need to navigate beyond the futile contested terrain (or "boxing ring") between a false sense of personal fulfilment coming from obedience to those various rules and regulations imposed to provide limits to our natural egocentricity, and genuine fulfilment from finding our true selves in God by surrendering personal desires and ego.[26]

Here is an implicit critique of Scott's new institutionalist schema: neither regulative nor normative/cognitive institutions, with their emphases on providing instrumental knowledge about how to do and not do business, are able to frame genuinely the purpose of leadership endeavor. For Richard

Rohr, there exists a distinction between good power (or authority) and bad power. We are exercising bad power when our point of reference is our own ego, and when we seek to protect and promote those who through luck or judgment are already endowed with power. On the other hand, we are exercising good power when pursuing "growth hierarchies"[27] with the intention of promoting and protecting the interests of others—in other words providing something of genuine value. Spiritually supported leadership can therefore be embodied and visible to others as an example of love in action.

There is an almost limitless range of spiritual practice or discipline to explore within the confines of Christian tradition before considering other faith or philosophical perspectives. This is not least because Christians believe in the limitless creativity of the Holy Spirit in human lives. Central is the practice of prayer, which might be characterized as a two-way conversation with the divine and around which there are many variations of practice, tradition and experience to explore.[28] In my own experience, on many occasions as an academic leader, it is through spiritual reflection supported through the dialogue of prayer that I focus on God's perspective on others as people of infinite intrinsic value. This helps me to constrain inate human reactions based on tit-for-tat, pride or just disinterest, in favor of empathy, compassion and wider reflection on the position of the other. However, rather than focus in detail on particular practices or techniques, I want to conclude by highlighting two particular themes.

- The first is that in Christian spiritual practice *there is always a balance between the social or corporate and the private or personal.* Spiritual practice undertaken with others and, importantly, for others, as opposed on one's own for private benefit, would seem to be an essential ingredient for a leader to create a shared understanding of what the common good or public value looks like. It might be more of a struggle to acquire this understanding in isolation.
- The second is that there is often, some might say always, a balance between the present moment (*kairos*) and movement. For any leader there will be such opportune moments along the way—these reflexive moments are ends in the themselves and they are to be enjoyed and celebrated.

Returning to a critique raised earlier, spiritual practice can be enjoyed as an end in itself and not merely as a means to some other objective. This notion is central to the Christian idea that there is a tension between the present kingdom of God and its future fulfilment. The physical presence of Jesus at a particular point in human history is, for Christians, the supreme *kairos* moment.[29] On the other hand my personal development as a leader is dynamic, and different aspects of value, beyond the purely economic, intrinsic to oneself as well as extrinsic and public for others will be created over time. Leadership therefore becomes a sequence of ends and not just a means to a single end. For those with no particular faith perspective, the central message here is that we can all seek to enjoy and celebrate those moment of leadership which are life-affirming for others and formative for ourselves.

Personal Reflection

As I ponder the subject of "value", I am drawn into reflecting on my own experience over the past 15 years as a leader. Even though I am an academic, for most of the time through the second half of my career I have also found myself in positions of leadership. When I think back over the reasons why I chose higher education as a career, leadership was never part of the plan. Indeed, until my thirties it always seemed to be others who were chosen for leadership roles. Before that it was just a case of experiencing the privilege of being able to teach and research topics that I enjoyed, and the rewards of seeing students develop and mature and viewing my work eventually in print. The value of all of this was intrinsic and self-referential. Aside from occasional senior common room discussions about public policy and forays into the ethical implications of studying a subject that is framed uncritically in highly materialistic terms, that was enough.

I grew up in a strongly Christian educational context, and would perhaps identify a point in my late teens when that "received" faith became personal to me. But it wasn't really until I did find myself thrown into leadership that the transcendent nature of God became important to my sense of the value of what I did in the workplace and how I did it. As I became the head of a growing university business school, higher education in the UK was becoming rapidly more marketized and drenched in the language of private sector commercialism. We were "competing" for students, in the "market-place"; we had to be "differentiated" through research excellence and, slightly later, we had to become preoccupied with the "customer experience" and teaching quality.

At the time, I didn't find it easy to be locked into a relentless annual cycle of student recruitment, business planning and curriculum planning and delivery within budget. In fact, as international student numbers began to grow rapidly to meet the university-in-question's ambitions for growth and campus development, it became a continual game of catch-up. The game was one of fighting for resources to keep unmanageable pressure away from my generally hard-working and committed staff. It was hard to maintain a sense of value, and even harder to communicate this to a growing number of academic and professional support staff, rising in their scepticism about what "value" had become in higher education, and nervous that their value was no longer intrinsic but largely as an instrumental "human resource".

In all of this I had to find the means to keep a wider sense of perspective, and to find the space to meet my own desire for spiritual refreshment and re-centring. As someone with a "pragmatist" learning style[30] I had always found experiential and small group based activities a more rewarding way to explore my Christian faith. And yet, by contrast with traditional Sunday worship meetings, these were often ruled out by the demands of work. Two experiences came to my rescue, and I would recommend both to any emerging leader, regardless of whether or not they are a person of religious belief.

The first came as a result of my wife becoming tired of Friday evening "downloads" of my worries and anxieties. She advised me to start keeping a journal as an opportunity to reflect on events and activities. Reading back over the journal, which now covers a decade or more, much of it is full of the mundane and the far from notable experiences. But the material which is about my professional life reveals the wax and wane of a process of finding value and purpose in what I am doing. It records a great deal of angst with other people, some those for whom I had line management responsibilities, but the majority were my co-leaders or seniors. As I read back, the words written in private and left unspoken are hard and sometimes harsh. But they also allow me to be thankful. One of the great joys of having a Christian faith is in a divine source of unconditional love to whom I can be thankful for what happened and for what did not.

By a serendipitous turn of events, the second was when someone from outside higher education, who shared my own faith perspective, approached me to volunteer her (free) services as a leadership coach. One of the first questions she asked me concerned how I knew whether I was authentic as a leader. I can recall vividly this question coming as a "sucker-punch", because I had no idea if I was authentic or a fraud. To be an authentic leader felt encouraging and attractive but also very courageous. As we worked together I realised that authenticity is what allows a leader to encourage and to be courageous. With her support I was able to take some courageous decisions because I had gained a secure sense of my own spiritual identity and grounding. One such decision eventually was to move on, and to explore new opportunities.

It is often only when you move on from a role that people will tell you that you did a good job. In fact, to have a good chance of maintaining a sense of humility, it is no bad thing that people usually only highlight your virtues at your leaving party! But watching what happens afterwards can be hard for a leader. My journal entries over this time reflect this. It was important to be able to let go of success, and in particular to let go of people for whom you have had responsibility. In due course, the university employed an individual in my former role who turned out to be highly controversial, some might say "toxic". Because of particular events and actions, the story of this played out in the pages of the local and higher education media. A significant proportion of my former team, over a short period of time, moved on or retired early. When I saw what happened to the people in which I had invested, it would have been easy to be consumed by a sense of remorse, or at least doubt that I had made the right decision. What many organizations "value" can in fact turn out to be ephemeral. The integrity and professionalism of my former staff at the time appeared to count for little. However, as long as those individuals continue to flourish as human beings (and I know that nearly all are) then the value that I encouraged as a leader was not transitory.

Notes

1. Burns (1978).
2. For many commentators, it is clear that subsequent additional regulation has failed to make much difference, see Knights (2016).
3. See, for example, Rubin and Dierdorff (2013) and Mabey and Mayrhofer (2015).

4. Because the pursuit of profit is embedded in the legal constitutions of capitalist organizations, some important critiques question the extent to which it is in practice possible to reconcile this primary objective with other notions of value.
5. Sedlacek (2011), among many others, makes this point.
6. Poole (2015). See also Kidwell and Doherty (2015) for a recent dialogue between economists and theologians.
7. Schumacher's approach derives from Buddhist thinking (Schumacher, 1973). Other authors, such as Wilson (1997), compare and contrast different positions in Christianity, Judaism and Islam.
8. Knights (this volume).
9. Niebuhr (1934).
10. Brewer (2013).
11. Burawoy (2004).
12. Habermas (1984).
13. See, for example, Tourish and Tourish (2010).
14. And therefore justifying the transformation of what was in the past termed "personnel management" into modern human resource management practice.
15. This implies an openness to a wider range of post-secular perspectives than often implied by propenents of secular rationalism and offers the potential of fresh validity to religious and spiritual values in a Habermasian communicative rationality.
16. One such Quaker business leader, George Cadbury, went as far as to question the value of personal wealth, by stating before a committee of the Church of England that: "I have seen families ruined by it, morally and spiritually" (quoted in Cadbury, 2011 p. 179).
17. O'Donovan (1994).
18. It is worth pointing out that this is unusual more generally in British culture where there is an unwritten social and cultural convention that religious views remain private.
19. For an overview of alternative bases to leadership development, particularly in the context of moral and spiritual development, see Mabey (this volume).
20. The most recent edition of this is Scott (2013). The classic statement of institutions as devices for the regulation of undesirable economic activity and behaviour is found in North (1990).
21. The seminal academic statement on this is Granovetter (1973).
22. A wide range of literature could be cited here. See Mabey et al. (2016) for an extensive bibliography.
23. Case and Gosling (2010) adopt this description.
24. For an accessible introduction, see Plantinga (2015).
25. Perhaps the most commonly cited statement to this effect in the Bible is found in John, Chapter 1, verse 14, in which the writer explores the notion of the word of God as the creative force in the cosmos and then goes on to draw the conclusion that physical incarnation of Jesus is the presence of the word of God among humankind.
26. Rohr (2016).
27. Wilber (1995).
28. For further discussion and development, see Mabey (this volume).
29. The is the underlying Greek usage, translated as "time" or "moment" in Romans, Chapter 5, verse 6, where the author of one of the New Testament epistles describes Christ as arriving at the right time. The idea in Christianity that God's presence can be in the moment stands throughout Christian tradition and teaching as complementary to the belief that faith in based on historical accounts of Jesus's life and teaching, validated by other non-Christian accounts.

30. P. Honey and A. Mumford (2006), Learning Styles Questionnaire, Maidenhead, Peter Honey Publications Ltd.

Bibilography

Brewer, J. (2013) *The Public Value of the Social Sciences*. London: Bloomsbury.

Burawoy, M. (2004) Public sociologies: Contradictions, dilemmas and possiblities. *Social Forces* 82(4), pp. 1603–1618.

Burns, J.M. (1978) *Leadership*. New York, NY: Harper and Row.

Case, P. and Gosling, J. (2010) The spiritual organization: Critical perspectives on the instrumentality of workplace spirituality. *Journal of Management, Spirituality and Religion* 7(4), pp. 257–282.

Granovetter, M.S. (1973) The strength of weak ties. *American Journal of Sociology* 78(6), pp. 1360–1380.

Habermas, J. (1984) *The Theory of Communicative Action, Volume One: Reason and the Rationalization of Society*, trans. T.A. McCarthy. Boston, MA: Beacon Press.

Honey, P. and Mumford, A. (2006) *The Learning Styles Questionnaire: 80-item version*. Maidenhead, UK: Peter Honey Publications.

Kidwell, J. and Doherty, S. (2015) *Theology and Economics: A Christian Vision of the Common Good*. Basingstoke: Palgrave Macmillan.

Knights, D. (2016) The crisis of ethical leadership in financial services. In Storey, J., Hartley, J., Denis, J.-L., Hart, P. and Ulrich, D. (eds.) *The Routledge Companion to Leadership*. London: Routledge.

Mabey, C., Conroy, M., Blakeley, K. and de Marco, S. (2016) Having burned the straw man of Christian spiritual leadership, what can we learn from Jesus about leading ethically. *Journal of Business Ethics*, published online 17 February 2016., doi: 10.1007/s10551-016-3045-5

Mabey, C. and Mayrhofer, W. (eds.) (2015) *Developing Leadership: Questions Business Schools Don't Ask*. London: Sage Publications.

Niebuhr, R. (1934) *Moral Man and Immoral Society: A Study in Ethics and Politics*. New York: Charles Scribner's Sons, reprinted by Kessinger Legacy Reprints.

North, D.C. (1990) *Institutions, Institutional Change and Economic Performance*. Cambridge UK: Cambridge University Press.

O'Donovan, O. (1994) *Resurrection and Moral Order: An Outline for Evangelical Ethics*, Second Edition. Grand Rapids, MI: Eerdmans and Leicester: Apollos.

Plantinga, A. (2015) *Knowledge and Christian Belief*. Grand Rapids, MI: Eerdmans.

Poole, E. (2015) *Capitalism's Toxic Assumptions: Redefining Next Generation Economics*. London: Bloomsbury.

Rohr, R. (2016) *Things Hidden: Scripture as Spirituality*. London: SPCK, reprinted from Cinncinati: St Antony Messenger Press, 2008.

Rubin, R.S. and Dierdorff, E.S. (2013) Building a better MBA: From a decade of critique to a decennium of creation. *Academy of Management Learning and Education* 12(1), pp. 125–141.

Schumacher, E.F. (1973) *Small Is Beautiful: A Study of Economics as If People Mattered*. London: Vintage Books.

Scott, W.R. (2013) *Institutions and Organizations*, Fourth Edition. Thousand Oaks, CA: Sage Publications.

Sedlacek, T. (2011) *Economics of Good and Evil: The Quest for Meaning From Gilgamesh to Wall Street.* Oxford: Oxford University Press.

Tourish, D and Tourish, N. (2010) Spirituality at work and its implications for leadership and followship. *Leadership,* 5(2), pp. 207–224.

Wilber, K. (1995) *Sex, Ecology and Spirituality.* Boston: Shambhala.

Wilson, R. (1997) *Economics, Ethics and Religion: Jewish, Christian and Muslim Economic Thought.* Basingstoke: Palgrave Macmillan.

11 Leadership Development and the Cultivation of Practical Wisdom

Mervyn Conroy, Catherine Hale and Chris Turner

Key Questions

How can we cultivate practical wisdom in medical leaders so that they make wise decisions?
How could this help leaders in other contexts to lead more ethically?

Introduction[1]

Despite having professional lives that are rife with competing demands and relationships, questions have rarely been asked about what professionals need in order to be equipped morally (or otherwise) to deal with these. The most ethically challenging decisions in any organization are often cases in which there are multiple conflicting moral and functional goals that a leader feels bound to pursue. For instance, in medical settings, a consultant must weigh up the different benefits that they can pursue for their patients— should they seek to prolong life or ease pain in the palliative care setting? The good for a particular patient must also be weighed up against the good for others—for instance, who, out of a range of suitable patients, should benefit from an organ transplant when only one organ is available. Or, when five patients require emergency operations to save life or limb, who should benefit from being at the front of the queue? Even when it is clear initially what benefit or outcome to pursue, there are often multiple ways in which this outcome or an alternative can be reached—is it best, for instance, to prescribe a drug, advise on nutrition, advocate surgery or allow the patient to choose. This is often further complicated by co-morbidities such as obesity, high blood pressure, high cholesterol and so on.

When faced with such uncertainty, whether this be in a medical setting or otherwise, the response of many leaders, is to reach for the rule-book—that is, to make ever more intricate guidelines, protocols and procedures to determine what must be done in morally fraught situations. Over the last 25 years, 73 clinical guidelines could be found in PubMed in 1990 and 7.508 in 2012, indicating a significant growth in clinical practice guidelines.[2] However, in the face of this tide of ever-closer codification of good medical practice, many clinicians bemoan the loss of their professional autonomy with practitioners noting the inability of these guidelines to take into account the complexity of caring for patients with multiple comorbidities. In one reported instance, practitioners resisted (and, practically speaking, sabotaged) one system[3] that attempted to codify and constrain physicians' decisions. The paradox for leaders as they govern practice today is this: while these rule-based mechanisms are supposed to bring clarity, accuracy and consistency to decision making and make it easy to know what to do, leaders themselves experience the growth of rules, guidelines and procedures as alienating, confusing and even demeaning. They also recognize the artificial *work as imagined* perspective of these guidelines: they tend to oversimplify the complexity of the clinical situation, making patients single-pathology entities rather than the complex multifaceted (medically and socially) humans that they are.

In medical ethics, a large body of work exists on the virtues that enable good ethical decision making. The field of medical ethics singles out a number of virtues of the good doctor for attention; amongst others, these include empathy, care, truthfulness and justice.[4] According to medical ethicists like Pellegrino and Thomasma, however, practical wisdom (or what Aistotle called *phronesis*) "occupies a special place" among these virtues.[5] For some, *phronesis* is regarded as being "indispensable" to good medical practice because it coordinates all the different moral virtues that the doctor must bring to ethical decisions as part of wise moral action. There is also a growing body of work in the generic leadership literature that is addressing the issue of *phronesis* for leaders.[6] This takes us to the questions posed at the start of this chapter.

The authors are currently addressing these issues by researching doctors who take up a clinical leadership role either as consultants or General Practitioners (GPs).[7] Although the focus of our research is the medical community, the issues are relevant to any leadership role in a practice-based professional community in business, education, law and so on. In this chapter we summarize the dominant theoretical discourses,[8] the current challenges to those discourses and then we open new horizons for acting in this area. We explore what might be missing for this particular group of medical leaders as they navigate their way through pre-clinical education, clinical training and onto consultant or GP leadership roles. As with other professions, ethical leadership is frequently complex with the right decision for one patient not necessarily being the right decision for another.

One author[9] suggests that education within the professions (or professional education) does not support either the collective or individual development of virtues, and we are beginning to see indications that this could well be the case for medical education. Certainly what we find is that doctors get very little education and training that helps them cultivate their executive virtue, *phronesis*. In the final "new horizons" section, we suggest what form of research and outcomes might help leaders cultivate practical wisdom in order to make ethical decisions that are not just based on rules and guidelines offered to their professions. These include resources that engage the learner-leader at a psychological, emotional and personal level beyond a formulaic set of principles or guidelines for a given profession.

Dominant Theoretical Discourses

Theoretical discourses to leadership ethics fall into three types: outcomes based (consequentialist), rule or guideline based (deontological) and the "good person" or collective (virtue ethics). For example, in medical leadership ethics as outcomes based, the doctor's main ethical duty is to secure the best possible outcome for a patient (or a group of patients) by assessing the positive and negative consequences that result from any decision, intervention, treatment or policy. The rule-bound doctor's essential duties are laid out in a set of principles of medical ethics that they must absolutely uphold (regardless, sometimes, of the real consequences). For the "good person", based on Aristotle's principles, the main concern in medical ethics is not that the good doctor must do something in a particular way, rather it is that the doctor must show good moral character (or "virtue") in how they practice medicine. Virtue ethics holds that the right thing to do is what a leader of good character would do in that situation.

As mentioned earlier, one of the dominant ethical stances for many professions including the medical profession is rule-bound or what some refer to as deontological ethics; in other words, their profession is obliged to follow guidelines or a set of principles. There are, of course, some exceptions like the obligation of confidentiality that are outcomes-based or consequentialist. Overall, all professions, including medicine (where for example the General Medical Council) have issued guidance for medical leaders), have witnessed a huge growth in the number of policy documents in recent years/ This tells us that the profession recognises the need for more clarity around professional behaviors and decision making, but the less visible gray areas are still prevalent and no guidance—however good—can cover every context. So on the one hand we seem to have fewer ambiguous areas but how to apply the rules in difficult situations or where there is a conflict is as difficult as ever.

We argue that the culture of providing ever more rules has at least two unintended and unhelpful consequences. First, people switch off: there is too much to know and they are difficult to take in as they are rarely relevant at the time they are read. Second, people stop taking responsibility for what is the right thing to do—because all they have to do is follow the rules—so people lose the skill of practicing ethical judgment.[10]

Common Challenges to These Discourses

The main challenge to all three of the above discourses comes from MacIntyre.[11] His thesis is that we are living in a time "after virtue", that we have lost the narrative resources to make good ethical decisions in any practice community. He argues that this is due to the scientific, rationalistic neo-liberalistic (market driven) influences and individualistic effectiveness and efficiency interests that have become dominant since the *Enlightenment*.[12] For MacIntyre, the main driver of practice corruption is the prioritisation of the "external goods" of money, status and power over the "internal goods" of practice excellence, personal fulfilment and outcomes that contribute to wellbeing for all. The media is littered with national and international practice corruption scandals of this nature in all sectors, so we could argue that his thesis has some credence and has come to fruition (see Box 11.1).

Whether it is fraud or fragmented and competing moralities in these situations, the primary issue is one of ethics. To use MacIntyre's language: although the antecedent external goods and premise ideologies are different, corruption occurs when drives towards money, status or power (external goods) rather than practice excellence, job satisfaction or patient benefit (internal goods) becomes dominant. Hence, for leaders in any professional community the cultivation of debate, reflection and discussion on ethical decision making is timely, globally significant and beneficial.

When Aristotle first discussed *phronesis*, he perceived this as an individual's virtue. More recently this idea has been challenged, particularly by MacIntyre. His main concern in any practice based community is not that

---

Box 11.1   Health Care Corruption in the US and the UK

In the United States, we have seen the corruption to health care on a staggering scale. The United States spends more on health care than any other industrialized country but despite the extraordinary level of spending, very little attention has been given to corruption, fraud, waste and abuse in the US health care delivery system. Sparrow[13] suggests that fraud and corruption in the health care system exhibits all the standard challenges of white-collar professions, and he goes on to argue for enhanced ethical decision making on the part of professionals. The UK is apparently no better and in an attempt to stem the tide of corruption the Counter Fraud Centre and the City of London Police, Economic Crime Academy (CIPFA) launched a new professional accredited qualification to boost business and public sector defences against bribery and corruption in May 2016. The Certificate in Anti-Bribery and Corruption Studies, will equip counter-fraud, finance and regulatory compliance specialists with up-to-date knowledge of corrupt practices, legislation and investigation. This world-leading approach to professionalism came as global leaders gathered in London in May 2016 for a major summit on tackling corruption. Tiffen, Head of the CIPFA Counter Fraud Centre was quoted as saying at the summit, "Today's summit is putting anti-corruption high on the agenda around the world. We hope it will deliver a new era of international cooperation and information sharing".

an individual must *do* something in a particular way, it is that the community of practitioners work together to agree their practice virtues that bring "internal" goods for their practice, their own professional practice and for their patients. This also challenges the de-ontological stance of trying to define what the ethical rules are for any particular practice; this is because any such guidelines are contained in a communal narrative that engenders certain virtues and a continuous clarification of the purpose for their practices.

So rather than a rule-bound stance of defining virtues, like a set of principles to work to, we propose that each practice and context is unique and therefore only the practitioners themselves can work out what the virtues are for their professional group. MacIntyre argues this is a collective rather than individualistic process but we lack the moral debating resources[14] and philosophical and theological educational underpinnings.[15] This leads us to question whether this lack of moral debating resources and educational underpinnings apply in medical schools? Like other professional education faculties within some universities, have they become siloed due to market forces? For example, program affordability limitations may mean lost input from the philosophy and theological faculties as MacIntyre suggests. We argue that these "out of core" subject inputs are essential for cultivating the ethical decision-making mind and developing the executive virtue, practical wisdom. This conclusion is supported by authors from the medical ethics writing community.[16]

What's Next in the Medical Profession?

In medicine, the principles of medical ethics often do not themselves settle what a person should do in a particular situation—the principles themselves need context in order to be interpreted.[17] This argument again aligns with what MacIntyre puts forward around the need for practitioners themselves to define their practice virtues, rather than having them mandated. Moreover, the rules of medical ethics often make conflicting demands on the doctor and these rules need to be balanced as the situation requires. This balancing act takes the virtuous doctor out of simple rule-adherence and requires practical wisdom.

The way forward seems to be for a community of doctors to agree what they would do in that particular situation, based on their specific practice virtues. Furthermore, in defining their practice virtues there is also a need to refine them by engaging in ongoing moral debate with the other professionals who contribute to the care of patients, namely nursing, therapists, professions allied to health, social workers and the police. Each group would share the virtues for their specific disciplines and be willing to debate and refine these virtues based on a common telos (purpose) of working towards the well-being of patients and for wider society. However, MacIntyre suggests that the resources for such debate are currently lacking in our professional practices. So this is not just about the good character of individuals, as Aristotle suggests, but it is also about the facilitation by an ethical leader of moral debate with related practices.

So our preliminary conclusions are as follows:

- practical wisdom—or phronesis—can help leaders in medical and other professional contexts lead more ethically in at least here ways: An understanding that good and wise decision making for people who consider themselves ethical leaders goes beyond following a set of guidelines or rules or working out the consequences of their actions but also requires the ability to discern the relevant virtues with their colleagues.
- even when those virtues are discerned (e.g. courage, justice, prudence etc.), knowing where to act on each virtue continuum (vice to vice via a mean) requires the development of the *phronesis* that can be regarded as the adjudicating or executive virtue.
- *phronesis* needs to be cultivated over time to offer a way to balance competing demands, relationships, multiple conflicts and a range of functional goals to find an ethical decision point that will bring good outcomes for their discipline, the professionals who are part of their profession and the people they serve with their products or services.

The problem is that professional education in most universities (at whatever level) has been compartmentalized to such an extent that cross cutting subjects, like philosophy and theology, which help to develop ethical decision making, have been omitted from curricula.[18] In the next section we open up new horizons to thinking about leadership development in the area of phronesis and good decision making.

New Horizons in Leadership Research and Education

In this final section, we discuss how we are working with these ideas on three levels: in our own research using a novel, narrative approach; in our leadership development, with particular reference to a particular worked example of whistleblowing; and, thirdly, on a more personal level (for the first author), as an unexpected client of healthcare!

Some Research Examples

To date little research has explored empirically the ways in which phronesis (practical wisdom) is cultivated over a period of time within one professional community.[19] While a considerable scholarship has started to build around phronesis in medicine, this work has been almost entirely theoretical and while many researchers within medicine[20] have made the case for a reorientation towards phronesis in medical education, little has been undertaken to explore empirically what that might look like.

It is for this reason that we are pursuing a narrative study with medical students and doctors in the United Kingdom to begin to fill some of the gaps in our understanding of phronesis in medicine. The study is currently being conducted and attempts to answer the following research questions:

- What does phronesis mean to practitioners?
- To what extent is phronesis cultivated, maintained and molded over the educational and practice life of doctors in the UK?
- To what extent can phronesis be promoted through educational and practice interventions?

As we suggested at the beginning of this chapter, questions have rarely been asked about what professionals need to be equipped morally (or otherwise) to navigate a chaotic world of practice rife with competing demands and relationships.

Existing studies have tended to capture practical wisdom within one snapshot, within one organization or by considering one practitioner.[21] In our research, we are choosing to study three communities of doctors over three time periods: at the beginning of formal medical study; on placement at the end of formal study; and established medical professionals with five years plus qualified experience. This design will offer an opportunity to see if phronesis develops over time while enabling a varied discussion about moral resources and what the role of formal education is in equipping practitioners for the messy realities of practice. By asking doctors at different points in their careers about access to and use of moral resources, the study is interested to see what it means to doctors to make "good" decisions for the patient at hand; balancing care, compassion, quality, resources, capacity, medical outcomes and the wider well-being of the community.

The new horizon in this project involves an *artistic skyline* whereby participants will be involved in creatively shaping an original "soap opera" style series of video clips that will connect to an existing virtual community of health and social care practitioners, patients and the public.[22] The purpose is to engage them in providing an artistic interpretation through which they see the issues of phronesis in their practice arena. The soap opera and the way it links to the community will be debated with a broad audience of academics, practitioners, patients and policy makers and others with an interest in the field. The video series will offer an innovative, edgy resource to complement the many text based de-ontological recommendations that have emanated from scandal enquiry reports and social science based studies to date.

New understandings of the cultivation of phronesis in medical communities and its role in rebuilding public trust in the light of many scandals will be of interest to healthcare researchers, educators, practitioners and policymakers. The project aims to impact on the medical and professional education of doctors as a community, building stronger links between the medical

---

Box 11.2   Using Virtue Ethics and Phronesis in Research

In a prior study, I explored the ethics of leading change by using a narrative approach with practitioners.[23] Stories told by practitioners to a researcher may or may not be what actually happened; however, they contribute to the "pool of meanings" and support the social construction of ethics and decision making in a given professional community. In another study, we used MacIntyre's virtue ethics and the theory of phronesis to present a mapping what we called *virtue continuums* for a health and social care community.[24] The virtue continuums were based on the stories told by the participants and showed where on the continuums each of their stores was located, hence the claimed phronesis. This mapping showed for each virtue narrated by the community of practitioners there is a continuum from vice to vice via a median. What we have subsequently proposed[25] is that there is a median point for courage in each case, arrived at via conducting a moral debate with fellow practitioners on the corruptions observed and collectively working towards wise action.

---

community and the public and rebuilding public confidence in the medical profession. The main impacts will be to increase the effectiveness of health services and enhancing health and wellbeing, all within the time-frame of the research. The lead author already has some experience of working in this way (see Box 11.2).

Introducing Phronesis to Leadership Development

In a recent leadership development workshop, participants were discussing the issue of how to deal with unacceptable practice. There was general consensus that keeping schtum or rationalising corrupt acts as justified would both be at one vice pole of the virtue continuum of courage with whistle-blowing at the other vice pole (Conroy, 2015). Both are extremes that from a virtues ethics perspective are unlikely to benefit the individual, the collective or the practice. The "phronesis" or practical wisdom element was seen to be the ability to collectively find the median point on a virtue continuum—for any particular context—that will bring (internal) goods for the individual (e.g., job satisfaction), improve outcomes and experience for patients and contribute to practice excellence.

What became clear from the workshop with the community was how useful it was for medical professionals to be able to see the virtue continuums presented and where the stories indicated decision points on the continuums. Their response to seeing this depiction of *phronesis* was typically, "I realise now I need to move in another direction with a given virtue continuum to make a better decision". In other words, they were using the constructed picture of virtue continuums to help them improve their decision making based on their own understanding of their practice. This is very different to giving health and social care practitioners a set of ethical guidelines or deontological principles to work to.

So using the example of whistleblowing, how do leaders find a median point on the courage continuum at which they could still find a way of resisting the corruption to practices but not risking all with an act of whistle-blowing? Anderson urges us to not to ask of a social institution: "What end or purpose does it serve?' but rather 'Of what conflicts is it the scene?"[26] In other words, the individual and the meaning of individual action are framed by the wider culture in which the action takes place. What I do now in my work with health and social care leaders is track their practice dilemmas, rife with competing demands and relationships, back to their ideological roots and differing standpoints. Once they understand that they are wittingly or unwittingly supporting a standpoint that could lead to practice corruptions then they became angry at becoming "emplotted" in an ongoing and emergent narrative that they did not identify with. Courage to resist is found through externally facilitated peer group reflection, moral debate and collective action rather than individual whistleblowing.

This approach tallies with the recommendations made by Anand et al.[27] They found that when corruptions come to light there is a tendency to "blame rogue individuals or isolated groups, arguing that they do not represent the otherwise pristine organization. In cases of collective corruption, such scapegoating misses the point that individuals and systems are mutually reinforcing" (ibid, p. 50) We see this in the Robert Francis's Report[28] into the failings at the Mid Staffordshire Foundation Trust. The Kings Fund[29] say, "It is clear that the causes of the Mid Staffs scandal are deep and complex, and the solutions are equally diverse".

In the report, a single Trust and senior individuals in the trust are heavily criticized for creating a "culture of the trust was not conducive to providing good care for patients"[30] instead of looking at the ideological roots that have led to much wider system corruptions that these people were just a part of. Anand et al. (2004) suggest it is better to involve external change agents to support education and connection between staff and external networks because insiders are often part of the system and continue to be susceptible to the rationalizations associated with corrupting influences on practices. Anand et al do not elaborate on the nature of the education and connection so virtue ethics offers an option to gain clarity on the type of connection and education that would contribute to maintaining ethical practice. The seminar series suggests a reframing of leadership ethical education with its emphasis on individuals towards externally facilitated collective peer group reflection and ethical debate that develops proficiency in virtue ethics understanding and the application of phronesis.

Personal Reflection

On a more personal note, the lead author was recently involved in a serious cycling accident and had to spend three months in hospital recovering from brain surgery, multiple head bone fractures and other post-operation complications including pneumonia. After coming round from an induced unconscious coma and then a conscious coma, what I experienced was a team of health care practitioners led by a neurological rehabilitation consultant demonstrating practical wisdom. Thankfully, I made a full recovery, and I am now back working full time and loving my work like before. The consultant concerned agreed to be interviewed as a "black-belt" in phronesis for the author's project and spoke about his approach. His approach with the author was to listen to what I was concerned about and support me in a way that conveyed his experience with other cases like mine. He even spoke about another academic he had treated and what happened to him. The DVLA told me I would not be able to drive for 18 months. The consultant kindly wrote to them and I was back driving in six months. What the author discovered during the interview is that the consultant had recently been promoted into a significant leadership position for the hospital Trust as a whole. What he demonstrated are the internal goods and benefits of applied practical wisdom: those that are on the receiving end of their services or products feel honored and grateful and those people who are able to apply practical wisdom and develop practice excellence become sought after for leadership roles in their organization. What leader would not want to see that as an outcome from their work?

For me, the experience of the accident and recovery affected my own development as a leader. It caused me to reflect on and rethink a few things about what is important in my life and career. I would say I am less willing to spend time on things that do not contribute to internal goods and I am more courageous in proposing and taking what I think is the right course of action to bring social justice. For instance, I have recently highlighted an issue raised by participants in our recent research study about ethical purpose for the medical community. Is it to bring the best possible outcome for any individual patient or wider society?

Notes

1. This chapter gives a more detailed outline of a presentation made at the 5th ESRC seminar series (www.ethicalleadership.org.uk/news/8/15/Seminar-5-Virtue-Ethics-and-Christian-Values-in-Health-and-Education.html) on a project entitled "Phronesis and the Medical Community".
2. Upsher (2014).
3. The UK National Health Service's "Choose and Book" out-patient referral system. See Greenhalgh et al. (2012).
4. Carel and Kidd (2014).
5. Pellegrino and Thomasma (1993, p. 83).
6. For example Shotter and Tsoukas (2014).

7. www.birmingham.ac.uk/schools/social-policy/departments/health-services-management-centre/news/2015/03/phronesis-and-the-medical-community.aspx
8. Here and throughout, we use the word discourse to refer to the language, artifacts, thinking and assumed way of behaving in a given field. The beguiling feature of these "bubbles" is that we are often unaware of operating within them.
9. MacIntyre (2009).
10. See Derrida (1978) although he makes it fundamental—rather than a possible—outcome.
11. MacIntyre (1981).
12. The Enlightenment period stretches roughly from the mid-17th century through the 18th century and was a dramatic revolutions in science, philosophy, society and politics moving from a medieval culture of "myths" to modern Western ideas based on scientific "facts".
13. Sparrow (2006).
14. MacIntyre (1981).
15. Macintyre (2008).
16. See Dawson (2010) and Montgomery (2006) and Kaldjian (2014).
17. Pellegrino and Thomasma (1993).
18. See, for example, Mabey and Mayrhofer (2015), Macintyre (2009).
19. Kotzee et al. (2016).
20. e.g., Kaldjian, 2014; Montgomery, 2006).
21. For example, Shotter and Tsoukas (2014).
22. This artistic element which will animate the findings of the research. The participants will be involved in creatively shaping an original "soap opera" style video series and other social media that will integrate with an existing virtual community of health and social care practitioners, patients and the public based on a fictional town (Stilwell) in England.
23. Conroy (2010).
24. Conroy et al. (2012).
25. Conroy et al. (2014).
26. Passmore (1962).
27. Anand et al. (2004).
28. Francis Report (2013) Francis's brief was "to examine the operation of the commissioning, supervisory and regulatory organisations and other agencies, including the culture and systems of those organisations in relation to their monitoring role at Mid Staffordshire NHS Foundation Trust between January 2005 and March 2009, and to examine why problems at the trust were not identified sooner and appropriate action taken".
29. Kings Fund (2017), available from: www.kingsfund.org.uk/press/press-releases/our-response-final-report-mid-staffordshire-nhs-foundation-trust-public-inquiry
30. Guardian (2013), available from: www.theguardian.com/society/2013/jan/30/final-report-mid-staffs-scandal-devastating-nhs

Bibliography

Anand, W., Ashforth, B.E. and Joshi, M. (2004) Business as usual: The acceptance and perception of corruption in organizations. *Academy of Management Executive* 18(2), pp. 39–53.

Annas, J. (2011) *Intelligent Virtue*. Oxford: Oxford University Press.

Carel, H.H. and Kidd, I.J. (2014) Epistemic injustice in healthcare: A philosophical analysis. *Medicine, Health Care and Philosophy* 17(4), pp. 529–540.

Conroy, M. (2010a) *An Ethical Approach to Leading Change: An Alternative and Sustainable Application*. Basingstoke: Palgrave Macmillan.

Conroy, M. (2010b) Leadership of change narratives: What are we missing? In Grint, K. and Brookes, S. (eds.) *The Public Sector Leadership Challenge*. Basingstoke: Palgrave.

Conroy, M. (2015) *Phronesis and the Medical Community*. University of Birmingham. www.birmingham.ac.uk/schools/social-policy/departments/health-services-management-centre/news/2015/03/phronesis-and-the-medical-community.aspx

Conroy, M., Clarke, H. and Wilson, L. (2012) *Connected Health and Social Care Communities. AHRC*. Available from: www.ahrc.ac.uk/documents/project-reports-and-reviews/connected-communities/connected-health-and-social-care-communities/

Conroy, M., Kotzee, B., and Paton, A. (2017) A methodology to research phronesis. In *Medicine: A Social Science and Arts Hybrid*. HEC Forum (accepted/forthcoming).

Dawson, A.J. (2010) Toward the 'Fair Use' of empirical evidence in ethical arguments: vaccination, MMR and disagreement. In Häyry, M. (ed.) *Arguments and Analysis in Bioethics*. Amsterdam: Rodopi.

Derrida, J. (1978) *Writing and Difference*. London: Routledge.

Francis, R. (2013) *Report of the Mid Staffordshire NHS Foundation Trust. Volume 1: Analysis of Evidence and Lessons Learned*. London: The Stationary Office.

Greenhalgh, T., MacFarlane, F., Barton-Sweeney, C. and Woodward, F. (2012) 'If we build it, will it stay?' A case study of the sustainability of whole-system change in London. *Milbank Quarterly* 90, pp. 516–547.

Kaldjian, L. (2014) *Practicing Medicine and Ethics*. Cambridge: Cambridge University Press.

Kotzee, B., Paton, A. and Conroy, M. (2016) Towards an empirically informed account of 'phronesis' in medicine. *Perspectives in Biology and Medicine*, 59(3).

Mabey, C. and Mayrhofer, W. (2015) *Developing Leaders: Questions Businesss Schools Don't Ask*. London: Sage Publications.

MacIntyre, A. (1981) *After Virtue: A Study in Moral Theory*. London: Duckworth.

Montgomery, K. (2006) *How Doctors Think: Clinical Judgement and the Practice of Medicine*. Oxford: Oxford University Press.

Pellegrino, E. and Thomasma, D. (1993) *The Virtues in Clinical Practice*. Oxford: Oxford University Press.

Shotter, J. and Tsoukas, H. (2014) In search of phronesis: Leadership and the art of judgment. *Academy of Management Learning and Education* 13(2), pp. 224–243.

Sparrow, M.K. (2006) *Corruption in Health Care—The US Experience*. TI Global Report on Corruption, pp. 16–22. London: Pluto Press.

Stilwell. (2016) *Welcome to Stilwell Virtual Community: A Unique Dedicated Environment Developed By the University of Cumbria*. Available from: www.stilwell education.com (accessed December 2, 2016).

Upsher, R.E. (2014) Do clinical guidelines still make sense? *Annals of Family Medicine* 12(3), pp. 202–203.

Vignette

How Can We Be Fully Human at Work?

Phil Jackman

This question was posed by one of eight participants in a teaching/research project exactly half way through at the time of writing. The purpose of the project is for two facilitators and eight participants from business and education to work together over a three-month period to better understand, experience and promote resilience. One of the challenges of ethical leadership is to resist riding roughshod over individual integrity. Employees frequently arrive at training courses wondering whether they really want to be there. If the training course is of a kind that asks deep and personal questions, there is a risk that employees will feel affronted.

Resilience is a quality required by employees across multiple sectors, such as the aftermath of a dangerous rescue operation, living through an acute financial crisis or responding to an adverse OFSTED report. Moreover, it is a goal that is clearly in the interests of both the organization and the individual within it. Our intention is to explore whether such a course can not only increase spiritual self-awareness among the individuals participating, but also whether this translates into enhanced resilience and integrity at an organizational level.

As we surveyed the current literature, I had the feeling that something quite significant was missing. Philosophical schools and folk traditions around the world have been teaching for centuries that the wise, moral and disciplined life will be the strong and resilient life. One of the most well-known examples is the picture described by a Jewish sage called Jesus. The picture is of a wise man who built his house on a rock, which, unlike his neighbor's house with sandy foundations, then withstood the storms. It comes at the conclusion of one of the most famous speeches of all time, known as the sermon on the mount. Heed my words. says Jesus, and you will have a resilient life. So, what words?

In the second half of his speech, Jesus touches on issues which echo contemporary resilience research, such as discipline and low fear of failure, but at the heart of his "manifesto" following his poetic and startling declaration of who is truly well off, he sets out something entirely absent from the literature, which could be summed up under the heading of moral courage, adapted by me as a set of alternative responses in the schematic below.

Presenting issue	Response A	Response B	In a word
Difference	I want to kill you	I want to understand you	EMPATHY
Attraction	I want to control you	I want to love you	FAITHFULNESS
Shame	I want to hide from you	I want to be honest with you	TRANSPARENCY
Offense	You owe me	I want to cancel your debt	FORGIVENESS

So here is my dilemma. How can I as a follower of Jesus teach and explore resilience with no reference to moral courage, without which, Jesus suggests, our lives will sink? How can I be fully human without engaging with this idea in my work of teaching? Yet, here in the 21st century, West there is no longer a consensus that the words of Jesus should carry special weight or authority. If I introduce Jesus into a course, the context of which is neither religious nor theological, will I be seen as inappropriate at best? If I introduce Jesus's ideas anonymously simply as a set of moral possibilities to consider on their own merit, then I can be justifiably criticized for not properly acknowledging my sources.

We could approach the question from another direction. Why do the majority of resilience models seem to stay on the surface, and while there is tangential mention of faith, values and meaning, they seem to overlook moral courage as a major component in their diagrammatic representations[1]? It is clear that the majority of research is carried out within scientific disciplines such as Psychiatry, Epidemiology, Developmental Pathology and Organizational Psychology. They therefore tend to stay close to what is measurable, providing "clear evidence" to support certain interventions. There appears to a reticence to move too deeply into the more fluid territory of the humanities, and especially the controversial territory of morality, which for many people in the Western workforce has a historic connection to one religion or another.

As it turns out, I need not have worried. When we presented the above table to the group they unanimously considered it more or less self-evident that moral courage is connected to resilience. Not only so, but there seemed to be a consensus that the four moral options highlighted by Jesus would lead to greater resilience than their alternatives, with one participant articulating that Islamic State is therefore not a resilient organization and will, in time, implode. This could be debated, but the point to note here is that a helpful and engaging discussion ensued, assessing Jesus's ideas—utterly radical in his time—not on the basis of who said them, but on whether they seem to ring true and connect with life in the 21st century. Having begun on day one of our course emphasizing the importance of empathy and listening, trust in the group has grown to the point where we can have this discussion with no feeling of religious coercion or spiritual totalitarianism. All voices and opinions are valuable.

Following this discussion, I had a rather unusual experience. As I was sitting in a wooded area enjoying the sun and writing in my journal the first draft of my thoughts above, a man walked out of the woods, smiled warmly and engaged me in conversation. It transpired that he was a presenter for South Asian local radio, and I spent the next hour listening to him pouring out the woes of the Kashmiri community, which was losing its cohesion and historic integrity. He moved on to the problem of non-reporting of rape within Asian families, and how this needed to change. In the space of an hour he had described a community which had lost its identity and vitality and attributed this in part to the negative effects of a shame-honor culture that habitually buries bad news in order to protect family reputation.

I therefore feel freshly energized and empowered to press the conversation deeper in our next course session together. We may notice that in supporting the response "I want to be honest with you?" over "I want to hide from you?" we are preferring a Western view to an Eastern one, truthfulness over family honor, running the risk of cultural imperialism. But as I now have two examples of Easterners critiquing their own Eastern culture (Jesus and my Kashmiri friend) I feel emboldened to open up the conversation. Jesus will thus be explicitly present in the room once more, but neither meekly nor coercively, and I hope that we as a group will be able to take that in our stride, recognizing that not all cultural values have equal weight and that via healthy dialogue and critique on ethical issues we can develop our resources of resilience and grow in our spiritual self-awareness.

Note

1 See, for example, https://thewellbeingproject.co.uk/ and http://atriagroup.org/ resilience-overcoming-stress-fatigue/. http://energy-excellence.com/inspiration/ resilience-model-2/ refers to integrity and serving others, but these are very "safe" areas compared to the more radical comparisons that Jesus makes.

Index